BEHAVIOURAL SCIENCE
IN MEDICINE

Behavioural Science in Medicine

Helen R. Winefield, PhD

and

Marilyn Y. Peay, PhD

Lecturers in Behavioural Science
Department of Psychiatry
University of Adelaide
Australia

UNIVERSITY PARK PRESS

Baltimore

First published in 1980 in North America by:
University Park Press
233 East Redwood Street
Baltimore, MD 21202

© Helen R. Winefield and Marilyn Y. Peay 1980

Library of Congress Catalog Number: 79-92423
ISBN: 0-8391-4108-4

First published in 1980 in Great Britain by:
George Allen & Unwin (Publishers) Ltd and
Beaconsfield Publishers Ltd

George Allen & Unwin (Publishers) Ltd
40 Museum Street, London WC1A 1LU

Printed in Great Britain

Preface

Behavioural science courses have been introduced into medical curricula in the last couple of decades, in response to a growing realization within medicine that an understanding of human behaviour is vital for successful practice. Technological advances have not overcome the fact that it is the whole person who decides when to seek treatment and whether to follow medical advice or not. A major challenge to medicine consists of persuading people to accept and cooperate with the sophisticated treatment and care which is now available. Increasingly too, patients are asking for information about their own treatment and a voice in what is to be done, with maternity care currently providing a dramatic example.

As yet there has been a gap in the availability of text books for the new behavioural science courses. Psychology books for example are too detailed in some areas, and too cursory about other areas relevant to practice, while medical books have not included enough of the basic scientific rationale to satisfy students. Our experiences over several years of teaching behavioural science to medical and dental students prompted us to write this book, where we have aimed to integrate material from many behavioural sciences, and to present both the scientific foundations and the applications to clinical practice in parallel. We hope that this approach will help students and practitioners in many health-related areas in addition to medicine. We have tried to write a book which suits a variety of needs, from the beginning student to the postgraduate, and from professionals to interested lay people. Further details of how the book can be used to achieve these goals, and of the topics covered, can be found in the first chapter.

Our efforts have been greatly assisted by many people. Behavioural science students at the University of Adelaide have for the past several years provided us with feedback and encouragement. Colleagues, especially Professor I. Pilowsky, have supported our attempts to develop and present a clinically relevant behavioural science course which remained true to its theoretical origins, on which this book is based. We are also greatly indebted to Professor

Margaret Christie (Director, School of Studies in Psychology, University of Bradford), Professor Murray Wexler (Director, Division of Psychology and Allied Behavioural Sciences, University of Southern California School of Medicine), Dr John Hall (Principal Clinical Psychologist, South Glamorgan Area Health Authority), and Dr Ruth Porter (Deputy Director, The Ciba Foundation), all of whom read and commented critically upon early drafts of this book.

As a final point, the issue of how to refer to people in the sexist English language has caused us some difficulties. Sometimes it just is not possible to avoid the singular third person pronoun. As two women writing about a field where about a third of students and over half the consumers are also female, we have settled for the simple generic 'he' with poor grace, and hope that readers will forgive the clumsiness of 'he or she' where we particularly wanted to avoid implications of sex-typing.

Helen Winefield
Marilyn Peay

Contents

Chapter 1

Why Behavioural Science?

During the last decade courses in behavioural science (sometimes under modified titles) have been added to preclinical medical curricula all over the world. The majority of students have had no prior formal study of human behaviour. This chapter therefore constitutes a brief overview of what the subject includes and why it has been accommodated within already overburdened courses. At the end of it are our suggestions for the use of this book.

WHAT IS BEHAVIOURAL SCIENCE?

Behavioural science courses teach the contributions in knowledge of those social sciences most relevant to human behaviour in health and illness. They have arisen partly out of disenchantment with the technocratic, reductionist view of medicine previously current, which implied that illness was simply a matter of bodily disorder. As remarked by Millon (1975) in the preface to his book of readings (p. vii)

> Now, with growing success in the control of infectious diseases and marked advances in laboratory diagnosis and treatment, medicine has entered an era in which increasing attention is being given to behavioral events that promote and complicate physical illness, and which undermine the effective implementation of many remarkable technological advances.

The search for understanding of such events transcends traditional academic subject-boundaries. Psychology, sociology and anthropology have offered most, and other fields as disparate as history and ethology have also been explored for assistance. A core of subject matter has emerged which represents the consensus of professional opinion about how the diverse and at times conflicting viewpoints of these different disciplines can most helpfully be sifted, and their relevance to medical practice made plain (Winefield 1980).

It has to be recognized at the outset that the scientific study of human behaviour is, compared with our knowledge of less personal events such as physics and chemistry, at a relatively primitive stage of development. We still find claims to psychological expertise, and corresponding use and abuse of psychological terms, boldly put forward by individuals with no formal training, in a way which is not true of the more refined physical sciences. There is still in process a search for measuring instruments, and for the correct questions to ask, which is not typical of the elementary levels at least of other sciences. We all have some experience in observing and trying to predict and even control the behaviour of people around us, yet when we turn to social science for more detailed information, a collection of generalizations, or sometimes over-specific and contradictory experimental results, are what is frequently found. The underdevelopment of the subject can be seen as a consequence not only of its comparative newness, but also of its complexity and personal relevance. This complicates the scientific process by making experiments both harder to carry out and harder to interpret.

On the other hand, the challenges inherent in studying ourselves need not inspire pessimism. Although the task is not easy, the payoffs for success are great (see e.g. APA Task Force report, 1976). A psychologist called to serve on a government subcommittee devising policies on organ and tissue transplants has recently (Saks 1978) reported eight areas of psychological knowledge which he discovered, somewhat to his surprise, to be relevant to the discussion. At what age might a child be regarded as mature enough to give informed consent to the donation of his tissues? What were the effects on potential donors, and on the likelihood of their consenting, of the long series of tests and briefings before tissue-match was confirmed? What would be the psychological consequences, to the individuals concerned and their families, of choosing to donate or not to donate, their tissues?

This example of a medical problem with many social and psychological aspects is not unusual. The interdependence of mental and physical well-being, at the level of both individuals and of social institutions, is further illustrated by the fact that 'between 20 and 50 per cent of the physically ill suffer from concurrent psychological disturbances, and vice versa, and that at least one-half of patients attending medical outpatient clinics present somatic symptoms in the absence of demonstrable organic pathology' (Lipowski 1976, p. 16–17).

We can now proceed to review some areas of human behaviour of crucial relevance to medicine, and to see what contribution behavioural science has to offer in each.

AREAS OF BEHAVIOUR OF SPECIAL INTEREST TO DOCTORS

Compliance

All the technological expertise medicine has to offer is of no use if patients do not follow instructions, take medicine as prescribed, present themselves for checkups or special investigations, and generally comply with the doctor's expert advice. Yet on many occasions, perhaps the majority, patient **compliance** is unsatisfactory. There seem to be a number of elements affecting the extent to which compliance occurs (Ley and Spelman 1967). One is the straight-forward cognitive one: patients can't follow instructions if they did not understand them in the first place or did not remember them. The anxiety associated with being ill can hinder both, as can language difficulties (including those which occur when both patient and doctor speak good English but the doctor uses medical jargon), failing memory with age, or distraction. A doctor who understands how information is received and processed, in people of different age and intellectual levels (see Chapters 4 and 5), is in a good position to reduce the influence of this source of non-compliance.

Another influence upon compliance rates is the motivational one – how well the patient trusts the doctor to know what is best, wants to please the doctor, and feels confidence in the doctor's predictions about the consequences of different courses of action. Here the whole question of behavioural influence and control is relevant, as well as the emotional correlates of different styles of interaction between the purveyor and recipient of health care (Chapters 7, 10, 14 and 15).

In addition to these motivational factors, aspects of the patient's social environment which make it more or less difficult to carry out the doctor's instructions must be considered. In the face of social pressures, even highly motivated patients may falter from the course advocated by the doctor. For example, a patient who must change his or her dietary, smoking or drinking habits may have great difficulty in doing so, when the previous unacceptable but more satisfying ones are still maintained by the family, or form the basis of major social activities. Likewise, heart attack patients who have always held jobs involving strenuous physical activity may find it very difficult to reconcile the doctor's demands for the elimination of such activity with the necessity of earning a living. It is extremely important that doctors recognize the effects of the social environment on behaviour and attitudes, and help patients to find realistic ways of adapting their lives to medical necessities. The mere statement of a prescribed course of action, without the recognition and discussion of the social forces acting against it, may not be sufficient to induce compliance.

This issue of patient compliance or non-compliance has become even more important given the recent trends in medical practice. Most medicine today is practised not in hospitals, but in settings where there is a greater chance of relatively long-lasting contact between the patient and doctor. In addition, because the nature of illness in our society is changing in favour of chronic and frequently preventable conditions, the relationship between doctor and patient is less often one of passivity, or even of child-like obedience, on the patient's part. These kinds of relationship still occur when patients are unconscious in an emergency, or need some drastic treatment such as surgery (Szasz and Hollender 1956). In the greater proportion of cases however, especially in general practice and many of the specialties, the active participation of the patient is needed in a treatment regime mutually acceptable to patient and doctor. Reproduction, parenthood, physical and mental handicap, ageing, psychological disorders, allergies, drug addictions and alcoholism, diabetes, heart disease and hypertension, are just some examples of the health problems requiring such a mode of doctor-patient relations. The achievement of a mutually trusting and cooperative doctor-patient relationship is discussed in Chapter 10.

Preventive medicine
Many of the most common causes of premature death, such as accidents, suicide and lung cancer, are related to voluntary and therefore, in principle at least, modifiable behaviours. Often the doctor is the most appropriate person to make recommendations about preventive measures (such as changes in diet, drug use and life style), to those individuals in his or her care.

A wider preventive role is also available, in that doctors are well placed to act as agents for change in all sorts of health-relevant community and governmental policy decisions. In other words, even doctors in private practice (as well, obviously, as those whose actual career is in public health), may find themselves wishing to persuade non-patients to some course of action. Often more can be achieved by implementing a change through higher levels of the decision-making process, than at the individual level. Examples are the reductions in physical morbidity and mortality due to enforcement of compulsory wearing of car seat-belts, or protective apparatus in mines and factories. Information about group processes, social influences and the attitude change process is helpful equipment for this effective and political application of the doctor's expensive training (see Chapters 14, 15 and 18).

Behaviour modification
Apart from improving compliance with treatment and preventive instructions in patients, and effecting preventive measures in decision-makers who are not patients, there is yet another way in which skills dependent upon an understanding of behavioural science are relevant to medical practice. It is that there is a growing armoury of therapeutic techniques which involve direct manipulation of behaviour. Sexual difficulties are a very clear example of a 'body problem' which will be brought to the doctor, and for which the treatment of choice is not drugs but behavioural change. Ignorance, poor communication and anxiety are the causes of the great majority of sexual problems. Therefore the treatment is usually purely a matter of teaching more adaptive behavioural patterns (e.g. of relaxation and communication between partners, see Chapters 10 and 12). Many other physical and mental problems, if we may for the moment overlook the dualism implied by that description, are most effectively treated behaviourally. Obesity, insomnia, headaches and other chronic pain are examples, as well as the more traditionally 'psychological' problems such as depression, phobias, childhood behaviour disorders and so on, all of which are discussed in detail in Chapter 12.

In other areas of medicine strong clues exist about behavioural aspects of health and illness, but the understanding has not yet been fully translated into clinical practice. For instance, for many years there have been indications that cancer and heart disease, as well as many other psychosomatic and psychiatric diseases, do not strike randomly. Some individuals seem to be at particular risk, whether due to personality pattern, or life experiences, or some combination of the two (see Chapter 7). The elucidation of such factors, and a better understanding of how they relate in turn to the physiological characteristics of those individuals, is a major challenge for behavioural science at present. Answers would facilitate early detection, prevention, and perhaps even cure of the illnesses involved.

The implications for the doctor's role may turn out to be far-reaching. The number of close friends a person has, for example, has been found to be relevant to how well that person can cope with the stresses and frustrations of life, and how likely is the response of illness. Social skills training methods are available; should doctors see their implementation as a responsibility?

Definition of 'illness'.

The state of being 'sick' is a socially recognized one, although societies differ in what exactly that state comprises and implies (see Chapters 17 and 20). The sick person adopts a definite role with its own set of behavioural obligations and privileges. Admittance to the **sick role** is the province of the doctor. The doctor alone is qualified in our eyes to decide whether a given set of symptons and complaints constitutes sickness or not, and many consultations have just this purpose. Sometimes the benefits of admittance are very clear, as in worker's compensation or sick leave applications. Conversely, there are many people who do not seek admittance to the sick role despite suffering physical symptoms.

The evaluation people make of their own state of health, and their subsequent actions (e.g. to consult a doctor, self-medicate or ignore it), is altogether known as **illness behaviour** (Mechanic 1966, and see Chapters 11 and 17). We know that illness behaviour differs according to sex and socio-cultural background, but the dynamics of how it is learned and maintained are not yet established. Presumably similar developmental processes operate, as in other forms of socialization such as sex-typing and conscience development (Chapter 9). The variations in illness behaviour training in different families and social classes affect the use of and demand for health care facilities (Chapter 19).

Professional efficiency

We need scientific understanding of the behaviour of one other group of people apart from the patients, community leaders, and parents and friends of patients considered so far. This other group is the medical profession itself. Medicine is a demanding career and rates of drug addiction and suicide amongst doctors are high (Bowden and Burstein 1974). How can learning of appropriate 'detached concern' (Lief and Fox 1963) be facilitated, and how can professional satisfaction be maximized? The sociology of medicine (Chapter 19) and the psychology of personal adjustment (Chapters 9 and 10) may be able to assist with such questions. The fact that medicine is most commonly a team effort between doctors, nurses and workers in many related fields, and that it tends to be carried out within durable institutions such as hospitals and clinics, also affects the interpersonal skills required by practitioners (see Chapters 16 and 18).

USE OF THIS BOOK

We have tried to make this book suitable for use at different levels of depth and prior familiarity with the subject areas of behavioural science. Although the text is designed for the preclinical student with little or no background in the scientific study of human behaviour, we have aimed to include sufficient documentation to make the book useful as a reference source for deeper explorations by new students, and at later stages of the course as well, including at postgraduate level. The time available for the course will have an important influence on how many of the suggested readings are assigned to students by different instructors, and what use is similarly made of the discussion questions. Although medical students are our main intended readers, students of related health professions such as social work, dentistry and nursing may, we hope, find here much of interest and of value.

THEORETICAL ORIENTATION

It seems only fair to describe the author's biases at the outset. This book reflects our teaching of a behavioural science course which is well accepted by our students, and which has evolved over several years to fit the needs we perceived in those students.

Its main aim is to provide a general knowledge of human behaviour, both individual and social, that will be generally applicable to all phases of medical practice. In other words, it is meant to serve as a source of background knowledge, as well as acting as a foundation for specific applications of its subject matter to medical practice. Without a respectful introduction to the background disciplines, and the means by which they pursue knowledge, students are ill-equipped to evaluate new claims and to continue their own education independently after graduation, both of which are essential for modern doctors. Thus we have tried to strike a balance between the 'applications' and their underpinnings.

The emphasis of this book differs greatly from those of introductory psychology or sociology texts, because of our intended readership. Medical relevance is our focus, and many traditional content areas of the parent disciplines have correspondingly been omitted or given cursory attention. The many specific applications of behavioural science to medical practice which can be productively studied at the preclinical level have been described throughout the text, where appropriate.

Some surprise may perhaps be felt that the psychophysiological aspects of behavioural science have not been more stressed in a medical textbook. The reason for their omission is precisely this pedagogic context: physiology, biochemistry and so on will assuredly be taught to our readers elsewhere. The behaviour of the whole person through the lifespan and in the normal environment, as a subject of study in its own right, tends to be neglected in the rest of the curriculum.

Another relative omission which may need explanation is our concentration on normal behaviour and its dynamics, rather than on the abnormal. This emphasis reflects our belief that 'the abnormal' refers to a section of the continuum of individual variability which can be diagnosed, and comprehended, only in the perspective provided by 'the normal'. A behavioural science course should be seen, not as a diluted introduction to psychiatry, but as a foundation for all medical practice.

A cognitive behaviourist viewpoint has been favoured at the expense of the psychoanalytic one perhaps more familiar to medicine, and social psychology stressed relative to pure sociology. These choices reflect our opinions and tastes about which approaches to the understanding of human behaviour are likely to prove most effective in the education of future doctors. In addition, we hope that consistency in theoretical orientation will add a helpful continuity of perspective to our book without decreasing its scope.

Lastly, given our cognitive behaviourist point of view, we felt that a text would be incomplete without a discussion of the research methods used in behavioural science. Although a detailed treatment of data collection and analysis is beyond the scope of this text, an introduction to these issues is provided in Chapter 2. Students and instructors may prefer to tackle this material at a later stage as appropriate, and proceed straight to the substance of the book in Chapter 3.

SUMMARY

Behavioural science is newly introduced into medical curricula and here we have sketched some of its applications to practice. Compliance by patients, preventive medicine, behaviour modification, health service usage and professional efficiency are some of the broad areas where doctors need to understand the principles of human behaviour. In the following pages we aim to provide the conceptual tools and information which will assist in this search.

TERMS AND CONCEPTS

This section of each chapter will provide a check-list of terms and concepts from the chapter which may be new to you, and which you should be sure that you understand. Each appears in bold type upon its first use in the text. Some are new words, but frequently these terms will consist of familiar words which have a different, specialized meaning in the behavioural science context.

Most chapters will produce longer lists than does this introductory one. Use them to check your mastery of the material and for revision purposes.

compliance
sick role
illness behaviour

FOR DISCUSSION

1. Gather what evidence you can, for example by talking to doctors, observing medical treatment, and talking to recipients of medical care, about the need for a scientific study of human behaviour. Use the behaviours listed in this chapter as a starting point for your investigation.
2. Sample the scientific literature on the interface of medicine and the social sciences, by reading in recent issues of journals such as

Social Science and Medicine
Journal of Psychosomatic Research

Preventive Medicine
The General Practitioner
Journal of Consulting and Clinical Psychology
Behaviour Research and Therapy.

SUGGESTED READING

These suggestions will be taken from the References provided, for each chapter. You may also find it useful to list here other assigned or discovered sources.

APA Task Force report: brief and comprehensive.
Millon: a useful collection of readings. The editor's introductions to each section are recommended at this stage.
Christie (see Winefield ref.): a collection of reviews of behavioural science areas of particular relevance to medicine.

REFERENCES

APA Task Force on Health Research 1976. Contributions of psychology to health research: Patterns, problems, and potentials. *Amer. Psychol.* **31,** 263–74.

Bowden, C. L. and Burstein, A. G. 1974. *Psychosocial Basis of Medical Practice: An Introduction to Human Behavior.* Baltimore: Williams and Wilkins Co.

Ley, P. and Spelman, M. S. 1967. *Communicating with the Patient.* London: Staples Press.

Lief, H. I. and Fox, R. C. 1963. Training for 'detached concern' in medical students. In H. I. Lief, V. F. Lief and N. R. Lief (eds) *The Psychological Basis of Medical Practice* 12–35. New York: Harper and Row.

Lipowski, Z. J. 1976. Psychosomatic medicine: An overview. *Modern Trends in Psychosomatic Medicine* **3,** 1–20.

Mechanic, D. 1966. Response factors in illness: The study of illness behavior. *Soc. Psychiat.* **1,** 11–20.

Millon, T. (ed) 1975. *Medical Behavioral Science.* Philadelphia: W. B. Saunders.

Saks, M. J. 1978. Social psychological contributions to a legislative subcommittee on organ and tissue transplants. *Amer. Psychol.* **33,** 680–90.

Szasz, T. S. and Hollender, M. H. 1956. A contribution to the philosophy of medicine: The basic models of the doctor-patient relationship. *Arch. Int. Med.* **97**, 585–92.

Winefield, H. R. 1980. Behavioural science in the medical curriculum: Why and how. In M. J. Christie (ed.) *The Psychosomatic Approach in Medicine I. Behavioural Science Foundations.* London: Wiley.

Chapter 2

Tools in the Study of Human Behaviour

Throughout this book we will be describing how human beings behave. But, how do we *know* how they behave? We all observe people in our everyday lives and, based on these observations, we all develop our own ideas of how people behave and why. Often, however, the ideas held by different people do not agree very well with each other, mainly because any one person's ideas are based on idiosyncratic experience with particular people. It is important to understand that the study of human behaviour is a matter for scientific investigation, not armchair speculation or the subjective experience of one's everyday encounters with others. Consequently, the study of behavioural science, like the study of any other science, requires an understanding of the research techniques most commonly used. This chapter focuses on those aspects of research design of particular relevance to the study of people and their behaviour, including their needs and ideas.

We will first look at different methods of collecting data, and then briefly consider data analysis techniques and the interpretation of results. Many of the principles are common to all scientific investigation and will not be discussed at great length. However, we hope that you will gain from this chapter an ability to evaluate the claims of others: for example, to have discovered a new method to control weight or smoking, or a new insight on the variables affecting medication compliance. Sensitivity to the issues and pitfalls of human behavioural research should also help you understand why knowledge about many aspects of behaviour is difficult to obtain, or subject to different possible interpretations, or both. Lastly, although this chapter will not be sufficiently detailed for use as a 'how to do it' manual, it will introduce you to the concepts and principles relevant to gathering data about human behaviour for yourself.

RESEARCH TECHNIQUES

Behavioural scientists assess human behaviour in settings ranging from the 'real world', i.e. the normal, everyday environments that people find themselves in, to the highly artificial and unfamiliar laboratory. Research techniques also vary in the degree to which the researcher manipulates or intervenes in the situation in which behaviour is studied. These can range from unobtrusive observation of the seating pattern in a doctor's waiting room, to the complete structuring of the environment found in some sensory deprivation experiments, such as where the subject is submerged in a tank of water (see Chapter 4). Survey research, where subjects respond to questions posed by the researchers, falls somewhere in between: individuals are responding to questions about 'real life' issues in a natural environment, but the stimuli to which they are responding (i.e. the questions) are structured by the researcher.

Regardless of the techniques used, the main aim of the research is to test a hypothesis or to answer a question about behaviour. In some cases, the researchers will have developed specific hypotheses that are to be tested. These hypotheses may be derived from fairly complex theories or may be expectations based on the empirical work of others. In other cases, however, where there is no *a priori* reason to predict one result or another, the researchers will be trying to answer a question about behaviour, such as 'are females more satisfied with their GPs than males?', 'at what stage can children separate from mother without tears?' or 'under what conditions will people change their minds in the course of group discussion?'

In either case, the researcher will study a **sample** of subjects who are assumed to be representative of the population whose behaviour is being investigated. The **population** is defined by the researcher as perhaps all human beings, all pensioners, all public servants, all people in a certain geographical area, all hospitalized females, or whatever group is under investigation. In most cases, a sample is used because it is impossible for practical reasons to study every member of the total population.

This sample should be a **random** sample. In general we can say that a sample is random when every member of the population has an equal chance of being included in the sample. Randomness is extremely important because the final aim of research is to discuss conclusions about the entire population, and not merely about the sample. To the extent that the particular sample studied is not representative of the total population, the results of the research cannot be generalized to the population.

Random sampling of subjects from a large population is more difficult than it may appear. Your first idea may be to get a list of all the members of the population from which a random sample can then be selected. However, obtaining or compiling such a list for a large population, i.e. the residents of London, is a difficult if not impossible task. You may be tempted to use an existing list such as the telephone book or electoral rolls, but these usually exclude sections of the population, such as those without telephones or those who have recently moved. To the extent that people excluded differ from those included, your sample will not be representative of the population. This applies also to those who cannot be contacted or who refuse to participate. Therefore it is important that samples be fully described, so that readers can judge to what extent results can be generalized.

OBSERVATION IN NATURAL SETTINGS

Observation is one of the most elementary and least sophisticated ways of studying behaviour. When using this technique, the researcher simply observes the behaviour to be studied in the appropriate setting, as unobtrusively as possible. If people are aware that they are being observed, they may modify their behaviour, which means it is no longer representative of how people in general behave in this particular situation. For instance, patients and staff in a hospital ward who know they are being watched for research purposes may behave differently from those who are not being observed.

Systematic records of the behaviour observed, preferably by independent mechanical means such as videotape, guard against distortion of the data through inadvertent selectivity of recall. The videotape provides a permanent record which can then be analysed completely at a later time. Unfortunately, in some situations, it is not possible to make notes, tape-recordings or videotape without being noticed by those you are studying. Bias in observation can be reduced by the use of independent records made by two or more observers, which can then be checked for agreement and also, if necessary, by observers who are trained beforehand to look for the same things.

In order to formulate generalizations on the basis of observation, the observations must constitute a random sample of all possible observations of the behaviour in which you are interested. For example, if you were studying doctor-patient interaction in cardiac wards, you would need to observe a random sample of doctors, patients, interaction occasions (e.g. at different times of the day) and cardiac wards.

It is important to remember that the technique of observation only allows you to make generalizations about overt behaviour; it tells you nothing about the internal states that may accompany or perhaps cause this behaviour. Using our example of cardiac wards again, you can determine the average distance from the bed that doctors stand to address a patient, and whether they stand closer to more severely ill patients, but not why they vary.

The advantage of observation in natural settings is that the behaviour observed is natural and uncontaminated by the researcher's restraints. The corresponding disadvantages are the researcher's lack of control, inability to study motives and attitudes, and risk of biasing the results by his presence or recording techniques. Ethical problems may also arise in that subjects probably have not given their consent to participate in the research, and may consider the observations to be an invasion of their privacy.

SURVEY RESEARCH: QUESTIONNAIRE AND INTERVIEWING

Questionnaires and interviews are used extensively in **survey research**, and frequently as part of the laboratory procedure in some experiments (see next section). Sometimes questionnaires are administered in the context of an interview and sometimes simply given to the subject to complete alone.

The aim of the questionnaire or the interview is to elicit as accurate an account as possible of what the subject thinks or, in cases where observational techniques are impractical (e.g. number of cigarettes smoked per day), what the subject does. Prompting the subject to answer questions accurately and openly is not as easy a task as it might first appear. Lack of attention to the principles of questionnaire construction or interviewing techniques, when studying the sample, will yield results that may not be representative of the population.

Open-ended questions allow the subject to formulate an answer in his own words, and **fixed alternative questions** require that the subject choose which of a number of given alternatives best expresses his own response. Open-ended questions enable the researcher to obtain detailed and complex information from subjects that may not be reflected in responses to fixed alternative questions. However, substantial time and effort is required to categorize and code open-ended questions before analysis can begin. Conversely, responses to fixed alternative questions are easily prepared for tabulation, but may be limited or even distorted by the particular alternative answers that are provided.

Wording is important: questions must be unambiguous. Consider the following item, 'The present warnings on cigarette packages are inappropriate'. When a subject agrees with this statement, it could mean that the subject is against the warnings on cigarette packages or that he believes the warnings should be stated more strongly. In this context the meaning of the word 'inappropriate' is ambiguous.

'Double-barrelled' items like 'Smokers should give up smoking because it is harmful to their health' are also ambiguous because they ask the subject to respond to two statements but only give him one opportunity to respond. The subject may believe that smokers should not give up smoking, regardless of the reason, or that they should, but not because it is harmful to their health, but because it annoys non-smokers (or for other reasons). The solution to this problem is to present the subject with two items, the first of which asks for his agreement or disagreement with 'Smoker should give up smoking', and the second of which asks the reasons for his response to the first.

Questions must not make implicit assumptions—that the subject will share the basic attitudes or possess information (for example from newspapers or television) that the researcher has. The reluctance of some subjects to disagree or admit ignorance when implicit assumptions are made is one illustration of the general effect of **social desirability** on responses. Most of us try to 'look good' in front of others, particularly if they appear to have more knowledge or in some way seem superior, and to maintain our self-image and esteem. Subjects being surveyed are no exception. Clearly, admission of ignorance is not consistent with 'looking good'. Neither is disagreement with the implicit position taken by the interviewer and manifested in the wording of the questions.

Therefore another important principle of questionnaire construction (and of survey research in general) is that the biases and opinions of the interviewer must not be perceived by the subject. Although some biases may readily be hidden from the subject, by avoiding implicit assumptions and also by avoiding value-loaded language (e.g. referring to smoking as a 'filthy habit'), the social desirability or undesirability of some positions will be very clear to the subject, and its effect on responses correspondingly difficult to eliminate. This effect is not confined to attitudinal items but applies to reported behaviour as well, such as number of cigarettes smoked per day, number of pregnancies, or amount of alcohol consumed.

In an interview, the opinions of the interviewer can be revealed to the subject not only through the wording of the questions but also by the verbal and non-verbal cues inadvertently provided by the interviewer during the interview. When the interviewer reacts to a subject's response by saying 'yes' or nodding, or with a look of surprise or disdain, he may be influencing the subject's subsequent responses.

The interview procedure itself must be constant over interviews. Inquisitive subjects who ask for additional information about the survey, further clarification of a question, or even for the interviewer's opinion, pose a difficult dilemma for the interviewer, who must remain friendly and receptive but not provide some subjects with more information than others. In these situations interviewers should repeat or rephrase what has already been said, giving as little additional information as possible, and under no circumstances give their own personal opinions.

The advantages of survey research lie in the opportunity to study cognitive and motivational variables in addition to the overt behaviours observable in natural settings. The drawbacks consist of the possibilities for distortion of responses, as discussed above.

THE EXPERIMENT

The laboratory experiment is perhaps the most sophisticated research technique used by behavioural scientists. Assuming that the behaviour being studied can be studied in the laboratory, this technique has many advantages. These centre around the fact that the researcher has much more control over the research situation than with other techniques. On the simplest level, we can ensure that the distractions, unanticipated events and so forth, which can potentially disrupt observations and survey interviews, do not occur. But more importantly, the researcher can control and therefore hold constant all of the variables except the one or ones he wants to test. This enables the researcher to establish reliable causal relationships rather than merely associations among variables.

Let us suppose that we wish to study the effects of a new drug on the performance of a manual task, such as operating a driving simulator. The variable we manipulate, in this case the amount of drug administered, is our **independent variable.** The variable that we then measure, that we anticipate will be affected by our independent variable – in this case, ability to perform a manual task – is our **dependent variable.** On the simplest level, we may test the effects of the drug by administering a certain constant dosage to some subjects but not to others. Then we can compare their performance on the manual task to see if the drug makes a difference. This is a simple experiment with two conditions: 'drug' and 'no drug'.

On a more complex level we may want to assess the effects of various dosages of the drug on manual task performance. Let us arbitrarily choose three dosage levels: low dosage, moderate dosage and high dosage. Furthermore, we may suspect that the effects of the drug on task performance may be different for males and females. If this is the case, we then have two independent variables–level of drug dosage and sex–yielding six experimental conditions as indicated in the diagram below.

		Drug dosage		
		Low	Moderate	High
	Male	Low Male	Moderate Male	High Male
Sex				
	Female	Low Female	Moderate Female	High Female

Ideally, only drug dosage and sex of subject will vary; all other aspects of the experimental situation will be constant, such as conditions under which the drug is administered, instructions and information given to subjects, and conditions under which the task is performed. Then, the performance of the subjects in each condition can be compared, and differences in manual task performance due to drug dosage, to sex or to both can be assessed. We may find that as drug dosage increases, task performance deteriorates, and that this relationship exists for both males and females (drug dosage effect); that over all drug dosage conditions the performance of females is better than males (sex effect); or that female performance improves with higher drug dosages while male performance deteriorates (interaction effects).

In addition to the experimental design, we must consider the source of our subjects and their assignment to experimental conditions.

Ideally, as with observation and survey research, we should have a totally random sample of the population of people whose behaviour we wish to study. In laboratory experiments this ideal is often impossible to achieve because of practical considerations: not everyone in the population is equally willing to participate in psychology experiments. Consequently, researchers must use volunteers, or frequently first-year psychology students who have been required to participate in experiments as part of their course. Such samples are hardly random with respect to the general population, and the particular characteristics of such samples must be taken into account when generalizing results.

Once the sample of subjects is procured, they must be randomly assigned to the experimental conditions. In the example given above, the random assignment will be made within sex: i.e. females will randomly be assigned to one of the three dosage levels, as will males. However, if the second independent variable was not determined *a priori* but was manipulated by the researcher (e.g. if it were practice versus no practice at the task, instead of male versus female), then subjects would be randomly assigned to all six conditions.

Much of the meticulous care that is taken in designing and carrying out laboratory experiments is to ensure that the *only* factors that vary are the independent variables, and that any differences in the dependent variables can be unequivocally attributed to the independent variable(s) studied. In the example given above, the two independent variables were totally crossed with each other. If they had not been, and we had instead used two groups, females – low dosage and males – high dosage, we would not be able to determine whether drug dosage, sex or both were responsible for any observed differences in task performances.

The random assignment of subjects to conditions serves much the same purpose. It increases the likelihood that individual characteristics, which are not controlled for in the experiment but which may affect the behaviour under investigation, are distributed over conditions rather than being concentrated in one condition. Suppose that overall level of coordination were related to performance on our task. We would hardly want all of the subjects with good coordination in one condition, as this could distort our results and lead us to erroneous conclusions about the effects of the drug on our task.

Control groups
The use of **control groups** is another technique for eliminating

alternative explanations (those other than the independent variables) for the results. Control groups can be used in different ways depending upon the experimental design. For instance, in our experiment we may find at each of the three levels of drug dosage, females are better at performing our task than males. We may then be tempted to conclude that the task performance of females is less affected by the drug than that of males. However, we have no way of knowing how males and females perform this task without any dosage of the drug at all: females may be generally superior to males, in which case our conclusions would be incorrect. In this experiment there should be two control groups, one male and one female, who go through the same experimental procedure as our other subjects, but receive no dosage of the drug. In this way we can correctly interpret any sex differences that occur in subjects who have had some dosage of the drug.

Another popular use of the control group in medical research is in the assessment of the **placebo effect.** Often a drug has the desired effect on a patient not because of its chemical properties but because the patient believes in the drug's effectiveness. When new drugs are tested, it is important that one group of subjects actually receives the drug and that another group, the control group, believes that it has received it but actually gets some inert substitute, such as an injection of a saline solution or sugar tablets. Then the effects of the biochemical action of the drug, as opposed to the psychological effect of receiving a drug, can be assessed. Controls for placebo effects are necessary in other studies as well. Contact with professional helpers and the corresponding expectations of being helped have generalized therapeutic effects, which may amount to an extremely effective treatment (probably by means of anxiety reduction, at least in part).

Thus in studies exploring the efficacy of various behavioural therapies (described in Chapter 12), it is desirable to have a 'dummy treatment' group who get the same amount of contact with the therapist, and have the same expectations of benefit, for comparison with both the treatment group and the untreated controls.

Control groups are also used in experiments where some manipulation, such as listening to a speech advocating regular blood pressure checks, is preceded by and followed by a questionnaire assessing the subject's attitude towards the issue. The effect of the speech on attitudes is then determined by comparing pre-test and post-test responses. However, without a control group of subjects who complete both questionnaires **without** listening to the speech, one cannot assume that attitude change in the direction advocated in the speech was in fact caused by the speech: completing the first questionnaire may have prompted the subjects to rethink their attitudes, resulting in the change.

The advantage of the experiment is the ability to investigate *causal* relationships by systematic exploration of the effects of the variables in question. The disadvantages flow from the subject's awareness of being studied, and from the artificiality of the setting, which may alter the subject's normal responses from what they would be in the 'real world'. Some will try to guess the experimental hypothesis (which is rarely divulged beforehand), and then try to 'help' the experimenter by acting as what they imagine to be 'a good subject'. Others may delight in being 'bad subjects'. Either behaviour is no help at all to the experimenter.

In some laboratory situations, subjects tend to surrender much of the autonomy and decision-making power over their own behaviour that they would normally exercise in the real world, thus placing the experimenter in a very powerful position. This is particularly relevant to studies of compliance (see Milgram's work, Chapter 14). **Experimenter effects** consist in unconsciously influencing the outcome in line with the experimental hypothesis and the experimenter's expectations, as has already been discussed in relation to interviews. Rosenthal (1966) established that the most conscientious experimenters can affect the results towards conformity with their hopes or expectations, by inadvertent cues such as different degrees of attention or approval to different responses. The use of 'blind' procedures, where the person administering the treatment, and the one who assesses the results, are kept in ignorance of which treatment is expected to work best, is a precaution against experimenter biases and expectancy effects.

Field experiments allow the researcher to study behaviour in the 'real world' while maintaining some control over the variables that may affect this behaviour. 'Real world' situations are manipulated or structured by the researcher, and the behaviour of the 'subject', who is unaware of the manipulation or that an experiment is in progress, is then observed. Although this technique has methodological advantages, it does pose ethical problems (see the end of this chapter).

ANALYSING THE DATA

Having gathered the data, how can it be organized and interpreted? The first step is to summarize the findings in a way which reduces the detail to comprehensible form and allows the researcher to see the main trends. Then, depending on how exact the quantification is, various statistical tests can be applied to help you to decide whether apparent differences, for example between groups receiving different treatments, are either reliable or fortuitous.

On any measure of physiological or behavioural characteristics, people are likely to show a great deal of variation, both between individuals and within the same individual on different occasions. Some of this variation may be due to the effects of the variable in which you are interested, and the rest to a host of unknown other factors. Statistical tests can help you sort out the sources of variation into those in which you are interested (the independent variables), and those due to chance, errors of measurement and so on. **Statistical significance** is usually claimed if there is only a 5 per cent or 1 per cent probability of your results being due to chance alone. The **probability level** (expressed as $p < .05$ or $p < .01$ respectively), that is the probability of the results arising due to chance alone, is thus the key result of the statistical test.

Correlation is one statistical technique which reveals to what extent two variables (such as smoking and heart disease, or the IQ scores of twins) go together. It is necessary to remember that correlation by itself is no proof of causality.

Numbers vary in their exactness. Some represent real measurement (such as age or test score), while others only describe categories (ordered into ranks, such as primary/secondary/tertiary educational achievement, or just into discrete categories such as male/female, or 'attended'/'did not attend' antenatal classes). Different types of statistical tests are required for the different ways that the numbers have been used. As you will see, many important social and behavioural characteristics of people cannot as yet be quantified with much exactness.

Although we would like to provide details of statistical analysis of data here, we are restrained by limitations of space and by the availability of excellent treatments of the subject elsewhere, for example by Robson (1973), Levitt (1961) and Runyon and Haber (1971). It is important to your ability to evaluate reported research results critically, and to your ability to investigate things for yourself, for you to master the principles of statistical analysis.

The availability of computers and also of packaged computer programs such as SPSS (Nie *et al.* 1975), which do not require the user to have mastered computer programming first, have greatly expanded the kinds of statistical analysis which behavioural scientists can feasibly plan.

RESEARCH EVALUATION

Science, as a cumulative social enterprise in search of knowledge, relies heavily upon communication between the researchers. The scientific and professional journals are the main means of communication and therefore the best place to look, when you want to know what are the frontiers of thought in any given subject. Recent papers, in acknowledging the efforts and contributions of past workers in the area, provide a fruitful source of references which may be followed up in turn. Books may review an area of knowledge which is more consolidated, as the publication lag between research and printing is usually considerably longer than for journal articles. It is desirable therefore that you should develop competence in assessing the reports of other people's research results (as well as in conducting and reporting on your own researches).

The principles that we have discussed in the previous section should enable you to make a competent evaluation of the methodology used. Although, as we stated before, a detailed account of statistical methods is beyond the scope of the book, the statistics used in any study should be carefully scrutinized to determine whether they are appropriate to the data.

Two additional points should be emphasized, given that a relationship between independent and dependent variables has been reported. First, have the researchers eliminated alternative explanations for the relationship? Can their results be explained by other theories, or by methodological deficiences resulting from lack of control groups or samples that are not random? And secondly, what is the practical and/or clinical significance of the result? With large enough numbers of subjects, very small group differences or correlations may reach statistical significance, although for everyday purposes very little information is actually being conveyed. If method X increases the rate of patient compliance with medical instructions from 35 per cent to 42 per cent, for example, it is clearly not the final answer. Another aspect of this question is the length of the follow-up period. Unfortunately, adequate information about the *durability* of the treatment effects is even rarer than that about their efficacy. In behavioural manipulations especially, for example control of alcohol intake, it becomes crucial to know how lastingly the more adaptive patterns have been established.

ETHICAL CONSIDERATIONS

Methodological issues have been the primary concern of this chapter thus far. Of equal, if not greater concern, are ethical considerations. In any sort of research in which human beings are used as subjects, their rights and the long term and short term effects of the research procedures on them must be very carefully considered. Some research procedures would not be expected to produce detrimental effects, such as administering a questionnaire on television viewing habits. Others, however, such as testing the effects of stimulus deprivation on human development by randomly selecting infants to spend three months in an isolation chamber, would most certainly be considered harmful, and therefore should not be used. Where to draw the line between 'not harmful' and 'harmful' is a question that arouses considerable difference of opinion. For example, some researchers have considered it acceptable to lead subjects to believe that they were administering painful electric shocks to another subject (see Chapter 14), or to put subjects in an extremely realistic 'live-in' simulated prison experiment (see Chapter 17), while others, despite the fact that subjects volunteered for these experiments and that they were 'debriefed' afterwards, are horrified that such research was ever conducted. This question is further complicated by the fact that different subjects will react differently to the same procedure. Nonetheless, even when research procedures are considered to be relatively innocuous, steps must still be taken to protect the rights of subjects, for example by obtaining their *informed* consent to participate, and ensuring that the data they provide are confidential and will not result in injury to them in the future.

Organizations such as hospitals, and medical and psychological associations, provide detailed guidelines for ethical research with human subjects, (e.g. see APA 1973). Many decisions about the rights of present and future subjects are difficult, for example when ethical considerations conflict with methodological ones. To mislead subjects about the stressfulness or possible after-effects of participating in an experiment might be convenient, but it is not ethical. Ethical considerations must override methodological ones in research in behavioural science. These issues apply whenever people are used in research, in medicine as well as in behavioural science. (See Veatch and Branson (1976) for a discussion of human experimentation in medical research.)

SUMMARY

Research in behavioural science proceeds through techniques such as observations in natural settings, surveys and experiments. Guidelines to the advantages and weaknesses of each of these have been discussed, and elementary statistical tools and concepts introduced, in a way which is aimed to make students competent in evaluating research reports. Ethical considerations are outlined.

TERMS AND CONCEPTS

sample
population
randomness
survey research
open-ended versus fixed alternative questions
social desirability
independent } variables
dependent
control group
placebo effect
experimenter effects
field experiment
stastical significance
probability level
correlation

FOR DISCUSSION

Select one or more reports of original research in an area of behavioural science which interests you, perhaps from the journals listed at the end of Chapter 1. Carefully analyse the good and bad methodological aspects of the study. How much faith would you put in the reported results? Design a study which would correct any methodological faults you have found. What is your opinion of how the research met ethical demands?

SUGGESTED READING

Robson: a comprehensive if basic introduction.

REFERENCES

Ad hoc committee on ethical standards in psychological research 1973. *Ethical Principles in the Conduct of Research with Human Participants.* Washington: American Psychological Association.

Levitt, E. E. 1961. *Clinical Research Design and Analysis in the Behavioral Sciences.* Springfield: Charles C. Thomas.

Nie, N. H., Hull, C. H. Jenkins, J. G., Steinbrenner, K. and Bent, D. H. 1975. *SPSS: Statistical Package for the Social Sciences* (2nd edn). New York: McGraw-Hill.

Robson, C. 1973. *Experiments, Design and Statistics in Psychology.* Harmondsworth: Penguin.

Rosenthal, R. 1966. *Experimenter Effects in Behavioral Research.* New York: Appleton Century Crofts.

Runyon, R. P. and Haber, A. 1971. *Fundamentals of Behavioral Statistics* (2nd edn). Reading, Massachusetts: Addison-Wesley.

Veatch, R. M. and Branson, R. (eds) 1976. *Ethics and Health Policy.* Cambridge, Mass.: Ballinger.

Chapter 3

Predispositions in Human Behaviour

One question which constantly arises as we contemplate the behaviour of the people around us, and occasionally our own, is *why?* The search for reasons for particular pieces of behaviour, or indeed for failure to behave in certain ways, is one of the central themes of all psychological theories. These theoretical systems, however, differ greatly amongst themselves in the causes of behaviour which are stressed as of paramount importance, as will become clear in Chapter 11 when personality theories are introduced.

The issue of motivation, what makes people do what they do, is clearly a vital one in any attempt to predict and influence behaviour, and will be studied from different angles throughout this book. In this chapter, we look in some detail at those sources of behaviour which may prove to be relatively inborn and free from environmental effects. Other parts of the book (especially Chapters 6, 9, 13, and 14) will consider those influences of the outside world which shape and control behaviour, both in the experience an individual accumulates and in the effects of other individuals.

How much of our behaviour is predetermined by innate factors and how much is acquired? We shall see that even to put the question in these simplified terms is misleading. From conception onwards there is an interaction between the biological 'given' and the individual's environment. For illustrative purposes it may be helpful to think of the determinants of human behaviour as being arranged along a continuum ranging from inborn to socio-cultural. At the latter end, behaviour would show a great deal of variability according to where the individual resides, how he was treated as a child, and what his friends and family consider to be normal. Behaviours such as taking vitamin pills, or playing golf for recreation, are examples. A behaviour such as the individual's performance in the school room will be closer to the middle of this continuum, being partly determined by external factors such as father's occupational status and the extent to which academic achievement is encouraged and expected at home, and partly by more internal factors such as the inherited component of that person's intelligence. At the 'inborn' or biological end of the range of behavioural determinants, which we consider in this chapter, there are such things as the infant's first smiles, and the likelihood of serious mental illness in adulthood. The influences to be taken into account here fall into two main groups – species-specific determinants of behaviour and genetic determinants of behaviour.

SPECIES-SPECIFIC DETERMINANTS OF BEHAVIOUR

Birds build nests and sing, spiders weave intricate webs, and dogs bury their bones, all without any apparent chance to learn how. The question of whether human behaviour is guided by equally rigid instincts has a long history in psychology. The maternal, mating and herd 'instincts' are cliché terms used in common language to describe our behaviours, albeit in a rather circular way. Consideration of customs in a variety of cultures shows that there is great diversity of human behaviour across different social groups, even in such basic matters as fighting, sex roles and child-rearing. The argument for human **instinct,** strictly defined as a well-organized pattern of behaviour, unlearned yet universal amongst members of a species, was destroyed by anthropological evidence (see e.g. Mead 1950). It became difficult to speak of a maternal instinct in humans when contrasting the very permissive, indulgent behaviour of Arapesh mothers with the resentful, irritable child-rearing methods of Mundugumor women. Recent work in **ethology** however suggests that some elements of human behaviour may be a function of species-membership, but that these elements are in the form of *predispositions* to learn and to respond in certain ways, rather than in the form of long fixed sequences of motor activity.

Interest in the whole question of species-specific behaviour has been revived by the careful observations and investigatory methods of ethologists, biologists who study animal behaviour in its natural surroundings. Study of courting rituals in the stickleback fish provided a classic example of this approach (Tinbergen 1951), which is characterized by painstaking non-participant observation and description of natural behaviour sequences. Rather surprisingly perhaps (but perhaps not if you think of the difficulties and discomfort of long term fieldwork), the systematic application of this method to humans is a relatively recent development, and one greatly aided by tape recorders and telescopic cameras. Later, when able to form hypotheses about the significant environmental triggers or 'releasers' for the set piece of behaviour, often called a **Fixed Action Pattern,** ethologists may test their ideas by deliberate manipulation of the environment in one limited but crucial way, and observe the result. Goodall (1971), for example, provided bananas at her camp site. This changed some normal patterns of troop movement amongst the chimpanzees she was studying, but gave her the opportunity to watch other behaviours at close hand (e.g. competition, and frustration when the 'free' food was not made available). Tinbergen found by lowering a series of different models into his fish tank, that the sexually aroused male stickleback will charge any object which is red, and disregard all other cues such as shape and fish-likeness. One very restricted sign from a complex perceptual array, i.e. the **sign stimulus,** is sufficient to release a stereotyped pattern of behaviour which has not been learned even by observation.

There has naturally been great interest in exploring the implications for the human species of this new set of ethological concepts and techniques. Several writers have discussed evidence of Fixed Action Patterns and their releasers, in ordinary (i.e. non-laboratory) human behaviour, and it seems realistic to conclude that these concepts do have relevance to the study of our motivations. In humans the links between sign-stimulus and Fixed Action Pattern are weaker and more variable between individuals than is the case in lower animals, due to the overriding effects of experience and learning. We are probably the most adaptable and creative species of animal, and our lack of rigid instincts is not surprising. On the other hand, it would be surprising if we had total freedom from some propensities to respond to certain stimuli in certain ways, given our continuity, in evolutionary terms, with the other inhabitants of Earth. Again, it is relevant to take into account the relatively greater development and dominance of the cortex over the lower brain centres in humans, and our correspondingly greater ability to inhibit or suppress 'natural' reactions.

That we walk in a certain way and sense a certain range of odours, sights, sounds and so on – all due to the way our bodies are put together – is not what is being discussed here, although the insight that 'anatomy and physiology are fossilized behaviour' (Jones 1975, p. 85) is an intriguing one. Rather, our concern here is to tease out those behavioural tendencies which may be a) common to all members of the human species, and b) likely to be relevant to our two main assets as a species: our ability to live in cooperative, coherent and durable social groups, and our versatility in inventing and manufacturing things to help us survive, sometimes luxuriously, in a wide variety of environments. Even more so than with animals, the search for *similarities* in natural behaviour of all members of our species is both recent and difficult, as discussed by Eibl-Eibesfeldt (1970) and Jones (1972).

GROUP-LIVING SKILLS

Bond-formation
The human propensity to form lasting emotional relationships with others is of clear importance in the maintenance both of social groups, and of the smaller group, called the family, which provides a nurturant and stimulating environment for infants who are physically helpless and slow-growing compared to the young of other species. In fact, as we shall discover in greater detail later (Chapter 9), there is considerable evidence that deprivation during infancy of experiences of stable, affectionate relationships can harm the individual's capacity to form such relationships with others in his own adulthood. Infant-parent attachments are then a logical place to look for instances of the sort of preprogramming in question. Lorenz (1943, discussed by Eibl-Eibesfeldt, pp. 431-3) suggested that the large head, fat cheeks and stumpy, jerky limbs of the human baby (the 'kewpie doll' configuration) together form a constellation of stimuli which releases nurturant and protective responses in adults. Certainly these are the features exaggerated by greeting card designers who want their drawings to be seen as cute and appealing. It is also a truism, to parents especially, that the vocalizations made by babies have very powerful effects on other people, whether they be the gurglings of pleasure or the howls of distress or rage.

Crying and smiling by infants have both been carefully studied in recent years (Schaffer 1971). Methods of observation are being constantly refined, and this more accurate information is making it clear that the communication between mother and baby is very much a *reciprocal* process. Far from being passive and dependent, babies are rather effective initiators and shapers of interaction with adults, who adjust their responses accordingly.

One potent social signal, produced by all very young babies, is the smile. Whomsoever the baby smiles at feels delighted, honoured and recognized, and is likely to respond in a similarly positive way. Thus the infant gains both a protector and a stimulator or teacher, both of which are essential to wellbeing and future development. The fact that blind babies smile too, and that their smiles show a similar developmental path of greater and greater specificity, until they smile only at familiar figures and show distress in the presence of strangers (Fraiberg 1975), is convincing evidence for the innate nature of this early behaviour. It may be conjectured that those babies, who for some reason fail to smile, are more likely to be the victims of adult aggression.

As noted, with increasing age the baby smiles more and more selectively. While at two to three months two eye-like dots on a sheet of paper are a sufficient stimulus, by five months a more detailed representation of a face, which includes a smiling mouth, is necessary. From about seven months on, only real human faces, *and* ones which the infant recognizes as familiar, can elicit a smile. This sequence provides a good example of how the effects of learning quickly overlay innate mechanisms, to produce in the end a behaviour which, although it is vital for communication with attachment figures, will vary according to features of the environment – such as how regularly and sensitively a desirable consequence follows it.

Another aspect of rapid, predisposed early learning may have to do with tactile contact with other members of the species. Ethologists use the concept of **imprinting** to describe the tendency of some very young animals, mainly birds but also others such as guinea pigs and sheep, to follow the creatures which provide certain crucial cues during a specific period of maximum receptivity known as the **critical period.** A newly hatched gosling or duckling will follow practically any moving object it sees. After the first few days of life it no longer follows new objects. The timing of the critical period for the acquisition of this imprinting response, and the crucial aspects of the stimulus – for example whether it consists of visual or auditory cues – vary between species and even according to conditions of rearing in the same species. In nature there is an obvious survival value to newly hatched birds of staying close to their parents, which is what imprinting achieves. There is also evidence that adult sexual behaviour is likely to be directed towards members of the same species as the imprinting object.

The two most interesting considerations with regard to imprinting, for our purposes, are these. First, that many animals show a clear predisposition to acquire behaviours in infancy which have high survival value, and which determine directions and preferences in adult social behaviour. Secondly, that imprinting has a strong innate component, being unaffected by punishment as ordinary learning would be, but maximally affected by the age and maturation of the individual. While it is readily apparent that human infants do not imprint in the same ways as ducklings do – the only following movements they can make are visual not motor, and moving objects which they see early in life may well not be their parents – nonetheless some things in the formation of early attachment bonds between babies and their caretakers are reminiscent of the imprinting phenomenon. The apparent preprogramming of infants to pay attention and respond to smiling faces has already been discussed. Physical contact by holding and cuddling may also prove to be vital early experience, with a disproportionate effect on later ability to feel and show affection towards others. In 1958 Harlow reported that infant rhesus monkeys preferred to spend their time in contact with a towelling covered cylindrical object than with a bare wire one, even when they received their nourishment at the latter. This finding cast doubt on theories of infant-mother attachment which were based solely on the mother's ability to meet the infant's need for food. It suggested that characteristics of hers with less direct relevance to physical survival might be just as important for bond formation. While Harlow's work places emphasis on the tactual stimulation which the mother provides, visual and verbal stimulation have also been indicated as important by researchers such as Bowlby (1971) who are concerned particularly with human infants (see discussion of attachment, Chapter 9).

Experiments depriving babies of tactual stimulation, or severely modifying the form in which it is available, cannot of course be carried out for ethical reasons. As is often the case in trying to understand the dynamics of human behaviour, one can start from the clues provided by animal behaviour and must then proceed to study the rare cases of deprivation occurring naturally in our own species. This means a dependence on small samples and retrospectively collected information, and is most undesirable in terms of reaching firm conclusions about the generality of the recollections and observations made. Vital details may be unobtainable, or may be distorted in the retelling due to memory deficiencies or motivational factors in the reporters. The relatively rare human infant who has suffered from parental neglect, to the extent of being deprived of physical contact, will also have been deprived of much other normal stimulation: not only social but perceptual and motor experiences, and probably nutritionally too. These circumstances make it virtually impossible to determine the relative importance of any single factor, such as bodily contact. We shall see in Chapter 9 that the *continuity* of the person who provides such contact to the baby is a further important variable. For the moment it is relevant to note that the first two years of life are thought to constitute a critical period in emotional development. Good experiences during this time appear to give some immunity to separations later, while a lack of adequate 'mothering' at this stage may preclude the development of a healthy adult capacity to form deep and lasting relationships with others, including becoming a satisfactory parent. Unmothered monkeys made inadequate mothers themselves (Harlow and Harlow 1962), and many 'child-batterers' are found to have suffered severe emotional deprivation during their own early childhood.

Communication

A lot of the preceding discussion, dealing with social signalling and the development of attachment bonds between people, could also have been included as instances of communication. The 'prewired' nature of human behaviour is again evident here. Gestures such as nodding and shaking the head have different meanings in different cultures, but Eibl-Eibesfeldt provides examples of apparently species-specific signals that always have the same significance; these are the rapid eyebrow raise-and-lower of greeting, and the pattern of advance-and-retreat eye contact of flirtatious girls. Other observers of Western culture have written in detail of the 'body language' employed to qualify the words we actually say to each other. Fast (1971) describes the stance of the sexually assertive man, with hips forward and thumbs in beltloops, or the crossed legs and folded arms of the nervous woman. However, our interest at the moment is in communicatory techniques which appear without learning in all members of our species, and once again the early years of life provide the best opportunity to look for such predispositions.

Babies of all social groups and classes cry when they are distressed by hunger or cold, and possibly too by lack of bodily contact. Crying is present from birth, even in deaf babies, and shows a similar progression from reflex to voluntary control as does its more welcome counterpart, smiling. By six to eight weeks of age, infants will cry when their mother leaves the room, and in a few weeks more, in order to summon her. The caretaker can do several things to terminate this very aversive stimulus. Sometimes the sight of the caretaker's face, or the provision of something for the baby to suck, will be adequate. Rhythmical rocking is also effective, and is frequently self-initiated in neglected children. Physical contact such as picking the baby up serves a dual purpose, as the baby can see more interesting things and has a chance to observe and learn.

Fashions change in the advice given to mothers on what to do about a crying baby. Until about the middle of this century, Western mothers were encouraged to interpret the baby's cry as an attempt to impose his or her will, which if acceded to would produce a 'spoiled' infant tyrant. The current view (e.g. Murray 1975) is to regard crying as a natural expression of legitimate needs, not only for feeding or nappy-changing, but for stimulation and physical contact. Bell and Ainsworth (1972) found that infants whose mothers tended to ignore their cries during the first year cried more, and were less competent at communicating in other ways at one year of age, compared with babies with more responsive mothers.

As crying decreases in frequency, after the first three months or so of life, other vocalizations gain more prominence. Cooing sounds appear at six to eight weeks in all babies, including deaf babies with deaf parents. After the first three months, babbling is clearly affected by the environmental response. In normal family-reared children it begins to form part of the infant's capacity to attract and hold the attention of others, whereas in the institution child who never succeeds in that purpose, spontaneous vocalizations decrease. It is hardly surprising therefore that language development shows similar delays, in settings where it has little instrumental value due to lack of adult response.

Before nine or ten months of age, all infants sound alike. After that there is growing distinctiveness in the sounds produced by children growing up in different language environments. By the age of four years the child has virtually mastered the complexities of both pronunciation and grammar in his native language. This remarkable feat of memory and understanding, which allows the child to construct and to comprehend meaningful yet completely novel utterances, has been seen as evidence for prewiring of the human brain for linguistic competence (see Chapter 5). Certainly the evolutionary significance of language to our species is clear upon a brief consideration of how human cultures depend on shared information, transmission of ideas, values and attitudes from one generation to the next, and on the accumulation of knowledge by means of written and spoken records. Furthermore, the possession of language furnishes us with a system of symbols which assist all the higher mental processes, such as reasoning, memory and planning, discussed further in Chapter 5.

If language itself were completely innate, we would all presumably speak the same one. Once again it seems to be a question of a propensity to develop certain biologically useful skills, rather than of a fixed predetermination of behaviour, as we explore the possible role of innate motivational dynamics in human life.

PERCEPTUAL SKILLS

Although the light-sensitive retina of the human eye is two-dimensional, we perceive three-dimensionality; a world of depth as well as width and breadth. There is some suggestion that capacity for depth perception is another innately determined human skill. The **visual cliff** (Gibson 1970) is a piece of apparatus consisting of a heavy sheet of glass, covering a patterned surface which drops away suddenly under one half of the glass. As soon as they can move about, human babies show extreme reluctance to cross to the 'deep' side of this apparatus, as do chickens and goats who can move about independently on the first day of life. However, as parents are aware, whatever innate depth-perception capacities the infant may have are not in fact sufficient to protect him or her from the risk of injury.

The ability to coordinate information about the outside world and the internal sensations of balance and limb position (**proprioceptive feedback**), allows us to develop many complex sensori-motor skills, such as writing, and playing musical instruments and sport. Being able to carry out such complicated actions is very useful to us as a species, and it appears to depend both on physical maturation and on the accumulation of experience. Those born with sensory defects such as blindness or deafness have obvious adaptations to learn; those deprived of varied sensory stimulation early in life, through environmental poverty, may also be disadvantaged in developing problem-solving skills (Wachs, Uzgiris and Hunt 1971).

Other motives and behaviour patterns which are apparently universal to all members of the species and are unlearned, such as needs for food, warmth and sex, are often referred to as primary or biological drives. These are much less likely to be overlooked as important activators of human behaviour than the social and perceptual motives considered so far. The most interesting aspect of these 'primary drives' to a student of human behaviour is their great susceptibility to the effects of learning, in the way any given individual chooses to express and fulfil or not fulfil them. They, and species-specific predispositions to learn some connections more readily than others, will accordingly be discussed in more detail in Chapter 6. Burghardt (1973) and Hess (1970) give excellent reviews of the growing ethological influence in individual and developmental psychology respectively.

BEHAVIOURAL GENETICS

Having now explored some of the possible innate motives in human nature, with a view to discovering which bits of our behaviour, if any, are predetermined by membership of the human species, we may now turn to the question of which bits of our behaviour, if any, are predetermined by virtue of inheritance. Is it true for instance that bad temper is passed from parent to child in the same way as, say, eye colour? Some preliminary thought needs to be given to the reasons for the relatively slow rate of accumulation of knowledge in this field, where everybody has their own theory and indisputable facts are few and far between.

OBSTACLES TO RESEARCH

First, it is essential to face the obstacle posed by the extreme immaturity, cerebrally and behaviourally, of the human newborn. Even before birth occurs, the environment is affecting the biological substrate, perhaps irreversibly. These prenatal effects will be discussed in more detail later. At present it suffices to be aware that no gene can be imagined to determine behaviour in isolation from other, non-genetic, influences. Parents provide the environment as well as the genes, and such factors as the level of nutrition, the values and goals of the family, and the characteristics of the wider society, will all interact with the basic potential provided by inheritance. The determination of the contribution of heredity to intelligence shows this problem clearly: amount of protein in the diet, elaborateness of the speech commonly used at home, and teachers' expectations of academic success, have all been shown to affect measured intelligence (see Chapter 8). And all are at the same time more directly related to family income than to parental intelligence. Thus there is a necessary and constant contamination of the 'pure' genetic determinants of human behaviour.

A second major problem is the relative crudeness of our attempts to quantify human psychological characteristics. 'Bad temper' for instance, to return to our earlier example, is on closer observation an extremely vague term. It seems to imply some tendency towards overt expression of frequent irritable feelings, perhaps by verbal abuse of others, perhaps by physical violence, perhaps neither or both. We cannot in fact say that Tom is seventy-five per cent as bad-tempered as his father, with the sort of confidence necessary for genetical analysis. If we turn to some behavioural index of bad temper, such as being arrested for assault, people will at once object that arrests and bad temper bear only an imperfect relationship to each other, and that the one cannot therefore be taken as a measure of the other.

Although this chosen example may seem rather naive, it does illustrate the problems which arise in determining inheritance of psychological characteristics. The relationship which school performance or a test score bear to intelligence, or that which receiving psychiatric treatment bears to mental illness, are the same kind of relationship which being arrested for assault bears to bad temper. Although intelligence and serious mental illness are the two psychological characteristics for which measurements are the most precise even these measurements remain relatively crude (see Chapters 8 and 11).

Other problems in behavioural genetics research concern the genetics side more than the behavioural. It is difficult to establish the exact genetic constitution of a given individual, except by studying his parents, his offspring, and their offspring. Human matings may or may not be random for the characteristic in question: e.g. people do not choose their mates on the basis of whether or not they can taste the chemical PTC, but on the other hand intelligence and personality factors may be crucial. The ethical barriers to human experimentation, the impossibility of keeping people in controlled environments, and the length of time between generations, are all added problems and go a long way towards explaining why so much research is carried out on animals, even though fruit flies and mice can provide only very limited illumination about people.

GENETIC DETERMINANTS OF INTELLIGENCE

It is in the area of heritable intellectual retardation that some of the clearest evidence in behavioural genetics has been gathered (McClearn and DeFries 1973).

Several biochemical deficiencies, of which the best known is **phenylketonuria** (PKU), may result in mental subnormality. Affected persons lack a particular enzyme without which toxic substances accumulate in the blood. The early detection procedures which are now routine, and the possibility of avoiding deleterious effects on the nervous system by early institution of a special diet, mean that greater numbers of people who are homozygous for the condition (and who may therefore either transmit it to their children or provide a hostile uterine environment for unaffected offspring), are now reaching reproductive age uninstitutionalized, and becoming parents.

Chromosomal anomalies are responsible for another large category of mental retardation and behavioural consequences, the prime example here being the sex-linked conditions (see Money 1975). In **Klinefelter's syndrome,** (usually XXY genotype), affected individuals are males with small testes and low sex drive, and about half are retarded. In the last decade there has been a great deal of research on the 'supermale' XYY genotype, after it was first noticed amongst men who were very tall and instutionalized for violent criminal behaviour (Jarvik, Klodin and Matsuyama 1973). Although this genotype may predispose to over-aggressiveness, possibly through the social and psychological effects of extreme height, some XYY males nevertheless fail to demonstrate violent propensities. Field and Faed (1974) neatly illustrate the possible interweaving of genetic and environmental influences in their case report of a delinquent XYY boy of fourteen.

Sufferers from **Turner's syndrome** are short, sexually infantile females (genotype XO) who have highly specific defects in problem-solving ability, in the area of reasoning about spatial relationships and in number skills.

Down's syndrome (trisomy 21) is the most common of several non-fatal autosomal anomalies all resulting in physical abnormalities, severe mental retardation and, sometimes, reduced life expectancy. With several of them there is a clear association with maternal age. The number of Down's infants born would be reduced by more than half if there were no new mothers older than thirty-five.

The great majority of intellectually handicapped people in our society are not victims of one of the abnormalities described so far, but of lesser degrees of retardation with a clearly familial incidence. The role of inheritance in intelligence, or perhaps more exactly the *relative* role of inheritance in comparison with environmental influences, such as nutrition and educational opportunity, has been hotly debated during the last few years (see Chapter 8). Comparisons of **monozygotic** (MZ: identical) and **dizygotic** (DZ: fraternal) twins, reared together or apart, have been numerous, as have studies of the degree of correlation in test scores between parents and natural versus adopted children, and so on. Progress in understanding may accelerate in view of the recent realization that total score on an 'intelligence' test is probably far too gross a measure to be really useful. Specific abilities such as verbal fluency, memory, and spatial and quantitative reasoning, may be a more appropriate area to test for heritability of mental characteristics.

INHERITANCE OF SEVERE MENTAL ILLNESS

Psychosis is the summary term used to describe distinctively 'insane' behaviour in which there appears to be a qualitative difference from the normal in the psychological processes of thinking, learning and emotion. Although definitional problems abound, especially in borderline cases, there is fairly satisfactory evidence for genetic influences in the development of both schizophrenia and related serious mental illness, particularly manic-depressive psychoses (see Chapter 7). However, although the incidence of schizophrenia is higher amongst blood relatives of a known case – and this is true whether they have lived in the same household or not – whether the predisposition will be expressed still varies according to environmental conditions, such as stressfulness and the adequacy of psychological support.

Alcoholism is another serious medical and behavioural problem for which there is strong evidence of a genetic predisposition (DeFries and Plomin 1978).

FRONTIERS OF BEHAVIOURAL GENETICS

For an increasing number of heritable defects, accurate forecasts can now be made concerning the likelihood that a given child, conceived but not yet born, will be affected. **Amniocentesis** is a new technique whereby a sample of the amniotic fluid provides information about the chromosomal make-up of the foetus, at an early enough stage of pregnancy for therapeutic abortion to be possible. Genetic counselling has thus made a considerable advance over the earlier period, when only the odds of having an affected child could be calculated, and the prospective parents were left to make decisions on that basis. The routine availability of such advance warning, for women at risk of bearing a stigmatized child, could reduce the frequency of such births and their accompanying demands on the family and society. Awareness of the increased risk of Down's syndrome in children born to women over thirty-five, for instance, may be one factor in the current trend towards an earlier end to childbearing. If, on the other hand, women all began to reproduce young, the incidence of diseases which have a later onset, such as schizophrenia, might increase.

The idea of deliberate manipulations of the gene pool to 'improve' human genetic stock has been regarded with equally great optimism and suspicion by different thinkers. The 'racial purity' programmes of the Nazi party, involving the extermination of a wide variety of ideologically undesirable members of the community, damned forever in many minds the idea of improving the health or adjustment of a social group by selective breeding. A slightly different question arises in the case of artificial insemination by donor, where it would be theoretically possible for the sperm and ova of 'superior' men and women respectively to be preserved for this purpose. There are philosophical difficulties, however, in deciding which eminent members of society should be afforded this honour, and of the likely end result of selecting artificial parents on the grounds of their intelligence, creativity, happiness, or whichever other qualities might be thought desirable.

OTHER EARLY ACTING INFLUENCES

CONSTITUTIONAL DIFFERENCES

From birth, individuals differ in how active they are, how good tempered, how long they will pay attention to one thing, and in which physiological system they show responses to stress – the gastro-intestinal tract, skin, respiratory apparatus or cardiovascular system. The exact extent to which these congenital (i.e. present at birth) differences are inherited is not quite clear. All the factors mentioned will make a difference to what sort of baby the parents find they are dealing with, and how well or badly their expectations about their baby are fulfilled. Mismatches between, for example, the activity levels of parents and child can place strains upon the relationship from the start. Although it is widely accepted that early childhood experience has significant long term effects, exactly how and when it does so is still being explored by researchers (see e.g. Mussen, Conger and Kagan 1974).

EARLY ENVIRONMENTAL EFFECTS

Although our heritage as members of the human species, and as members of a specific family, may predispose us to learn or to respond in certain ways, it is important to remember that even at the moment of birth there has been a significant period of interaction between the genetic material and environmental influences. The womb is rhythmically noisy and allows the unborn baby a certain amount of movement. More important, however, as an influence on development, is the chemical composition of the mother's blood. The placental membranes are not an impermeable barrier, and therefore any drugs (including tobacco) that the mother may take during pregnancy, or at the time of the labour and birth, may affect the foetus. X-rays, illnesses such as rubella or syphilis, malnutrition, and Rh incompatibility between the mother and baby can all have harmful effects. Emotional upset in the mother also changes her blood chemistry, and has been shown to increase the irritability of the foetus (Sontag 1966).

Whether the mother feels happy or resentful about her pregnancy will affect not only her emotional state during it, but also the way she is likely to treat her new baby. Extreme neglect is one obvious example of environmental factors influencing development, but so far it is not known exactly to what extent lesser degrees of impatience or disinterest towards the baby may prejudice cognitive and emotional development.

During the delivery process itself the main danger to the infant is lack of oxygen to the brain (**anoxia**), often due either to too much pressure on the head or to failure to start independent breathing. Anoxia kills brain cells and can result in paralysis, mental retardation, or various milder conditions (often referred to as **minimal cerebral dysfunction**), characterized by clumsiness and poor concentration. All of these can limit the child's potential, or make adjustment to life more difficult.

Delivery difficulties, prematurity, and all the other prenatal complications discussed, are three or four times more likely to affect working-class than middle-class women. After birth too, the food eaten at home, the amount of appropriate sensory and linguistic stimulation of the child, and the availability of medical care, are all likely to vary in homes of different socio-economic status. As well as these physical differences, the environments of individual children will differ in the sorts of behaviour which are regarded as 'normal' or 'abnormal', including the sorts of goals and expectations the individual should hold. In the light of this multiplicity of influences, it is hardly surprising that our understanding of biologically-based determinants of human behaviour is a relatively underdeveloped area, with fascinating possibilities for both research and practice in medicine and allied social and biological sciences.

SUMMARY

Although humans do not show the rigid instinctive behaviour seen in other species, there is evidence of species-specific predispositions to learn and to respond in certain ways. This is particularly so in the areas of behaviour concerned with group-living skills: a) bond formation (infant smiling, need for physical contact) and b) communication (expressive gestures, infant crying, language); and with perceptual skills: a) depth perception and b) coordination of information from inside and outside the body, and between different sensory systems.

Despite serious difficulties in collecting and interpreting facts, genetic determinants of human behaviour are beginning to be understood, with most information so far concerning the inheritance of intellectual ability and serious mental illness. Amniocentesis and other advances make efficient genetic planning more of a possibility, and the demand for knowledge more pressing. The role of inheritance tends to be obscured by the many pre- and post-natal environmental influences which affect development.

TERMS AND CONCEPTS

instinct
ethology
Fixed Action Pattern
sign stimuli
imprinting
critical period

visual cliff
proprioceptive feedback
phenylketonuria
Klinefelter's syndrome
Turner's syndrome
Down's syndrome
monozygotic
dizygotic
psychosis
amniocentesis
anoxia
minimal cerebral dysfunction

FOR DISCUSSION

1. Collect some instances of use of the term 'instinct' in the media. What meanings does the term seem to have, and how much explanatory force?

2. How is human ethology different from anthropology, and what areas of knowledge about people are likely to be illuminated by each?

3. Recall and share the experience you have had with very young babies. If you haven't had much, perhaps you should try to arrange for some. Watch particularly for:
   - crying and smiling by the infant: the initiating stimuli and terminators,
   - your own emotional responses.

4. How would you advise a new mother to cope with the baby's crying? Why?

5. What is the place of behavioural genetics in genetic counselling?

SUGGESTED READING

Hess: a concise and useful introduction.
Burghardt: slightly more technical.
Eibl-Eibesfeldt, especially Chapter 18: slightly more technical.
Mussen, Conger and Kagan, Chapter 3: good introduction.
McClearn and DeFries, Chapters 8, 10 and 11: useful for those with some background in genetics.

REFERENCES

Bell, S. and Ainsworth, M. 1972. Infant crying and maternal responsiveness. *Child Development* **43**, 1171–90.

Bowlby, J. 1971. *Attachment and Loss* **1** *Attachment*. Penguin: Harmondsworth.

Burghardt, G. M. 1973. Instinct and innate behaviour: Toward an ethological psychology. In *The Study of Behaviour: Learning, Motivation, Emotion and Instinct*. J. A. Nevin and G. S. Reynolds (eds), 322–400. Glenview, Ill.: Scott, Foresman & Co.

DeFries, J. C. and Plomin, R. 1978. Behavioural genetics. *Ann. Rev. Psychol.*, **29**, 473–515.

Eibl-Eibesfeldt, I. 1970. *Ethology: The Biology of Behaviour*. N.Y.: Holt Rinehart & Winston.

Fast, J. 1971. *Body Language*. London: Pan Books.

Field, M. and Faed, J. W. 1974. 47, XYY chromosome constitution, physical growth and psychological disturbance – a case study. *J. Child Psychol. Psychiat.* **15**, 323–7.

Fraiberg, S. 1975. The development of human attachments in infants blind from birth. *Merrill-Palmer Quart.* **21**, 315–34.

Gibson, E. J. 1970. The development of perception as an adaptive process. *Amer. Scientist* **58**, 98–107.

Goodall, J. 1971. *In the Shadow of Man*. London: Collins.

Harlow, H. 1958. The nature of love. *Amer. Psychol.* **13**, 673–85.

Harlow, H. F. and Harlow M. K. 1962. The effect of rearing conditions on behaviour. *Bulletin of the Menninger Clinic* **26**, 213–24.

Hess, E. H. 1970. Ethology and developmental psychology. In P. H. Mussen (ed.) *Carmichael's Manual of Child Psychology* **1** (3rd edn) 1–38. New York: Wiley.

Jarvik, L. F., Klodin, V. and Matsuyama, S. S. 1973. Human aggression and the extra Y chromosome: Fact or fantasy? *Amer. Psychol.* **28**, 674–82.

Jones, N. B. 1972. *Ethological Studies of Child Behaviour*. Cambridge: University Press.

Jones, N. B. 1975. Ethology, anthropology and childhood. In R. Fox (ed.) *Biosocial Anthropology* 69–92. London: Dent.

Mead, M. 1950. *Male and Female*. Harmondsworth: Penguin.

McClearn, G. E. and DeFries, J. C. 1973. *Introduction to Behavioural Genetics*. San Francisco: W. H. Freeman.

Money, J. 1975. Human behaviour cytogenetics: Review of psychopathology in three syndromes – 47, XXY; 47, XYY; and 45, X. *J. Sex Res.* **11**, 181–200.

Murray, A. D. 1975. Infant crying and communication. *Aust. Psychol.* **10**, 303–8.

Mussen, P. H., Conger, J. J. and Kagan, J. 1974. *Child Development and Personality*, (4th edn). New York: Harper & Row.

Schaffer, H. R. 1971. *The Growth of Sociability*. Harmondsworth: Penguin.

Sontag, L. W. 1966. Implications of fetal behaviour and environment for adult personalities. *Annals of the New York Academy of Sciences* **134**, 782–6.

Tinbergen, N. 1951. *The Study of Instinct*. Oxford: Clarendon Press.

Wachs, T. D., Uzgiris, I. C. and Hunt, J. McV. 1971. Cognitive development in infants of different age levels and from different environmental backgrounds: An exploratory investigation. *Merrill-Palmer Quart.* **17**, 283–317.

Chapter 4

Knowing the World: Perception

Perception is the whole process by which information about the outside world impinges on the sensory organs and is then decoded and interpreted by the brain, resulting in a conscious experience. It is one aspect of cognition – all the mental activities which enable us to know and make decisions about the world.

In this chapter we concentrate on the psychological aspects of perception. The physiology of the sense organs will doubtless form part of your curriculum elsewhere, so here the focus is on how perception is affected by experience and motivation, and what it means to the person when there is some dysfunction in the perceptual process. This may be due either to deficient sensory apparatus or to problems at the interpretative end. We also give special attention to the perception of pain and physical discomfort, which is the most frequent reason why people consult a doctor.

SENSATION AND PERCEPTION

Vision dominates other senses in our species, and is the sense upon which we place greatest reliance if there is any conflict in the input data. 'Seeing with my own eyes' is the ultimate test of reality. Hearing also tells us about more or less distant events, and through the auditory channel we can process large amounts of information with great efficiency. Much less complex, but no less highly valued, information about nearer events comes to us through smell (olfaction), taste (gustation) and the skin (tactile experience). The way in which these latter types of stimulation affect emotional responses is a fascinating but poorly understood area. Certainly smell has often been claimed as a potent sexual releaser, by neuro-physiologists as well as by perfume manufacturers, and Montagu

(1971) has compiled a thought–provoking book on the intense – psychological significance of the skin and touching.

Proprioceptive feedback tells us about our own bodies. **Kinaesthesia** is the information we get about the position and movements of our muscles, tendons and joints, from nerve endings there. **Static sensitivity** or balance informs us about how we are oriented in three-dimensional space (e.g. up, down, leaning, accelerating), and is mediated by the semicircular canals of the ear. **Interoceptive** stimuli arise from the internal organs of digestion, respiration and circulation. Although these are of great importance in a person's experience of his or her current state of health and emotion, little research has been carried out by psychologists on the mechanics and individual differences normally apparent in this perceptual mode. Mechanical recording and display of information about internal processes through biofeedback (see Chapter 6) has opened up the possibility of learned control of blood pressure and muscle tension, for example, therapeutic purposes.

The human body is programmed to perceive *changes* in the internal and external environments. Unchanging stimulation tends to produce **habituation** of the receptors involved, such that we are no longer conscious of the sensory experience. An unfortunate example of this is the cook who cannot fully enjoy his or her own culinary products due to adaptation of the olfactory system during time spent cooking. Where there is maximum monotony of stimulation, as in **sensory deprivation** experiments carefully minimizing the sensory input (Zubek 1969), distortions occur both in perception and in problem-solving capacity.

The neural pathways which transmit sensory information to the brain for decoding are complex, and at once remove the possibility of any rigid one-to-one correspondence between our percept (conscious experience) and 'reality'. Sensitivity and attention both limit our capacity to perceive. First, our sensitivity is such that only changes of a certain magnitude will be perceptible. Above the **threshold** level at which a stimulus can be perceived at all, such as the brightness of a light source in a dark room, increments occur in units called 'just noticeable differences', usually abbreviated to **j.n.d.**s. The size of the j.n.d. is determined, at least over the middle ranges of stimulation, by the size of the change in relation to the original level of stimulation (such that the brighter the light, the greater a change will be needed in order for the difference to be noticeable).

Secondly, perception is determined by *attention.* The vast majority of sights, sounds, smells, and skin and proprioceptive sensations pass us by without becoming part of our conscious awareness. Perhaps you can stop to imagine how chaotic and distracting mental life would be without perceptual selectivity. We may as a species be set to attend particularly to size, repetition, intensity and contrast, and to certain patterns of stimulation; apart from that, previous experiences and current motivational state are prime influences.

EFFECTS OF THE ENVIRONMENT, MATURATION AND LEARNING

Animals have been reared from birth in environments offering enriched or impoverished amounts of stimulation, in the search for clues to the relative importance of early experience in human development (Sluckin 1971). Dogs failed to show normal avoidance responses to pain-producing stimuli, such as a pinprick or a flame, if they had been deprived in puppyhood of normal tactual experience (Melzack and Scott 1957). As usual, direct evidence from humans is sparse, but White (1971) was able to show improvements in acquisition of grasping skill in babies provided with a visually stimulating environment, compared with those whose usual dull surroundings in an orphanage were not altered. People who gained sight in adulthood for the first time, due to cataract removal, proved to Senden (1960) that the ability to make sense of visual information is a learned one and may be exceedingly difficult to learn after early childhood. Once again a critical period for certain experiences is implied.

Babies seem predisposed to perceive depth and object **constancy,** as shown by experiments such as the visual cliff described in Chapter 3, and others where an ingenious design allowed Bower (1966) to test young babies for how similar they perceived cubes of varying real and retinal sizes to be. The newborn's focal length is fixed at 20–22.5 cm (8–9 in.) (the normal distance between the eyes of mother and baby in the feeding situation), and everything beyond this must appear blurred. Over the first three months babies learn to control the eye musculature to focus efficiently on objects at any distance. Novelty, black-white contrast and movement are the most powerful determinants of infant attention, which of course means that human eyes and faces are very interesting and rewarding objects to look at.

By aptitude and study people can learn perceptual discriminations of increasing sensitivity, as shown by wine-tasters. Also, we can learn different ways of coordinating sensory information, for example the adjustment made to wearing lenses which invert visual data.

More interesting for the understanding of normal perceptual dynamics is the whole area of perceptual expectancies and constancy. Within limits we see things as constant in size, shape, brightness and colour despite changes in viewing distance, spatial orientation and illumination. The perspective effect in drawings and paintings, so noticeable by its absence in primitive and children's art, relies on a calculated use of distance cues of which we are not ordinarily aware such as the convergence of parallel lines. Examples of normal visual 'illusion', such as in the figure below, give us some evidence of how we learn to perceive what is familiar and expected.

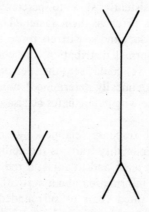

The Muller-Lyer illusion. To those raised in a 'carpentered world', the vertical line on the right appears to be longer than that on the left. Gregory (1966) suggests that this demonstrates the operation of size constancy adjustments normally made respectively for the outer and inner corners of buildings.

Resolving ambiguity by relying on past experience, as exemplified by the perceptual constancies, is a useful cognitive short cut which will occasionally lead to mistakes. In the diagnosis of illness it requires a positive effort to remain alert for, and even to seek out, evidence which disconfirms our first hypothesis. Habits of perception and the associated emotional responses also become important in the field of person perception, as we shall see in Chapter 16, where accent or skin colour may call forth a stereotyped pattern of response. Social situations are particularly likely to involve the sort of ambiguity, coupled with the need for its quick resolution, which encourage us to fall back on our prejudices.

EFFECTS OF CURRENT NEEDS AND PERSONALITY

Again, especially in situations of restricted information, what is perceived will be influenced to some extent by the motivational condition of the perceiver. 'Not wanting to know' can literally decrease the likelihood of finding out. Illustrative experiments on this **perceptual defence** syndrome have flashed words briefly to subjects, who found it much harder to read emotionally charged words than neutral ones (Dixon 1966). There was controversy, however, about the reliability and size of this effect, with a tendency to find that although some people are consistently slow to perceive 'dirty' or anxiety-arousing words, others perceive them faster. These types have been characterized as **repressors** and **sensitizers** respectively and, at least at the extremes of the normal distribution, the concept seems to have some validity. Thus we could see the person who suffers from 'hysterical' (i.e. non-organically determined) blindness as an extreme repressor, while the one who hallucinates accusatory voices may be an extreme sensitizer.

Another perceptual response, claimed by some investigators to reveal more general personality traits, is the ability to find simple line figures within complex ones, and to adjust a rod to a vertical position even when misleading information about verticality is being provided, by being seated in a tilted chair or surrounded by a tilted 'room'. People who can do these things have been labelled **field-independent** by Witkin *et al.* (1962), and are held to have a more analytical, independent approach to life in general than do conventional, uncritical **field-dependent** people. As with most personality measures, the clearest predictions can be made only about the relatively small number of individuals who gain extreme scores.

Although the connection with Freud's concept of repression (active failure to perceive psychologically-threatening information) generated much interest and research effort, experimental work on the motivational and personality determinants of perception has been bedevilled by the following problem: perception can only be demon-strated via some further overt response, such as verbal report, which in turn is affected by situational factors. Thus many questions remain unanswered, for instance about the degree of consciousness involved in perceptual selectivity. It does seem true, however, that where perceptual conditions are less than optimal (e.g. where insufficient information is provided), expectancy effects assert themselves and people will respond in terms of their normal habits. **Projective** tests of personality are founded on that assumption (see Chapter 11): the objects 'seen' in an inkblot (Rorschach), or the motives attributed to a human figure (Thematic Apperception Test), are treated as clues to the testee's dominant preoccupations and modes of organizing and interpreting the world.

At this point it is appropriate to consider perception in the *absence* of what would normally be regarded as adequate evidence: 'extra-sensory' perception (**ESP**). The belief in telepathy, clairvoyance and prophetic visions, which is widespread amongst non-scientists, has proved difficult to validate under laboratory conditions. When proper controls for the effects of chance and for non-verbal communication are instituted, ESP effects are fragile. While the burden of scientific proof still rests clearly on the believers rather than on the disbelievers, many ordinary people will be impressed by one or two instances of what they interpret as ESP, overlooking other possibilities such as statistical coincidence, intuition (unaware sensitivity to non-verbal cues), or self-fulfilling prophecy effects (behaving in such a way as to increase the likelihood of predictions coming true). In a way, the ESP controversy illustrates rather neatly the human tendency to attend to novelty and the unexpected, and once a hypothesis is formed, to disregard discrepant evidence. You will perhaps appreciate how intimate is the relationship between perception and other forms of cognitive activity, such as memory and decision-making (see next chapter).

EFFECTS OF SENSORY DEFECTS

The blocking of normal perceptual processes, by deficiencies in the sensory reception apparatus, always has both social and cognitive effects. It is hard for those with normal capacities to imagine how radically different is the blind or deaf person's experience of the world. The age of the person afflicted is a crucial variable, as is the degree of deficiency. Sudden blindness is probably what adults fear most, but deafness before language has been acquired is almost certainly the most devastating handicap, as it affects the capacity to master or understand speech, and therefore places limitations on all the cognitive processes normally mediated by linguistic symbols. The child born blind or deaf often has to face, in addition to the handicap itself, parental responses of shock, depression and possible guilt, ambivalence, psychological withdrawal, oversolicitude, or denial of the problem. Such a family is clearly in a crisis situation and needs readily accessible counselling and special educational services. Fraiberg (1971) has described how rejected parents of a blind baby feel when the baby does not return their smiles, and the corresponding isolation and emotional deprivation which may blight the baby's chances for personal adjustment. (She also describes a successful intervention programme.)

More minor visual and auditory defects may still affect the sufferer's self-esteem, and the response of the social environment. Perhaps because it can easily be attributed to lack of attention, failure to hear seems to cause hostility, whereas shortsightedness may, in children at least, be the subject of ridicule. Anybody who has to face the loss of sensory capacities for whatever reason can be expected to undergo a painful grief reaction, severe in proportion to the suddenness and unexpectedness of the loss. Loss of visual and auditory acuity can lead to confusion in elderly people, or to pathological suspiciousness (paranoia), where a person gets the impression that others are trying to keep things from him by lowering their voices. In the next chapter we shall look in more detail at how perceptual information is used in cognition.

PERCEPTUAL DISORDERS

Illusions are misperceptions of a real stimulus, as when a child is convinced that leaves tapping his window at night are a monster trying to get in at him, or when a face in the crowd is mistaken for the friend for whom one is waiting. It may often be difficult to distinguish between perceptual illusions and perception distorted by needs and personality factors ('wishful thinking'), as described earlier. The classic 'visual illusions', such as the Muller-Lyer figure shown earlier, are slightly different in that the misperception is usual rather than exceptional, within a society.

Hallucinations involve perception in the absence of relevant external stimulation. Epileptics, for example, sometimes experience olfactory or gustatory hallucinations as part of the 'aura' which warns of an impending seizure. In bereavement, people may hear the voice or footsteps, or see the face, of the one who is being mourned. Sometimes visions may occur when falling asleep (hypnogogic), or in the process of waking up (hypnopompic). All these occur occasionally in well-adjusted people and, like dreams, only show us the depth of our ignorance about how the brain functions. Hallucinations may also occur during states of drug intoxication: LSD, mescaline and psilocybin are known as hallucinogenic drugs, and alcohol may be associated with unpleasant visual and tactual hallucinations.

In some cases hallucinations, particularly auditory ones, are a sign of serious mental disorder, and may characterize states of unrealistic suspicion known as **paranoia**, or of **mania** (hyperactivity and grandiosity). In these cases they tend to co-occur with **delusions** (fixed wrong beliefs), often concerning persecution and omnipotence respectively. Again we see the closeness of the link between perception and thought processes.

PAIN PERCEPTION AND CONTROL

Pain is a percept of obvious relevance to medicine, and dramatizes again the importance of non-physiological factors.

MEASUREMENT OF PAIN

Like other percepts, pain is a subjective and therefore essentially unverifiable experience. Its occurrence in another can only be suspected, never proved, although the observer's confidence that pain exists in another may be strong. Pain is communicated to others by a variety of means, including verbal report, wincing, flinching, groaning, moving away from the source of pain (or possibly, attacking it), and non-specific signs of physiological arousal (see Chapter 7) such as pallor, sweating, muscular tension, and changes in heart rate and gastric activity. All of the above behaviours can of course be conditioned (see Chapter 6) and can therefore occur independently of pain, whether voluntarily or not. The difficulties of measuring pain objectively have hindered research and have forced investigators to use subjective measures such as rating scales and maximum tolerance levels.

DETERMINANTS OF PAIN PERCEPTION

Like other percepts, pain is not an invariant and totally predictable response to a definable external stimulus, in this case tissue damage.

Pain is 'a psychological experience' (Weisenberg 1977, p. 1008), and can fail to occur where there is bodily damage, or can occur in its absence. In the excitement of battle or a sports match, wounds and injuries go unnoticed. A concerted redirection of attention such as occurs in hypnosis, or competing stimulation such as provided by biting the lip, hot or cold packs, 'auditory analgesia' and perhaps acupuncture, all demonstrate how pain may be reduced by diverting attention from it. Imagining pleasant scenes, or numbness in the stimulated finger, have also been found effective (Chaves and Barber 1974). Pain is often felt to be worse at night, when the sufferer has no competing stimulation, and arthritis is felt more severely by housebound than by employed victims.

Conversely, 'phantom limb' pain which is experienced as emanating from about thirty-five per cent of amputated limbs, and the sympathetic aches and pains, especially in the gut and teeth, which are frequently reported by husbands of women in or near labour (Trethowan and Conlon 1965), show that tissue damage is not a necessary precursor for pain. The non-correspondence of pain and tissue damage is a clinical problem, in that it reduces the reliability of pain control methods which simply interrupt the pain 'pathways', for example by drugs or surgery. The most influential theory of pain perception has been the one proposed by Melzack and Wall (1965), concerning how cognitive processes open or close the neurophysiological 'gate' of pain perception. Although since modified and subjected to serious criticism, this theory valuably continues to stimulate interest and research.

Pain experience is affected by learning as well as by attention. Different social and ethnic groups report different amounts and locations of pain (Zborowski 1969), and customs differ about the pain regarded as normal during childbirth in different societies across the world. This can partly be attributed to different cultural values – for instance to 'keeping a stiff upper lip' (White Anglo-Saxon Protestant). It may be partly a question of *willingness to report* pain, as well perhaps as learned interpretation of given sensations as painful, rather than differences in capacity to experience pain. This is a useful distinction to make: the **pain threshold** is the lowest point of intensity at which a stimulus is perceived as painful, while **pain tolerance** is the upper limit of what a person will voluntarily tolerate. The former does not vary a great deal on different occasions, and shows little variation between people, except that there is some tendency for greater sensitivity to be shown by women, old people,

Negroes and Orientals (Sternbach 1975). Pain tolerance on the other hand is easily manipulated by altering the individual's psychological state, by means of drugs, distraction, anxiety or motivation. **Pain expression** is the readiness to complain of pain, and is affected by personality characteristics (introverts for instance being more stoical than extraverts), and by cultural background as discussed above.

An obvious obstacle to our understanding of pain is the difficulty in carrying out experiments which are both ethical and valid. Painful stimuli used in the laboratory include electric shock, pressure on a finger, or immersion of the hand in icy water. Not only does the subject know that he can terminate the pain at any time by withdrawing his cooperation in the experiment, but the pain is being carefully controlled by an experimenter, and will end at the end of the experiment. The subject's situation is very different from that of somebody who suffers a prolonged, extensive pain which may be of unknown origin, not controllable by anyone, and possibly representing a serious threat to the pursuit of normal daily activities or even life itself.

The *meaning* of the pain experience to the individual is a central issue in pain perception, and one which must be constantly explored. The doctor needs to be aware of the relativity of attitudes towards pain; this will free him or her from the unthinking assumption that his own childhood-learned attitudes are 'right' in an absolute sense. It will make him better able to respect and understand the views of patients who feel it appropriate to express pain more (or less) freely, and to show greater or less anxiety about its future implications than he would.

As we have seen earlier in this chapter, all perceptions are organized to produce meaning, usually well before any conscious awareness is involved. We see objects as constant in physical attributes, despite many actual variations in the stimulation received by the retina, without ever being aware of learning or deciding to do so. Similarly, painful sensations are interpreted and organized at a preconscious level in a way which affects the final conscious percept. Positive meanings reduce the anxiety and the awareness of pain stimuli. Examples are the soldier whose wound means he will be sent behind the lines to recover in a hospital (and who therefore needs less morphia than a civilian undergoing a similar operation), the masochist for whom pain is associated with sexual pleasure, the 'operations addict' for whom pain is associated with attention and care from others, the woman in labour for whom pain means progress towards the birth of her much desired baby, or the martyr for whom pain means ecstatic closeness to God. On the other hand, negative meanings, or confusion and uncertainty, all of which intensify anxiety, increase pain. Anxiety may cause pain by itself, as when muscular tension lead to neck and back pains and headaches, or clenched jaws or tooth-grinding lead to facial pain. Anxiety may secondly increase pain by focussing attention on sensations which would not normally be counted as painful, sometimes even including those of the pulse or the digestive process. Thirdly, as parental disapproval, illness and other losses tend to be temporally associated with anxiety and with physical pain, they can all come to evoke each other by conditioning (thus e.g. threats of loss of love may cause physical pain).

PAIN CONTROL

Distinctions have been drawn in the past between 'organic' and 'psychological' or even 'imaginary' pain, with the implication that only pain for which there is an obvious neurophysiological reason counts as 'real'. Viewing pain as a perceptual response, and making the distinction between its threshold, tolerance and expression, allows for a much more sophisticated understanding of pain complaints, and also stimulates ideas about how to treat intractable pain. Pain expression is an operant behaviour (i.e. one which is affected in frequency by its consequences: see Chapter 6), and therefore under the control of environmental influences such as reward and punishment. Behavioural methods of pain control are being developed and are described in detail in Chapter 12. The strong psychological element in pain perception means that even surgical and pharmacological control methods vary in effectiveness according to the psychological state of the recipient.

Counter-irritation, in the form of pressure or electrical stimulation at certain peripheral and central sites, can decrease pain by blocking, according to the gate-control theory. The precise mechanisms of acupuncture are still not fully understood. The fact that electrical stimulation of the brain has an analgesic effect similar to that of morphine (to the extent of being counteracted by the same drugs), led to research which has isolated a naturally-occurring morphine-like brain chemical known as enkephalin (Hughes 1975). The presence of such powerful pain controllers in the brain itself begins to explain how pain is so dependent on psychological factors, and why, for instance, reducing anxiety and changing the meaning of pain can diminish the intensity of the experience.

Anxious people are more suggestible, and accordingly more responsive to the far-from-inert 'placebo' power of the doctor-patient relationship. Expectations of pain relief can become a self-fulfilling prophecy. Relaxation training aided by biofeedback has been used to reduce pain caused by muscular tension, but there are several other methods of anxiety reduction which need no special equipment at all. Reassurance about the availability of analgesic drugs actually leads to lower patient demand for them (Pilowsky and Bond 1969). A feeling of control, and of knowing what is going on and what to expect, is a very effective anxiety reducer for humans. Predictability and advance preparation for pain reduce its impact, a fact which is exploited widely from ante-natal education (Macfarlane 1977), to post-operative recovery (Cohen and Lazarus 1973).

SUMMARY

Perception involves reception and interpretation of information from both external (world) and internal (body) environments. This information about changes is necessary for the brain to function efficiently, as well as for our awareness of what is going on. Perception is an active and selective process, not fully determined by the physical parameters of sense data. Attention determines what is perceived, and is in turn dependent upon motivational and personality characteristics and on expectations developed from past experience. Defects in the sensory apparatus, of greater or less severity, mean a corresponding impairment in perceptual capacity which has both social and cognitive consequences. Perceptual disorders include illusions and hallucinations, and the latter can in some circumstances indicate serious mental illness. Pain provides a clear example of how the conscious experience is related to cognitive factors such as attitudes and the meaning of the situation to the individual, as well as to sensory input.

TERMS AND CONCEPTS

kinaesthesia
static sensitivity
interoceptive

habituation
sensory deprivation
threshold
j.n.d.
constancy
perceptual defence
repressors/sensitizers
field-independent/ -dependent
projective personality test
ESP
illusion
hallucination
paranoia
mania
delusion
pain threshold, tolerance, and expression

FOR DISCUSSION

1.   Give examples from your own experience of visual or other perceptual illusions, hallucinations or other 'misperceptions'.
2.   On the basis of talking to affected people, if possible, list the effects of sensory deficits of different types, severity and age of onset.
3.   What determines how much pain is felt? What determines what a person does about the pain he or she feels? Think about your own experiences as well as research findings. Why might there be differences between them?
4.   Psychological factors affecting the degree of pain felt during childbirth is one specialized question important to women of childbearing age and their medical advisers. Search the relevant literature for information. (You may use the *Psychological Abstracts* and/or *Index Medicus*, or your instructor may refer you to a recent article as a starter.)

SUGGESTED READING

Gregory: introduction to psychology of visual perception.
Weisenberg: comprehensive recent review of pain and its control by psychological methods.

REFERENCES

Bower, T. G. R. 1966. The visual world of infants. *Sci. Amer.* **215,** 80–92.

Chaves, J. F. and Barber, T. X. 1974. Cognitive strategies, experimenter modeling, and expectation in the attenuation of pain. *J. abnorm. Psychol.* **83,** 356–63.

Cohen, F. and Lazarus, R. S. 1973. Active coping processes, coping dispositions, and recovery from surgery. *Psychosom. Med.* **35,** 375–89.

Dixon, N. F. 1966. The beginnings of perception. In B. M. Foss (ed.) *New Horizons in Psychology* 45–67. Harmondsworth: Penguin.

Fraiberg, S. 1971. Intervention in infancy: A program for blind infants. *J. Amer. Acad. Child Psychiat.* **10,** 381–405.

Gregory, R. L. 1966. *Eye and Brain: The Psychology of Seeing.* New York: McGraw Hill.

Hughes, J. 1975. Isolation of an endogenous compound from the brain with pharmocological properties similar to morphine. *Brain Res.* **88,** 295–308.

Macfarlane, A. 1977. *The Psychology of Childbirth.* Cambridge, Mass.: Harvard Univ. Press.

Melzack, R. and Scott, T. H. 1957. The effects of early experience on the response to pain. *J. Comp. physiol. Psychol.* **50,** 155–61.

Melzack, R. and Wall, P. D. 1965. Pain mechanisms: A theory. *Science* **150,** 971–9.

Montagu, A. 1971. *Touching: The Human Significance of the Skin.* New York: Harper & Row.

Pilowsky, I. and Bond, M. R. 1969. Pain and its management in malignant disease: Elucidation of staff-patient transactions. *Psychosom. Med.* **31,** 400–4.

Senden, M. V. 1960. *Space and Sight.* (trans. by P. Heath) New York: Free Press.

Sluckin, E. (ed.) 1971. *Early Learning and Early Experience.* Middlesex: Penguin.

Sternbach, R. A. 1975. Psychophysiology of pain. *Int. J. Psychiat. Med.* **6,** 63–73.

Trethowan, W. H. and Conlon, M. F. 1965. The 'couvade' syndrome. *Brit. J. Psychiat.* **111,** 57–66.

Weisenberg, M. 1977. Pain and pain control. *Psychol. Bull.* **84,** 1008–44.

White, P. L. 1971. *Human Infants: Experience and Psychological Development.* Englewood Cliffs, N.J.: Prentice-Hall.

Witkin, H. A., Dyk, R. B., Faterson, H. F., Goodenough, D. R. and Karp, S. A. 1962. *Psychological Differentiation.* New York: Wiley.

Zborowski, M. 1969. *People in Pain.* San Francisco: Jossey-Bass.

Zubek, J. P. 1969. *Sensory Deprivation: Fifteen Years of Research.* New York: Appleton-Century-Crofts.

Chapter 5

Making Sense of the World: Thinking and Language

Having considered in the last chapter how information is received by the body and organized into a meaningful experience, we may now approach the question of how we process this information and use it as a basis for action. **Cognition** summarizes that process, and here we look in detail at the mechanics of thinking and language. Disorders in these two broad classes of cognitive activity, and indeed the range of normal individual variation therein, have important implications for adjustment and for communication.

THINKING

It is difficult to define thinking precisely enough to avoid overlap with other mental activities such as memory and fantasy, and perhaps not realistic to do so. Thinking always involves the manipulation of mental symbols representative of external 'reality', and may have a more or less directed, problem-solving character.

TOOLS OF THOUGHT

The material of thought may consist of verbal or non-verbal images, symbols and concepts. Creativity and imagination involve the manipulation of novel, non-representative images, or recombination of old ones in new ways. Although we are justly proud of our human capacity for creative problem-solving, and often regard it as one attribute in which other animals are clearly inferior, it is well to remember that it does not appear fully developed at birth, and that it is perhaps a rarer and more fragile skill, even in adults, than we may wish to believe.

An **image** is a sensory experience not based on immediate sense data; a re-creation 'in the mind's eye', or mental representation of a perceptual event. While most of us seem to form our clearest images in the visual mode, there is some evidence of specialization within different individuals. Beethoven's achievement in continuing to compose after his own deafness suggests peculiarly acute auditory imagery. Teachers need to be sensitive to such individual differences if they are to be maximally effective. Images may also involve the other senses, including that of kinaesthesia (for example, we can have an image of what it feels like to swim or dance).

An **eidetic** image is an amazingly detailed photographic-like re-creation, such that the letters of a long foreign word may be read off, or other fine detail reported, from a visual stimulus after substantial delay. This ability is more frequently found in children than in adults. Another oddity is **synaesthesia**, mixed modality imagery, where for example numbers or sounds may be 'seen' in terms of different colours.

Images form the basic tool of cognitive function. They help us to classify and describe new experiences by matching with past ones, they form the basis of memory, and may at times be evoked or recalled purely for the pleasure that results, as in reverie or poetry appreciation. Images commonly have emotional associations: smells in particular are notoriously evocative of the past. One kind of image with a particularly powerful emotional meaning is the **body image**, our cognitive representation of our physical self. Discrepancies between this image and reality are common during self-conscious adolescence, after physical trauma (amputation and phantom limbs), and in cases of both obesity and extreme thinness (anorexia: see Allebeck, Hallberg and Espmark 1976). As far as the individual is concerned, the body image is a true representation of reality, and therefore the outsider's different view is likely to be regarded as mistaken. Body images have powerful emotional associations: even in childhood we know what is the cultural ideal for a body of each sex (and therefore how ours deviates), and in addition we learn social conventions regarding who may touch different parts of the body (see Chapter 16), which have obvious relevance to the clinical encounter.

Other tools of thought are symbols and concepts. *Symbols* stand for something other than themselves. They are related to objects more indirectly than are images; for example a given colour will symbolize different emotions in different cultures, and different languages will refer to the same object with a variety of linguistic symbols (words).

Concepts, which stand for a class of objects or events with some attribute in common, vary in their level of abstraction. The ability to form and use abstract, high order concepts in a logical and flexible way is a valued cognitive skill which develops gradually through experience, and is vulnerable to the effects of brain damage and mental illness. As it is not complete until the end of primary school, at the earliest, any one who wishes to communicate with children, as well as those who seek understanding of brain function at different ages, needs to understand the stages of conceptual development (see below).

MEMORY

Sensation lasting about a quarter of a second is the first stage in the process of memory. If attention is paid and the event perceived, it will be stored in **short-term memory** for up to about 20 seconds. Names heard at a party, or a telephone number looked up for immediate use, show the operation of this storage facility, which is one of the mental functions most noticeably adversely affected in old age. Longer storage requires an active effort to learn, for example by rehearsal, association of ideas such as with mnemonics, or 'chunking' of information into meaningful units. Then material can be transferred to the **long-term memory** store, and when this occurs it is potentially recallable for ever, even though the person concerned may have consciously forgotten it. Whereas forgetting is a natural fate for material in the short-term memory which is not transferred to the long-term store, material which has been permanently stored can become inaccessible to recall (and hence for practical purposes, forgotten), if there are no appropriate *cues* to its retrieval. A chance association of ideas, persistent probing during psychotherapy, or electrical stimulation of the brain, may suffice to recollect the memory.

Much of what doctors tell their patients is forgotten, and instructions and advice more so than diagnosis. Ley (1979) concludes that recall can be aided if the doctor says the important things *first*, and is specific and concrete rather than vague and general in recommendations.

Recall of past experiences is often more difficult to check experimentally than recall of past performance at some learning task, which has therefore been studied fairly extensively in psychological laboratories. As with perception, details may be filled in on the basis of expectations, and recall prove to be contaminated by earlier or later experiences. The witness in the jury box and the psychotherapy patient giving details of childhood may both provide examples of this **retrospective distortion** of recall. The same phenomenon reduces the reliability for research purposes of people's reports of the past. Mothers' reports of how they brought up their children are often regarded as very suspect for this reason: when objective details such as birthweight are often forgotten, the ages at which milestones such as sitting and speaking were reached, or the details of how discipline was applied, are even more likely to be recalled inaccurately. Distortions tend to be at least in the direction of conventionality or what the reporter regards as likely to be accepted as normative by the person who asks the question. Most if not all of such distortion is not deliberate, and people may feel quite convinced of their own accuracy.

Recognition of some object or event as familiar, or relatively faster *relearning*, are other ways to test memory. **Déjà vu** (French: already seen) experiences are probably based on recognition in the present of similarities to forgotten events. Apart from memory, thought processes such as categorization, and hypothesis-formation and testing, are important in problem-solving. Research on cognitive processes was piecemeal and unsatisfying during the period when psychologists saw individual cognitive differences in terms mainly of 'intelligence' scores (see Chapter 8). Recently there is renewed appreciation of the primacy for the individual of his or her *own* view and interpretation of the world. The relationship between cognitive and overt behaviours is not clearly understood, yet it is emerging as a vital issue in applying psychological theory to clinical practice (see Chapter 12).

CONCEPTUAL DEVELOPMENT

Piaget is the Swiss psychologist responsible for drawing attention to the mechanisms by which children develop logical concepts and learn to understand the world. His is a rich and sophisticated philosophy, and its main principles will be briefly summarized here from the point of view of understanding how children think and how they differ from adults. As children are relatively often patients, doctors need to know how they think in order to facilitate efficient communication.

We saw in the previous chapter that young babies seem able to recognize an object as itself and constant, even though it is shown to them at different distances away from them, and thus has different retinal sizes. This phenomenon of perceptual constancy should be distinguished from the achievement of object constancy (also called **object permanence**), which is the appreciation that objects exist independently of perception. Before four to six months of age, babies behave as though 'out of sight, out of mind' is their guiding rule. If a toy is hidden, interest in it at once disappears. Fading images of mother's face cause no alarm (Bower 1971), whereas by six months they cause distress, presumably due to violation of the baby's understanding of object permanence.

During the first eighteen months to two years of life, knowledge is acquired through observing the results of one's own actions, before symbolic representation appears. All learning during this **sensorimotor** stage depends on perception, and on movements of an increasing purposeful nature. The baby actively tries out various manipulations, such as sucking and tasting, and reaching for looked-at objects (achieved by six months). He or she explores the noise-making potential of objects by trying things which work with others (such as dropping, shaking or banging them), and towards the end of the period demonstrates the beginnings of *symbolic activity* by deferred imitation, makebelieve play, and the first words of speech.

The **preoperational** period is characterized as one during which direct physical interaction with the environment is no longer always necessary, although there are considerable limitations on the facility with which mental representations of objects and events can be manipulated. A child in this stage, between two and seven years, can process only a small amount of information at a time and is readily deceived by appearances. Thinking lacks **reversibility**, the ability to mentally undo an action and imagine the result. The child lacks the concept of **conservation** – that quantities remain constant despite changes in appearance – and will claim that liquid poured into a taller glass has become more than it was when in a wider glass. This failure to *decentre* attention and take account of several variables simultaneously also results in difficulties in seeing other people's points of view; indeed even in understanding that their point of view may be different (**egocentrism**), and also in very limited understanding of causality and of time and space. Thus the preoperational child thinks in a way which is qualitatively different from an older person. It is relatively prelogical, intuitive, even magical. The problem is not just one of ignorance of facts, but of the whole capacity to reason effectively and flexibly. Koocher (1973) provides some examples of how the rigid, concrete cognition of preoperational children affects their understanding of the concept of death. 'Death' for a child is not necessarily the opposite of 'life', which may be attributed to any object in good condition, or which moves. Several subjects believed that dead things can be brought back to life by such measures as keeping them warm or giving them hot food. Only one of the preoperational subjects was able to express the concept that death is a natural process related to physical deterioration and accidents; the rest gave specific causes such as 'guns, bows and arrows, rat poison, and getting beat up'. Estimates of their own likely age of death varied from seven to three hundred years. The adult who has to explain the death of a relative, or even of a pet, to a child of this age will therefore need to check to see that the message has been received appropriately.

The **concrete operations** stage lasts from seven to eleven years. Now the child gradually acquires conservational concepts. By the end of the period he or she is no longer deceived by how things look, and has a reasonably accurate and generalized grasp of concepts such as space, time and causality. What is still lacking, however, and which does appear during the final stage of **formal operations** from eleven to fourteen years onwards, is a truly scientific, hypothesis-testing, 'what if' mentality, not constrained by available choices but able to consider all hypothetical possibilities. The development of this capacity has been linked to the adolescent's idealism, radicalism and concern for analysis and prescription for social institutions. Whether all adults ever reach this level of cognitive development, and there is some evidence that city-dwellers are more likely to do so than countrymen, it is clear that in relatively few everyday-life situations are we obliged to think at such a high level of logic.

Piaget's original formulations were based upon the long-term observation of a small number of children, using open-ended questions and a deliberately non-quantitative method. Much further research occurring during the last fifteen years or so has tended to vindicate his original findings. The *sequence* of stages he described appears without a lot of variation in children of different nationality, social class and intelligence. The chronological *age* at which each stage occurs does however vary with overall mental development. It can probably be hastened within narrow limits by providing an especially enriched or educationally-structured environment. Stages are cumulative and incorporate each other; there is no quick shortcut to bypass additive experiences.

The growing ability to reverse actions mentally and to decentre attention, and the decrease in egocentrism, affects many aspects of the young child's thought beyond his or her readiness for formal instruction in subjects like mathematics and science. Ideas about morality show a parallel refinement, from a primitive equation of naughtiness with punishment, through a stage of unquestioning conformity to 'rules', and finally to more subtle and flexible principles of an abstract kind (where for example lying or stealing might be justifiable in certain circumstances). An increasing time span, and greater sensitivity to other people's needs and points of view, make it possible to process more complex information about the consequences of actions.

The logical deficiencies of child thought are manifested again in adults suffering from cognitive disorders.

ADULT THOUGHT DISORDER

'Thoughts' can be regarded for therapeutic purposes as a kind of behaviour subject to the usual principles of learning and unlearning. Unpleasantly intrusive worrying thoughts can be replaced with more adaptive cognitions, as we will see in Chapter 12.

Under the influence of anxiety, all thinking tends to lose flexibility and scope. Threat concentrates attention very effectively, but sometimes so narrowly and fixedly that the best solution to the problem may go unnoticed (like the clever rejoinders we think of an hour too late). Normal adults are prone to motivated lapses in cognition as in perception, but these do not usually persist unchanged in the face of contrary evidence. A **delusion** is a false belief which is not modified by reason and contrary evidence, and is one symptom of serious mental illnesses such as schizophrenia or paranoia.

Apart from the *content* of thought, disorders may become apparent in its *processes*. Magical, intuitive and egocentric features may be obvious in our daydreams, but usually disappear when we are trying to think constructively. For the schizophrenic, such prelogical or **primary process** characteristics may dominate all the time, which of course removes the sufferer from contact with reality and renders him unable to manage his affairs independently. Other characteristics of schizophrenic thought are concreteness, and the intrusion of idiosyncratic associations which gives an impression to the outsider of 'cognitive slippage' (Meehl 1962). Deficiencies in the ability to evaluate hypotheses may lead to impulsiveness. There is controversy over the origins of these difficulties; a strong genetic component is implicated, although it is evidently neither necessary nor sufficient.

Damage to the brain, for example through injury, illness (e.g. syphilis) or alcoholism, tends to produce distinctive results on tests of neuropsychological function. Experienced clinical psychologists can help in the diagnosis of site and extent of brain damage through their assessments of cognitive functions such as memory, visual-motor coordination, reasoning and judgment. Senility and normal ageing also produce changes in cognitive capacity, which are discussed in Chapter 8.

LANGUAGE

LANGUAGE DEVELOPMENT

Babbling starts in all infants at about six months and at first sounds the same everywhere. Then it slowly begins to approximate the sounds of the surrounding language environment, until at nine to ten months the range of sounds narrows and the baby starts to practise sounds more deliberately. All over the world, consonants with the tongue at the front of the mouth (p, m, b, t) and vowels with it at the back (a, e), are the first ones mastered, and the first 'word' at about twelve months is usually a duplicated syllable such as 'mama'. These **holophrastic** utterances depend on context for their interpretation. In different situations, or with different intonation and associated gestures, 'mama' for example seems to mean all sorts of things, from 'I wish mother were here!' to 'mother, fix things for me!' From here on, the differential effects of the speech environment become increasingly apparent.

By eighteen to twenty-four months most children begin to combine words to express themselves in a way already far in advance of the cleverest parrot. These two-word 'sentences' are called **telegraphic** because they consist mainly of nouns and verbs, a few adjectives, and no prepositions, conjunctions, inflections or other inessentials. Intonation is still very important to distinguish meaning, for instance statements and questions tend to have the same word order (e.g. 'daddy car'). Meanings consist of demands, observations and questions about what is happening, and word order is that of the parent language. Language is in fact not random imitation but is rule-dependent from its earliest manifestations.

Vocabulary size grows slowly at first then increasingly rapidly after the second birthday. With a few relatively minor exceptions such as the use of the passive voice, grammar learning is fairly well completed by the age of four years. The remarkable achievement in memory and rule comprehension that this feat implies has led many workers to assume an innate, species-specific predisposition to acquire language (see Chapter 3). Learning theorists on the other hand have pointed out how much stimulation and training parents and others provide to foster speech, and what advantages there are to a child in being able to express wishes and otherwise communicate verbally. Skinner (1957) and Chomsky (1959) led the 'learning' and 'innate predisposition' sides respectively into battle; the most popular theoretical stance now that dust has settled would be a compromise position (see e.g. Dale 1972). The learning view, with its stress on the effect of the (potentially modifiable) environment, has many practical implications. A rich and responsive verbal environment (for example one where parents explain and describe at length, read stories to the child from an early age, and encourage a complex individualized style of speech in the child), is the precursor for academic achievement as we shall see later. Training proceeds by example as well as by direct tuition, as is shown in the early acquisition by most children of that word so unwelcome to parents, 'No'.

SPEECH DISORDERS

Slowness in learning to talk is one of the most common of the few developmental disorders for which parents of very young children seek expert help. It may signify deafness, mental retardation, a specific organic dysfunction such as aphasia, or merely unrealistic expectations on the part of the parent. **Autism** is a serious mental illness of early childhood characterized by withdrawal and failure to develop communicative language, or regression in its use with the onset of the disease, but is fortunately a rare condition. The acquisition of speech by deaf people requires very protracted and arduous training, as it involves learning to associate the ambiguous visual input of others' lip movements, with inexact kinaesthetic-tactual feedback, in the absence of any auditory information. Nevertheless as we shall see, cognition itself need not be permanently impaired by lack of verbal language facility.

    Aphasia refers to language and communication disorders due to brain lesions or congenital dysfunctions of unknown origin. The **expressive** forms result in the inability to speak, and the **receptive** forms affect comprehension of speech. Reading, writing and expressive gestures may also be affected. Neuropsychological tests can help to determine the extent and site of any damage to the brain, using the fact that language functions are localized in the dominant hemisphere, i.e. the one on the other side of the body to the dominant hand, in the adult brain. In children, specific difficulties in learning to use language or, more commonly, to read and write and sometimes to do arithmetic, must be carefully distinguished from the effect of environmental factors such as poor quality or discontinuity of schooling, and from emotional disturbance or overall mental retardation. There is a continuing controversy about the usefulness of labelling specific learning difficulties with the medical diagnosis of **dyslexia**, (see Applebee 1971; Francis-Williams 1970).

Stuttering usually appears between two to six years of age and involves disfluencies of speech which with increasing age tend to become overlaid by tension, blocking and avoidance rituals. Whatever the causes may be, and they remain unclear, by the time help is sought the emotional aspects need to be considered in treatment. As a preventive measure parents should be advised not to focus undue attention on the normal hesitations, repetitions, mispronunciations and garbling of preschool speech, but to show patience and tact while children struggle to express their complicated ideas.

The schizophrenic's divorce from the reality accepted by the rest of the sociocultural group is frequently reflected in disturbances of speech such as '**word salad**', the incoherent conjunction of apparently unrelated terms, and the use of **neologisms**, made-up words with a private and therefore uncommunicative meaning.

Echolalia, repetition of the last words heard, appears in states of psychotic withdrawal, as in childhood autism. The *rate* of speech can also be a diagnostic indicator; in depression it is likely to be slowed up and to lack tonal variation, whereas in states of agitation or mania there may be a high speed and almost continuous flow of connected but illogical speech called **flight of ideas**. Lack of speech (mutism) and the filling-in of memory gaps with imaginary events (confabulation) are other cognitive disturbances with diagnostic importance.

RELATIONSHIP OF LANGUAGE AND THOUGHT

Just as images are obviously related to perception and memory, so are concepts and symbols related to language. Indeed, in the early days of psychology when there was heavy reliance on introspection, controversy raged about whether language and thought could be regarded as distinct or not. The intimate association between them is shown by the preponderance of verbal symbols and concepts in most people's mental furniture. We depend upon linguistic symbols to help organize and understand experience and solve problems; each has a *meaning* which is partly public and universal (**denotative**), and partly private and subjective (**connotative**). A term such as 'neurotic', with its differing lay, professional and scientific connotations, provides a vivid example of this emotional halo. The **semantic differential** technique measures connotative meanings along the dimensions of evaluation (good-bad), activity (active-passive) and potency (weak-strong). These dimensions appear to account for most of the implicit overtones that a particular concept may have for a person. Studies of the effects of therapy, for example, might compare the before and after therapy ratings on pairs of adjectives known to reveal connotative meanings, applied to the concepts 'myself', 'my ideal self', 'my mother', 'my husband', 'sex', 'my son', 'my work', etc.

Language has an *intra-individual* function as well as an *interpersonal* one. Being able to name things and repeat instructions to oneself helps enormously in memory and problem-solving. **Verbal mediation** has been extensively studied through transposition problems, where the subject is required to learn, for example, that 'the smallest' triangle (rather than the one of a certain absolute size) is the one behind which food is to be found. Kindergarten children can solve this sort of problem without difficulty, although monkeys can't.

EFFECTS OF DEAFNESS

If most people depend so greatly on linguistic symbols to organize their mental life, what do deaf people do, who rarely master their native language completely? Although language development depends on cognitive development, the reverse is not necessarily true. Furth (1971) has found that deaf children are not intellectually handicapped by their lack of linguistic competence (only about ten per cent ever become literate, for instance). On Piagetian problem-solving tasks they perform comparably with hearing children, with any lags being attributable to their less rich stimulus-environment. Clearly it must be possible for deaf children to make use of the non-verbal language which they frequently do master (such as some form of signing), or even of completely non-linguistic symbols (imagery perhaps), in thinking. The dependence of most of us on words (especially those who spend a lot of time reading and writing) should not lead us to overlook adjustments possible in their absence.

BILINGUALISM

Bilingual persons are often more aware of the independence of object and name than those who only have one way to label a thought. **Coordinate** bilingualism refers to the separate and parallel learning (most effectively from different individuals) of two languages from early childhood. This leads to the development of two independent sets of meaning associations. **Compound** bilingualism on the other hand, which involves the grafting of one language to an already well-established other, never leads to quite the same fluency in the second language, which tends to retain traces of the first, for example in accent or sentence structure. A Canadian experiment has indicated some of the hidden, cognitive results of learning a second language. Children from English-speaking homes who were sent to French-speaking kindergarten and school not only became functionally bilingual by the fifth grade, while showing no lesser accomplishment in English than children in English-speaking schools, but also developed more tolerance and understanding for French-speaking fellow Canadians (Lambert *et al.* 1973).

LINGUISTIC-RELATIVITY

An interesting conjecture about the relationship between language and cognition advanced by Whorf (1956) and others proposes that our perceptions of reality are not only reflected, but are *shaped*, by the linguistic symbols available to us. This strong version of the **linguistic relativity** hypothesis asserts that people actually experience the world differently according to what language they speak. It is true that languages other than the European ones have different ways of dividing up the spectrum into distinct colours, for example, or many more terms for culturally important happenings (e.g. the oft-cited forty Eskimo words for different types of snow). Fabrega and Tyma (1976) have analysed how pain is referred to in English, Japanese and Thai, and suggest that such material provides a window on how pain is differently conceptualized by speakers of those languages. They implicitly espouse the weaker version of Whorf's hypothesis—that although the availability of linguistic symbols to represent something may not absolutely determine our experience of that thing, patterns of usage may nevertheless, like well-learned and largely unconscious habits, mould our usual perceptions and cognitions to an extent which creates different usual points of view amongst speakers of different languages.

APPLICATIONS TO CLINICAL COMMUNICATION

Language differences between the doctor and the patient may interfere with their communication. Migrant patients, or less expectedly those long residents who have never mastered English, due to social isolation within the wider new society (this applies in Australia to many middle-aged women from traditional Mediterranean cultures), clearly need interpreters. Migrant doctors may face similar problems, and even regional dialects may cause difficulty in some countries.

Possibly less apparent, but equally dramatic in consequences, is the gap in comprehension caused by the doctor's automatic use of his specific professional language or jargon. Boyle (1970) found that patients were more often wrong than right in their understanding of the location of organs such as the heart and stomach. About the only phrase upon which there was complete agreement between doctors and patients over meaning, was 'a good appetite'. As patients will rarely mention that they have not understood some term, avoidance of jargon and the choice of words appropriate to the cognitive and social level of the patient becomes a major communicative skill needed by doctors (see Chapter 10).

Social class differences are also commonly reflected in (and conceivably, perpetuated by) differences in language usage, even when all concerned speak the 'same' language. Accent is not what is being referred to; rather Bernstein (1970) and others have described systematic variations in the extent to which language is used abstractly and complexly by members of different social groups. He refers to working-class language as a **restricted code**, whereas middle-class is **elaborated.** In the latter, sentences are longer and grammatically more complicated, and more likely to refer to intangibles, intentions and emotional states. The possibilities for communication difficulties between doctors, who are usually by background and certainly by education middle-class, and their patients, many of whom speak a more restricted code, are obvious. Vocabulary development as the best single indicator of overall score on a verbal intelligence test, and the systematic social class differences in school achievement, will be discussed in Chapter 8.

SUMMARY

Images, symbols and concepts are the raw materials of thought, and memory the best understood of its many component processes. Children pass through identifiable stages in developing the capacity for logical thought and problem-solving. Anxiety renders all thought less flexible, and in schizophrenia disorders of both content and process are evident.

Failure of children to develop language according to the normal stages may have a variety of causes, as do speech disturbances in adulthood. Most of us depend heavily on the intra-individual, verbal mediation function of language to organize memory and problem-solving. Variations in how the 'same' language is spoken by people of differing backgrounds may present hazards to doctor-patient communication.

TERMS AND CONCEPTS

cognition
image
eidetic
synaesthesia
body image
short term and long term memory
retrospective distortion
déjà vu
object permanence
sensorimotor
preoperational   ⎫ stages of
concrete operations ⎬ cognitive
formal operations   ⎭ development
reversibility
conservation
egocentrism
delusion
primary process thought

holophrastic ⎫
telegraphic ⎭ speech

autism

expressive ⎫
receptive ⎭ aphasias

dyslexia

word salad

neologism

echolalia

flight of ideas

denotative

connotative

semantic differential technique

verbal mediation

coordinate ⎫
compound ⎭ bilingualism

linguistic relativity hypothesis

restricted ⎫
elaborated ⎭ language codes

FOR DISCUSSION

1. To what extent is an individual's body image relevant to how that person behaves socially?

2. Within the group, share your experiences concerning memory aids for students.

3. Gather evidence about and discuss the validity of the idea of social-class differences in modes of communication. How could any such differences affect doctor-patient communication where you might practise?

4. Consider how information about cognition in this chapter could be applied to enhancing the chances of patient compliance with treatment instructions.

SUGGESTED READING

Dale: introduction to language and its functions.

Ley: a summary of research on cognitive aspects of patient compliance.

REFERENCES

Allebeck, P., Hallberg, D. and Espmark, S. 1976. Body image – an apparatus for measuring disturbances in estimation of size and shape. *J. Psychosom. Res.* **20,** 583–9.

Applebee, A. N. 1971. Research in reading retardation: Two critical problems. *J. Child Psychol. Psychiat.* **12,** 91–113.

Bernstein, B. 1970. A sociolinguistic approach to socialization with some reference to educability. In F. Williams (ed.) *Language and Poverty: Perspectives on a Theme.* 25–61. Chicago: Markham.

Bower, T. A. 1971. The object in the world of the infant. *Sci. Amer.* **225,** 30–8.

Boyle, C. M. 1970. Difference between patients' and doctors' interpretation of some common medical terms. *Brit. Med. J.* **2,** 286–9.

Chomsky, N. 1959. Verbal behaviour. By B. F. Skinner. *Language* **35,** 26–58.

Dale, P. S. 1972. *Language Development: Structure and Function.* Hinsdale, Illinois: Dryden Press.

Fabrega, H. and Tyma, S. 1976. Culture, language and the shaping of illness: An illustration based on pain. *J. Psychosom. Res.* **20,** 323–37.

Francis-Williams, J. 1970. *Children with Specific Learning Difficulties.* Oxford: Pergamon.

Furth, H. 1971. Linguistic deficiency and thinking: Research with deaf subjects 1964–1969. *Psychol. Bull.* **76,** 58–72.

Koocher, G. P. 1973. Childhood, death and cognitive development. *Devel. Psychol.* **9,** 369–75.

Lambert, W. E., Tucker, G. R. and d'Anglejan, A. 1973. Cognitive and attitudinal consequences of bilingual schooling: The St Lambert project through grade five. *J. educ. Psych.* **65,** 141–59.

Ley, P. 1979. Memory for medical information. *Brit J. soc. and clin. Psychol.* **18,** 245–55.

Meehl, P. E. 1962. Schizotaxia, schizotypy, schizophrenia. *Amer. Psychol.* **17,** 827–38.

Skinner, B. F. 1957. *Verbal Behavior.* New York: Appleton-Century-Crofts.

Whorf, B. L. 1956. *Language, Thought and Reality.* New York: Wiley.

Chapter 6

Human Learning

It is time to consider in detail how human behaviour is shaped and modified by experience. In many ways this subject holds the key to any attempt to change behaviour for the better, whether it is getting people to eat more healthily, control their anxiety, or grow up responsible and happy. Its central importance to the practice of medicine is therefore clear. Because of the plasticity of human behaviour in comparison with that of lower species, we must understand how learning occurs if we want to implement any changes in the behaviour of ourselves or others. In this chapter we first consider the basic principles of how learning occurs. Then we review the kinds of event most effective in leading to behaviour change when made contingent upon the emission of particular behaviours. This area of human reinforcement, in the terminology of this chapter, can readily be seen to encompass much of the topic known as Motivation.

THE MAIN VARIETIES OF LEARNING

Several main varieties of learning are manifested in everyday life. Although much early work in psychological laboratories was carried out using animal subjects, in recent years especially there has been a vast investment of energy and brainpower in the human applications and principles which are our major concern.

LEARNING BY ASSOCIATION: CLASSICAL CONDITIONING

The first kind of learning to be extensively studied was reported by the Russian physiologist, Pavlov, in 1903. In his work on the operation of the digestive glands in normal-living dogs, he had noticed that salivation sometimes occurred before food was given to the dog, and he devoted years of study to these 'psychic secretions'. Salivation in the presence of food is a natural, reflexive and normally involuntary behaviour which today we call an **unconditioned response** (UCR). The food is the **unconditioned** (i.e. natural) **stimulus** (UCS). If some other stimulus occurs along with or shortly before (ideally, half a second before) the UCS, it will come to evoke the same response independently. In Pavlov's case, the sight of the normal food-bringer, or of the food, was initially noticed to elicit salivation. Bell sounds and lights were later found to have the same property if the temporal sequence was right. These are thus examples of a **conditioned stimulus** (CS), and the response evoked, in all important respects the same as before except in how it has been evoked, is the **conditioned response** (CR).

The manipulation consists of teaching the animal to make an existing, involuntary response to a *substitute* stimulus, by pairing the occurrence of the two stimuli. If the CS is repeatedly presented without the UCS, the CR will fade away, which is called **extinction**. In humans there seems to be a particular application of the principles of classical conditioning in the development of the physiological responses of emotion. Heart rate may accelerate, and skin con-ductivity alter due to increased sweating. Other reflexes such as blinking or sucking (in babies) may be demonstrated in the presence of stimuli associated with the usual causes for these responses. Perhaps you have experienced feelings of fright (for example a pounding heart) upon seeing or hearing the stimuli associated with a frightening experience. Many people develop fears of white-coated individuals or of hospitals, for this reason. Human emotional conditioning via the physiological response pattern (see Chapter 7) seems to be able to occur with many fewer learning trials than learning in the laboratory situation, and quite a variety of responses which we normally think of as outside our control have been shown to be conditionable. Asthmatic responses appeared upon introduction of a disconnected mouthpiece formerly associated with allergen-inhalation, in an experiment by Decker, Pelsen and Groen (1957). Other examples will be discussed below in connection with biofeed-back training.

Generalization and discrimination
Stimuli which are similar to the CS may also evoke the CR, in proportion to their similarity. This phenomenon of **generalization** can occur cross-modally; having been conditioned to salivate to the sound of a bell, a person may also salivate not only to the sounds of other

bells, but also to the sight of a bell, or the printed word *bell*. The complementary process is **discrimination**, wherein the subject is trained to respond only to the criterion CS; responses to other similar stimuli are extinguished by never being paired with the UCS. In this way we can investigate sensory acuity, for instance by seeing how often a CR such as blinking occurs, or what discrimination can be achieved between two tones of similar frequency. Pavlov found that when the discrimination task was too difficult, formerly patient and cooperative dogs became excited and distressed and began to behave in a disorganized way, which Pavlov referred to as an **experimental neurosis**. Generalization and discrimination learning are obvious adaptive mechanisms which increase the organism's flexibility in coping with an ever-changing environment.

Particularly through conditioned emotional responses such as anxiety and sexual arousal, which of course consist of patterns of autonomic activity (see next Chapter) as well as a conscious experience, there are many illustrations of how classical conditioning affects daily health and adjustment. Voluntary behaviours, however, are affected by a different sort of learning.

LEARNING BY CONSEQUENCES: OPERANT CONDITIONING

What determines whether a person will continue to behave in a given way, or will change? The answer lies in the consequences of the behaviour in question. Any action is made more or less likely to recur according to what happens after it. This principle formulated by Thorndike and Skinner, and explored further by many other psychologists, now sounds obvious, so thoroughly has it become part of the common conceptual armoury. Research is still proceeding upon its full meaning and its implications for the understanding, prediction and control (which furnish ascendingly convincing proof of scientific knowledge) of human behaviour.

Reinforcement is the occurrence of any event which alters the probability of the preceding response. A *positive* reinforcer increases the probability of the preceding response when it is presented, and decreases it when contingently taken away. If praise from the teacher increases the work rate of a school child, and being ignored by her is followed by a decline in the child's work rate, we can say that for that child the teacher's praise is a positive reinforcer. A *negative* reinforcer conversely lowers the probability of the preceding response (punishment), and its removal increases it.

The concept of reinforcement describes (rather than explains) the relationship between two classes of events. It allows prediction and control of behaviours, because reinforcers can be expected to show some generalization from one situation to another. To follow up the previous example, the teacher may be able to increase the frequency of not only arithmetic efforts, but also spelling, cleaning the blackboard, and even playing appropriately with other children, by following these actions with her praise. In order to shape Johnny's behaviour most effectively, his teacher needs to know a little more about the process. First, how can she reinforce arithmetic success or effort if the child never demonstrates any? Sometimes a new motor behaviour can be physically guided by the trainer – as a tennis coach may push your arms into the right motions for a good stroke, or as a parent or dentist teaches toothbrushing. But frequently this is not possible, and reinforcement of **successive approximations** to the desired behavioural goal is needed. The teacher is therefore going to have to make a careful analysis of Johnny's behaviour and decide exactly what skills he needs in order to be able to perform arithmetically. Perhaps the first thing he needs to learn is how to sit still and concentrate for two minutes. In this case the teacher may need to begin by reinforcing attention for thirty seconds and gradually extending the requirements, then carry out similar shaping of actual written output, perhaps at first reinforcing for sums attempted and later requiring greater and greater accuracy.

Certainly it is necessary to point out that the teacher's praise is not going to be an effective reinforcer for Johnny unless he likes her, wants to please her, believes she likes him, and so on. The personal characteristics of the reinforcing agent, and the relationship between the modifier and the modified, are not irrelevant and can not be left out of the equation by the modifier. Others may wish to describe what is going on in a different way, perhaps in terms of the child's self-esteem, expectations of success, achievement motive or something else. The advantage of the behavioural view is that it is relatively easier to specify what in objective terms is the target or desired behavioural outcome, what is the initial, pretreatment or **baseline** rate of occurrence, and how the rate is affected by intervention.

In early behaviourist writings by J. B. Watson a 'strict' form of behaviourism was promulgated, which advised that unobservables such as feelings, attitudes and wishes were impossible to deal with scientifically. Skinner (1953), although wary of using people's self-descriptions as valid data, proposed some ideas about how the 'private' events of thought and emotion could be made public and therefore accessible to scientific study. At present there is increasing recognition, by psychologists with a behavioural turn of mind, that covert behaviours (wishes, thoughts, etc.) can and sometimes should be therapeutically modified. This **cognitive behaviourism** will be discussed in greater detail in Chapter 12.

Positive reinforcement not only increases the frequency of the antecedent response, but tends to stereotype the movement pattern too, as with the successful golfer whose action becomes more and more standardized and predictable. Conversely extinction, at least when first instituted, has a disruptive, energizing effect: the antecedent response may be emitted in a more intense and variable form before it begins to decline in frequency.

As with classical conditioning, learning in the operant paradigm shows generalization. Responses similar to the target one may be strengthened or weakened, which is another important aspect of deliberate training programmes. The over-submissive individual who is being taught how to communicate more clearly and assertively must learn how to do this in natural social situations, as well as with the therapist. Generalization over time as well as over setting is another necessary component to successful therapy, which the trainer will do everything possible to achieve. This usually involves some sort of graduated transfer from the relatively contrived externally delivered reinforcers of the early stages of training, to self-maintaining 'natural' consequences, either self-delivered or delivered by the reinforcing agents in the person's usual social environment. Thus our arithmetic reinforcing teacher would work towards a situation where Johnny's new behaviour is controlled by the normal consequences of feedback on success, such as ticks and progress through the workbook, approval from parents and peers, and his own feelings of interest and competence.

The **discriminative stimulus** acts as a learned sign or cue that reinforcement will follow a particular response. In daily life we are constantly responding to non-verbal information about the mood, wishes, and other characteristics of those around us, and this sensitivity is a major aspect of social skill. Mistimed or misdirected overtures which lead to rejection are often the result of failure on somebody's part either to attend to, or to transmit clearly, these discriminative stimuli. Another example occurs when a parent is trying to decide whether or not a child needs medical attention. It often takes trial and error on the part of new parents to discover the discriminative stimuli in the presence of which the doctor will feel a consultation is justified (e.g. what level of temperature, stomach ache or loss of appetite reaches the criterion for a treatable symptom).

Schedules of reinforcement

Most of our behaviour is maintained by **intermittent schedules of reinforcement**. By contrast, new learning will occur most efficiently if reinforced continuously, that is with a reinforcer following every correct response. The response-reinforcement ratio can then be stretched gradually. Behaviour maintained by intermittent (or partial) reinforcement is more resistant to extinction than that maintained by continuous reinforcement. Schedules of intermittent reinforcement vary along two dimensions; whether the ratio of reinforcer to response is fixed or variable, and whether it depends on time or the number of responses. Each has different consequences for the behaviour so maintained, which it is necessary to understand when trying to alter the behaviour in question:

Fixed interval (FI) schedules reinforce the next response which occurs after a fixed period of time has elapsed. The normal result is that the animal learns to estimate the time period, and will not respond much until near its end, when output rate will rise until the reinforcement occurs, then fall off again. Students cramming before terminal exams is one unfortunate example of this schedule in operation.

Fixed ratio (FR) schedules deliver reinforcement after a fixed number of responses. It is the 'no work no pay' condition of sweatshops or payment on commission, and can lead to high output rates, often with a short pause immediately after the reinforcer is delivered.

Variable interval (VI) schedules deliver reinforcements after unpredictable time periods. Although the average length of the interval can be specified, the animal on this schedule cannot learn when the next response will be reinforced, and this leads to a much steadier response rate than with FI. Output will be fast or slow depending on the density of the schedule, but will be greater than with the same number of reinforcements on a FI schedule. There would therefore be considerable educational benefits of 'surprise' tests of student knowledge, and in industry of bonuses which were irregular rather than predictable (e.g. at Christmas).

Variable ratio (VR) schedules, which are the strongest of all, vary the number of responses needed to earn a reinforcement around some specifiable average. The prime example of the VR control of human behaviour is gambling. You have to bet (respond) in order to have a chance to win, and you can never tell which pull of the poker-machine lever or throw of the dice is going to make you rich. Under these conditions extremely persistent behaviour develops, even with a very high ratio of responses to reinforcement.

The steadiness in rate and resistance to extinction, as shown by behaviour maintained by VI and VR schedules, are due to the difficulty to the person or animal of discriminating when reinforcement has been withdrawn. Because long periods of time or effort will sometimes pass without reward – although at other times there may appear to be a 'winning streak' where consecutive responses are rewarded – any next response may be the 'lucky' one, and extinction ('loss of hope') will be very slow. The whining or tantrum-throwing child (or adult) who even just occasionally gains a victory by these means will be encouraged to continue to try them out.

It is also important to note that animals can mistake the reinforcement contingencies. Skinner originally induced *'superstitious'* behaviour in his pigeons by delivering food pellets regardless of what response they were making at the time, and he found that stereotyped patterns of neck-stretching or turning in circles became very strong in individual birds. A human parallel is the wearing of a lucky charm. Whenever reinforcement occurs in the presence of the charm, charm-wearing will be strengthened, and will come to occur so often that the likelihood of reinforcement occurring in temporal conjunction with charm-wearing is very high. We may even speculate that to the person convinced of the protective or luck-bearing power of such a charm, anxiety over its loss may in fact be responsible for some misadventure. Unpleasant events occurring in the presence of the charm (or other ritual) will tend to be forgotten, or attributed to other causes, or the charm will be credited with having averted an even worse outcome.

This kind of analysis has moved us some way from the original behaviourist framework. Where, how and also whether the rat or pigeon conceptualized the response-reinforcement relationship was necessarily regarded as an irrelevant and unanswerable question. In dealing with humans, however, with their great capacity to reflect upon and seek order and meaning in their experience, we cannot avoid the need to investigate these cognitive aspects of the reinforcement process. The connection which the individual *perceives* between the response and the consequence affects the behavioural outcome. So does the *meaning* to the individual of the reinforcement, for example whether positive reinforcers are seen as rewards or bribes, and negative ones as punishment or helpful information.

The different varieties of reinforcer effective with humans are discussed in more detail later in this chapter.

Punishment

The presentation of aversive consequences for a response is worth some study in its own right. Just as anything which the organism voluntarily seeks out can be regarded as a positive reinforcer, anything which is avoided or not sought can be regarded as aversive. Aversiveness can therefore be determined, not *a priori*, but only by its reducing effect on the frequency of the antecedent response. For some people, for example, things which are aversive to most of us, such as pain or humiliation, may through unusual learning experiences have acquired positive characteristics (as in cases of sexual deviation: see Chapter 10).

Only responses which occur, i.e. have some frequency greater than zero, and which are thus maintained by some positive consequences, can be punished. Therefore the effects of punishment will be superimposed upon those of positive reinforcers. Punishment can alter the frequency of the response but can not wipe it out from the behavioural repertoire; as with all reinforcement, extinction of the effects may occur when it ceases to operate. Response frequency decreases while aversive consequences continue to follow the response, or in the presence of the associated discriminative stimuli (like the proximity of a police car to the speeding motorist). *But*, given no change in the maintaining positive reinforcers, it is likely to rise again when punishment is withdrawn.

Punishment as a tool for behavioural control has drawbacks other than the temporariness of its effects. Presenting aversive consequences (pain, ridicule, etc.) can lead to fear and anxiety. These can disorganize and reduce the flexibility of behaviour, and lead to the learning of escape or avoidance behaviours (at the least, keeping out of range of the punishing agent), which may be maladaptive to the person's overall functioning ('neurotic'). Use of the other form of punishment, contingent withdrawal of positive reinforcers (exemplified by fines, ostracism, withdrawal of love), can also lead to undesirable emotional side effects, of which anger and resentment, with corresponding increase in the likelihood of counter-aggression, are the commonest. The use of punishment can also increase the chances of aggression in the victim in another way, by providing a model which may then be imitated in other situations. Various long term developmental studies have shown a high correlation between the amount and severity of physical punishment during childhood, with the amount and severity of antisocial aggressiveness during adolescence.

To be most effective as a behaviour suppressor, punishment should be immediate, severe and at least initially, continuous. Many of these recommendations are flouted in daily life. Yet punishment retains its popularity with parents, educators, law-and-order enforcers, and other sections of the community, and it is not really difficult to see why this is so. The short term suppression of the behaviour in question, and the demonstration of superior power, may both be powerful reinforcers of punishment-usage, to the user. In addition there is the constructive possibility, perhaps often under-utilized in prisons and families, that while undesired behaviours are temporarily suppressed, more acceptable alternative methods of gaining the same positive rein-forcers can be shaped and strengthened.

LEARNING BY WATCHING: OBSERVATIONAL LEARNING

The growing interest in how humans learn, as opposed to laboratory animals, has increased our awareness of the need to understand learning by observation, the third major category. Anyone who has ever tried to learn how to knit, hit a tennis ball, make pastry or change a fuse, or any other skill of which the elements are already present to some degree in the repertoire, will know that a demon-stration can be of far more immediate help than a list of instructions. This type of learning also operates in non-motor behaviours: values and attitudes may be learned in the same way. It is necessary here to distinguish between the *acquisition* of a response into the repertoire of behavioural possibilities, by a one-trial perceptual process, and the later *performance* of that response by the observer. Bandura (1969) has elucidated some of the conditions under which performance of the observed response is facilitated. Basically there are three important factors affecting imitative performance, or an attempt at it. The first is the **vicarious reinforcement** of the observer, in terms of perceived consequences to the **model** (observed one) of the behaviour in question. In an experiment where adult models displayed physical aggression towards an inflatable Bobo doll, child observers were more likely to show similar aggression later if they had seen the model praised and offered refreshments afterwards, than if the model had been scolded and criticized (Bandura and Walters 1963). Interestingly, the children who had not seen any consequences to the model of the aggression, interpreted that as acceptance of the behaviour, and showed moderate levels of imitative aggression. Not surprisingly, the second important determinant of imitative performance is the expected and actual consequences to the observer of the first imitative performance. Asking the children in the above experiment to copy the model's behaviour, and providing rewards for each successful imitation, wiped out the differences between groups who had earlier received different vicarious reinforcements. This again demonstrates the simple perceptual nature of the acquisition process, in contrast to the influences upon *performance*, of a learned response.

The third set of factors affecting observational performance is the characteristics of the model salient to the observer. Imitation will be greater if the model is perceived: a) as having desirable attributes such as prestige and power (therefore a neatly groomed man in a business suit can lead more other pedestrians through a 'Don't Walk' sign than can a tramp); and b) as similar to the observer in important ways, which perhaps increases the observer's expectation of meeting the same consequences as the model for the same behaviour.

In any situation where one is learning 'how to behave', that is where it is a question of fitting together actions which in themselves are relatively easy, rather than of perfecting totally new skills, observational learning is very important. There are two obvious examples of this situation. The first is the socialization process during childhood, where the child uses the same-sex parent (unless that person is very rejecting) as a model of what it means to be a woman or man; which behaviours are possible, which are expected, which are inappropriate and so on. Secondly there is the medical student, similarly learning a role and set of customs and expectations about being a doctor from practising doctors such as the clinical teachers. In each case socialization (note, a set of values and attitudes as much as a set of motor behaviours) proceeds best when there is **identification** with the model by the observer. This refers to a feeling of some similarity to the model and a wish for even more. Identification is a complex, at least partly unconscious process which it will be important to study further when we look at individual psychosocial development (Chapter 9). At present it is sufficient to realize its relation to observational learning, and the importance of the latter as an adjunct to conditioning, in understanding the dynamics of human behaviour.

AUTONOMIC CONDITIONING

Although so far we have distinguished classical and operant conditioning as involving involuntary (visceral) and voluntary responses respectively, it is not in fact always possible or profitable to hold rigidly to that distinction. The main example of this which is of current research interest, and of clear relevance to medicine, is the work demonstrating that normally involuntary responses such as heart rate, skin temperature, brain wave rhythms (EEG) and so on, can be modified by operant conditioning. The usual reinforcement for changes in the desired direction (e.g. lowered blood pressure) is informational feedback, derived by monitoring the physiological processes involved, usually with sophisticated technological equipment. The process is therefore known as **biofeedback**. As frequently happens in science, early work (by N. Miller and his colleagues) led to a period of great optimism (and considerable sensationalization by the popular media), which has been succeeded by difficulties in replication in independent laboratories, and a more cautious attitude now prevails towards possible therapeutic applications. The problems of establishing the validity of treatment methods based on biofeedback are those relevant to any treatment of any condition. We basically want to know a) what is the magnitude and reliability of the effect and how much difference is there in the responses of different individuals? b) for how long is the benefit maintained after treatment? and c) is the benefit due to the treatment as is claimed, or is it due to some non-specific placebo effect of attention, contact with the enthusiastic, hope, selective attention to and reporting of symptoms, etc? Almost all of the illnesses in which psychological precipitants are recognized as influential – migraine, asthma, hypertension, chronic pain and others – have been and are currently being studied within the context of biofeedback control efforts (see Blanchard and Young 1974; Miller 1978; also Chapter 12). We may expect that further careful work will yield techniques of wide utility to medicine within the next several years.

EFFECTIVE REINFORCERS FOR PEOPLE

We can now give more attention to the question of exactly what kinds of events act as reinforcers for humans when presented or removed after a response. This constitutes the area of *motivation*, but avoids the implication of various hypothetical 'drives' or need states. These, with a few obvious physiological exceptions, retain an *ad hoc* and largely *post hoc* descriptive flavour in our present state of knowledge. When brain function is understood much better than it currently is, the sites and neural pathways for these 'motives' may be definitively mapped. Until then we can gain considerable insight into (and possibly, prediction and control of) human behaviour by taking the more molar, behavioural focus.

LIMITS OF LEARNING

It is clear first of all, and worth discussing for the sake of perspective, that being a member of the human race has a special significance in terms of effective reinforcers. Other species have different sensory and motor capacities which affect the stimuli which may be attended to and the responses which may be made. More importantly perhaps, species-membership probably predisposes creatures to find certain kinds of learning easy or difficult. Rats, who have great gustatory sensitivity and relatively poor vision, readily learn to associate unfamiliar-tasting food with the (delayed) experience of nausea, and to avoid that food in the future. Yet they fail to learn the connection between distinctive-*looking* food and nausea, which quail on the other hand learn relatively more easily. It is impossible to train counter-instinctive responses: rats 'freeze' (become immobile) when afraid and cannot learn to avoid a signalled shock by running. Raccoons being trained for a 'piggy-bank' advertisement had to be replaced with pigs due to their insistence on rubbing the 'coins' together, as they usually do to their food (Breland and Breland 1961).

Learning which is ethologically natural may occur readily despite suboptimal conditions, for example despite delays far longer than the 0.5 second CS-UCS interval best in laboratory conditioning experiments. It can also be extremely resistant to extinction, in comparison with learning for which the animal is biologically unprepared or counter-prepared (Seligman and Hager 1972). For humans, such considerations may be especially relevant in areas of behaviour where our few species-specific predispositions are evident, such as in bond formation and in communication and sensory-motor skills (see Chapter 3). Genetic/constitutional differences, and variations due to different nutrition, or physical characteristics such as size, age and sex, may all affect learning too, although the available information tends to suggest a fairly great degree of behavioural plasticity in humans. That is, that learning experiences can do much to override innate and constitutional predispositions.

Prior learning experiences, and temporary states of fatigue or drug effects, modify a person's readiness to attend to stimuli. They may similarly affect his capacity to perform certain responses, as well as his expectations of the consequences. Taking all these possible sources of individual variation into account, let us now attempt to list the classes of event which operate as human reinforcers.

CLASSES OF HUMAN REINFORCEMENTS

Biological: food, water, warmth, air, sleep, avoidance of injury
All of these have been frequently used in laboratory studies with animals, and in the natural environment they control behaviour very effectively. Because of their survival-related nature there are ethical difficulties in using them experimentally or even therapeutically with humans, although arguably the next two types of reinforcer are equally vital to proper functioning. Another drawback to the use of these reinforcers is that, because of homeostasis, *satiation* may be relatively rapid (i.e. more may not always be better).

Social: physical contact, sex, attention and approval from other humans
Baby primates, as has been described before, like tactual contact with soft surfaces. If reared away fron conspecifics like Harlow's baby rhesus monkeys (see Chapter 3), or when conspecifics are temporarily not available like the infant who has been left in a crib to sleep, they seem to derive comfort from inanimate objects with the right feel. Attachment to a loving and stable other (who stimulates as well as usually nourishing and protecting) is a prerequisite for growth and development, both physical *and* psychological (see Chapter 9). Later in life, explicitly sexual urges are experienced and their satisfaction again involves other people. Evoking a sexual response in another person can act as a powerful reinforcer and is sought avidly by many people for much of their time. Sexual pleasure and orgasm themselves strengthen the antecedent responses in a way which usually leads to more expert performance, and sometimes to the acquisition of unusual

habits such as fetishism, masochism and other deviations from the norm. Human sexuality is too complicated to discuss fully here (see Chapter 10), but because of its meaning in overall psychosocial adjustment it fits into this category of reinforcer more happily than into the preceding one.

The reinforcing effectiveness of attention, especially of an approving kind from other members of our species, and particularly those members with whom we have some psychologically significant relationship such as parents, teachers and peer group, is similarly a very large subject which receives its deserved share of attention later in this book.

Cognitive: information and perceptual novelty

We saw in Chapter 4 how stimulus-deprivation is aversive and can affect mental functioning deleteriously, and how we seem to be 'set' to attend to change in the stimulus environment. All primates show a great deal of curiosity, especially when young, and seem to enjoy manipulating and exploring the environment for no other gain than that of novelty. Change, informational feedback or **knowledge of results** is an extremely effective motivator, especially in human behaviour, and any skill is acquired faster the more feedback is available about the adequacy of early attempts. Applications of this are widespread, from the schoolteacher's efforts to return corrected work as quickly as possible to the pupils, to the use of videotape, which allows the slowing, repetition, and close-grained analysis of a variety of skills from sport to interviewing and counselling. (See Goroll, Stoeckle and Lazare (1974) on this use in medical education).

Conditioned reinforcers

The categories of reinforcement so far discussed all share the feature that they are a natural rather than artificial consequence of the behaviour in question, and are intrinsically rewarding to all humans. Another class of reinforcers can be distinguished which have no inherent value in themselves, but which acquire reinforcing properties by association with natural reinforcers. Money is the classic example of this sort of **conditioned reinforcer**: in themselves the coins, paper, shells or whatever other medium of economic exchange is used, are valueless. However, because money makes other reinforcers available, or makes them available in a more elaborate or gratifying form, it acts (to anybody who has 'learned the value of money', significantly *not* to others such as very young children) as a very powerful reinforcer. We even see instances of the pursuit of money becoming such a well established habit that it is carried out well after more money is objectively no longer needed. Money-making has then become **functionally autonomous**, perhaps because it has become an important part of the person's self-concept, and is itself reinforced by the power, deference or status it confers.

Other examples of unpredictable results of 'reinforcing' events are readily found. Criticism may be sought out, if it is seen in informational terms, or as a sign of serious interest on the part of the teacher. Money may be treated as aversive, if it is seen as an attempt to devalue the giver or the gift. Thus we are forced at every stage to take the cognitive aspects of the reinforcement process into account – what the events have come to 'mean' to the person being reinforced and how the transaction is 'perceived'.

By the time an individual has reached adolescence, at the very latest, each one has a unique history of learning experiences. Moderately consistent behavioural patterns known as personality characteristics have been shaped, which include habits of **self-reinforcement**. Both by direct shaping and by observation we develop internalized standards of performance. Some of us suffer a great deal of unhappiness because these self-determined goals are unrealistically high or exacting. Others cause pain and despair to those around them due to unrealistically low standards for their own behaviour. When our actions match our goals, the positive feedback we get from the assessment of others or ourselves – 'that was a kind/clever/lovable thing to do' – constitutes positive reinforcement and enhances self-esteem. We can also control our own behaviour by manipulating the reinforcement contingencies, for example the overweight person who plans to buy new clothes when a certain weight is reached by dieting, or the student who denies herself a cup of coffee until a certain proportion of the essay has been written. It is the capacity for self-reinforcement which enables people to stick to their principles, despite social or other kinds of pressure; for example, people who are ready to suffer for their beliefs, or more commonly, the ability to persevere at something which shows no immediate payoff, and to delay gratification.

CLINICAL APPLICATIONS

It can readily be understood why setting out to induce a therapeutic change in behaviour is so complicated. Some reinforcers work with most of the people most of the time, but the best reinforcer for a particular behaviour in a particular individual may be something quite idiosyncratic to that individual. A careful analysis of the maintaining reinforcers is always required before change techniques can be contemplated. Very often, with the sort of maladaptive habits which restrict people's lives and happiness, anxiety-avoidance will be found to be an important reinforcer. The particular methods of unlearning and retraining which can be used to help such problems are discussed in more detail in Chapter 12. We may note here however that many symptoms of physical discomfort or dysfunction, such as headaches and hypertension, and also many habits detrimental to health, such as alcoholism, over-eating and smoking, are included in the sphere of behaviours treatable within the learning framework described here.

Other applications of learning theory to medicine involve the whole process of attitude formation, during childhood and in response to later social experiences. Attitudes towards physical wellbeing (what constitutes it and how to maintain it), and of how medical services should be utilized, are included in this process and will be discussed further, as illness behaviour, in Chapter 11. Finally, in every interaction between 'patient' and health professional, each commands a selection of reinforcers which can be used to modify the behaviour of the other. Behaviours in which the doctor is particularly interested were reviewed in Chapter 1. The interactions between the two will also be coloured by the past learning history of each participant. Health care efforts are therefore likely to be expedited at several different levels simultaneously, by an understanding of human learning.

SUMMARY

Classical conditioning refers to the learning of a new association between an involuntary response and an originally irrelevant stimulus. Its particular importance lies in the conditioning of emotional responses. Operant conditioning is the process whereby the probability of a response is altered by the consequences of its emission. Responses may be strengthened or weakened, and new responses shaped by successive approximation, by the systematic presentation of reinforcers. Those to which humans are most responsive can be categorized as biological, social, and cognitive. Learning can also proceed by observation, with performance being affected by both vicarious and direct reinforcement. Many usually involuntary bodily responses seem to be conditionable. An understanding of how people learn is central to all attempts to modify behaviour, and thus of key relevance to medicine.

TERMS AND CONCEPTS

unconditioned stimulus, and response
conditioned stimulus, and response
extinction
generalization
discrimination
experimental neurosis
reinforcement
successive approximations
baseline
cognitive behaviourism
discriminative stimulus
FI, FR, VI, VR schedules of intermittent reinforcement
punishment
vicarious reinforcement
model
identification
biofeedback
knowledge of results
conditioned reinforcers
functional autonomy of motives
self-reinforcement

FOR DISCUSSION

1. Using the principles explained in this chapter, train an animal to do or not to do something. Keep records of baseline frequency of the target response, the reinforcement contingencies used, shaping or chaining procedures, generalization of the response to other trainers and/or other environments, and resistance to extinction. What, if anything, might have made your efforts more successful?

2.   Observe some real-life interactions between patients and health professionals, if possible in a variety of treatment settings.

What reinforcers are available to each party? Take into account both positive and negative reinforcers available to both, and biological, social and cognitive varieties of reinforcement.

Which reinforcers seem to be the most effective in controlling behaviour a) at the time, b) in the long-term? (Consider the behaviour of both patient and health professional here.)

SUGGESTED READING

Skinner (1953); Bandura and Walters: the basic texts of the behaviourist approach to significant human behaviour.

Skinner (1975); Bandura (1974): interesting recent reviews by these leaders of what they perceive major issues to be.

REFERENCES

Bandura, A. 1969. *Principles of Behaviour Modification.* New York: Holt, Rinehart & Winston.

Bandura, A. 1974. Behavior therapy and the models of man. *Amer. Psychol.* **29**, 859–69.

Bandura, A. and Walters, R. H. 1963. *Social Learning and Personality Development.* New York: Holt, Rinehart & Winston.

Blanchard, E. B. and Young, L. D. 1974. Clinical applications of biofeedback training; A review of evidence. *Arch. Gen. Psychiat.* **30**, 573–89.

Breland, K. and Breland, M. 1961. The misbehavior of organisms. *Amer. Psychol.* **16**, 681–4.

Dekker, E., Pelser, H. E. and Groen, J. 1957. Conditioning as a cause of asthmatic attacks: A laboratory study. *Psychosom. Res.* **2**, 97–108.

Goroll, A. H., Stoeckle, J. D. and Lazare, A. 1974. Teaching the clinical interview; An experiment with first-year students. *J. Med. Educ.* **49**, 957–62.

Miller, N. E. 1978. Biofeedback and visceral learning. *Ann Rev. Psychol.* **29**, 373–404.

Seligman, M. E. P. and Hager, J. L. 1972. *Biological Boundaries of Learning.* New York: Meredith.

Skinner, B. F. 1953. *Science and Human Behavior.* London: Macmillan.

Skinner, B. F. 1975. The steep and thorny way to a science of behavior. *Amer. Psychol.* **30**, 42–9.

Chapter 7

Emotion, and its Relation to Health

The subjective, unverifiable nature of our feelings is a particularly challenging problem in the light of their relevance to health. In this chapter we consider the nature of emotional experience, the methods used to describe and measure it, and the complex interaction between feelings and physical function. The reciprocal influence of psyche and soma in human health is a vitally important subject for medicine, upon which much research is being carried out at present, and which this chapter begins to explore.

THE DEFINITION OF EMOTION

Although we all 'know' what it means to feel happy, sad, frightened or angry, and have also learned verbal labels for many different shades and combinations of these basic emotions, how can we know that another person is describing exactly the same experience when using the same label? Although this problem is basically an insoluble one, there are a variety of techniques for investigating that private experience. First, we have expectations about likely antecedents for the major dimensions of emotional experience. Secondly, each may give rise to different patterns of overt behaviour, both verbal and non-verbal, on the part of the emotional individual. Thirdly, the fact that emotions have physiological correlates may assist in definition, if these can be adequately measured. It is important to remember that in every case the extremes of the continuum will be most distinct and easily studied, and that the less intense forms and the subtler shades of feeling will be more resistant to scientific exploration. As the physiological correlates are not particularly distinctive we shall discuss them first, then look at the antecedents and behavioural correlates of four major dimensions of emotional experience.

PHYSIOLOGICAL CORRELATES OF EMOTION

By hooking a person up to sophisticated monitoring devices we can obtain a continuous record of heart rate, electrodermal activity (Christie 1976: electrical changes in the skin associated with sweating), breathing patterns, muscular tension and a host of other possible indices. However what all this tells us is not which emotion is being experienced, but to what degree there is emotional arousal. The emotional response is mediated largely by the autonomic nervous system (ANS) and the endocrine system. The ANS controls the glands and smooth muscles responsible for involuntary, self-regulating functions such as circulation and digestion. One branch, the **sympathetic**, is mainly responsible for what has been called the 'fight/flight' reaction of emotional excitement. The body is in a state of emergency preparedness for action: heart rate is accelerated and more blood sent to the muscles and brain, and less to the skin and digestive organs. The pupil of the eye is dilated, skin temperature is lowered by vasoconstriction followed by sweating, and the adrenal glands secrete hormones into the blood which further increase the arousal level. Adrenaline and noradrenaline (also called epinephrine and norepinephrine) intensify the effects of the sympathetic ANS, obtaining the release of sugar stored in the liver so that there is energy for quick action. There thus occurs the self-enhancing, stirred-up bodily state familiar to all of us in moments of fright or rage, experienced subjectively as pounding heart, clammy hands, 'butterflies' in the stomach and an urge to *do* something. This feeling takes a while to subside, because of the closed circuit formed by the ANS and endocrine systems. Death may occur as a result of prolonged extreme arousal, as when a wild animal goes into shock upon capture.

The **parasympathetic** is the other branch of the ANS and by and large has an opposite, calming and restorative role. It also acts more specifically, and less as a unified whole, than the sympathetic branch. Under parasympathetic influence (and most of the viscera receive both sympathetic and parasympathetic neural fibres), heart rate and blood pressure decrease, digestion is facilitated, and a state of relaxation and conservation of resources prevails, in contrast to the urgent mobilization of resources under sympathetic arousal. Although the two branches are usually antagonistic, and the state of the body reflects the balance between them, there are also more complex interactions. For example, the parasympathetic functions of urination and defaecation may be stimulated by sympathetic arousal, and the sexual response shows a combination whereby sympathetic arousal is necessary for ejaculation in men, but inhibits erection (one reason for treating impotence by means of anxiety reduction).

Sources of autonomic arousal
So far little has been said about what sorts of stimuli turn on the sympathetic arousal productive of these well-recognized autonomic components of our experience of emotion. Here we have to take into account the operation of the central nervous system (CNS), particularly the forebrain areas where the hypothalamus and limbic system sort out the significance to the organism of the perceptual input, and organize the appropriate emotional response. Although the brain is scarcely less mysterious than interstellar space, some clues to cognitive influences on emotional arousal are available, initially from experiments carried out by Schachter and Singer (1962).

One group (I) of their subjects was injected with adrenalin and told correctly to expect tremors and palpitations. Another group (II) was similarly injected and misinformed about what to expect (they were told numbness and aches). These two groups therefore had the same level of sympathetic arousal (induced by the adrenalin) but Group I knew the reason for their visceral arousal, and Group II did not. A third, control group was injected with an inert saline solution. All subjects were then observed from behind a one-way screen, for a twenty minute period during which they were joined by a confederate of the experimenters posing as another subject. Half the confederates acted in a high spirited, euphoric manner and half acted irritable and dysphoric. The dependent variable was the extent to which the subjects, in both overt behaviour during the twenty minutes and by questionnaire responses at the end, caught and imitated the emotional mood of the stooge.

Group I was not emotionally suggestible, and neither was Group III. But Group II subjects tended to report and demonstrate emotion in line with that displayed by the stooge. They experienced arousal, and had no explanation other than the environmental cues provided by the stooge's behaviour, which they then used to interpret their own feeling state. These results suggest that, in the presence of visceral arousal, the determinants of emotional experience are cognitive (and therefore depend on how the environmental situation is perceived and interpreted). We have in other words a two-stage or 'juke-box' theory of emotion: arousal is a necessary but not sufficient precondition, like activating the machine by putting in a coin, then cognitive factors determine the feeling tone, like pressing the button to select a record (Mandler 1962). If the arousal is due to strenuous exercise, or having ingested a drug known to have such effects, it will not be interpreted as emotion at all; if due to a perception of any sort of threat or other exciting or arousing situation, the emotion learned as appropriate, or in some cases predisposed by species-membership, will be experienced and reflected in behaviour.

Effects of level of arousal

The actual level of arousal seems to be a function of the reticular formation in the brainstem. For any task, there is an optimum level of arousal at which performance will be most efficient (this is known as the **Yerkes-Dodson Law**). This optimum intensity of arousal is dependent on the complexity of the task. Cooking is for some people an aversively boring activity, which is likely to be done inattentively unless the cook is additionally stimulated by the thought of the eater's appreciation or nutritional needs. Writing an examination paper on the other hand is a complicated cognitive task which can be disrupted by excessive levels of anxiety, as some unfortunate candidates are aware. We have seen beforehand that excessively low levels of arousal, as in stimulus deprivation experiments, are aversive and also disrupt cognitive performance.

On the whole, moderate levels of arousal seem to act as positive reinforcers, and extremes as negative. While real terror is extremely unpleasant, many people enjoy rollercoasters. Likewise many of us voluntarily subject ourselves to mildly frustrating situations such as sport, card games and detective novels. One important factor in the situation seems to be the extent to which the individual involved has *control* of what is going on. Uncontrollability of the situation (often combined with unpredictability) gives rise to feelings of helplessness which are aversive, cause a decline in performance efficiency, and can be stressful to the point of illness and death (Seligman 1975; see also next section).

Because of the primacy of cognitive factors in determining how an individual interprets his or her own emotional state, it is not suprising that emotions such as rage and fear cannot be reliably distinguished purely by measuring their physiological concomitants. We are forced therefore to return to a consideration of emotion as conscious experience, with two caveats. First, individuals may develop, through learning, consistent and characteristic physiological response patterns in particular emotional states, e.g. hypermotility of the gut in any anger-arousing situation, or hyperventilation whenever anxious. Secondly, emotional learning need not always remain a conscious process: in cases where an anxiety-avoiding response has been successfully developed, the anxiety may never be experienced. (Freudians would describe this as an *unconscious* dynamic, see Chapter 11.) Both these features of our emotional behaviour are very important to the field of psychosomatic medicine, the whole area concerned with the interaction of the physiology and the feeling.

SOURCES AND CONSEQUENCES OF EMOTIONS

If emotions cannot then be objectively distinguished according to the resultant pattern of physiological arousal, and if, as we have seen, perceptions and interpretations of the environment can impose their own definition of what emotion is being experienced, it is clear that cognitive and behavioural data become very valuable. We shall now review the assessment, antecedents and behavioural results (including covert, physiological responses) of four emotions. These have been selected as primary emotions, capable of being experienced by adults in many intensities and combinations, and as being of the greatest apparent relevance to health and illness, both 'physical' and 'mental'.

FEAR AND ANXIETY

It is usual to distinguish between these two emotions on the basis of whether or not the cause is an immediately tangible object. Where a person fears a tiger, in contrast to feeling anxious at the memory or anticipation of a tiger, the distinction is plain enough, but there are many everyday situations where it is more problematic. For example a person may be said to fear, or feel anxious about, the prospect of bad news. The interchangeability of the terms in this sort of case makes hard and fast distinctions difficult to maintain.

Antecedents
Fear usually results from aversive stimulation (such as pain or injury) or the threat of it (the relationship is not an exclusive one however

anger could also be a result). In humans, lack of information about events likely to affect one is aversive, and uncertainty often causes anxiety. Recall too that fear is readily conditioned: anxiety may be evoked thereafter by stimuli originally irrelevant to the fear response. The classic example is provided by little Albert, a baby taught by Watson and Rayner (1920) to fear small furry animals by having a loud noise presented simultaneously. The sources of fear do in fact change with age, as one would expect in view of developmental changes in cognitive capacity. Infants show distress, presumed to be fearful, when subjected to sudden changes in stimulation, such as loud noises or loss of support, and later, to separation from attachment figures (see Chapter 9). Primary school children fear ghosts and monsters, with more realistic fears such as of bodily injury and physical danger gaining preponderance as they mature (Bauer 1976). Fears of failure and social disapproval become paramount in early adolescence; in other words, threats of a more symbolic nature to self-esteem rather than to life and limb.

Behavioural results

Fear and anxiety, being in themselves unpleasant to feel, motivate avoidance of the threatening situation. The termination of anxiety powerfully reinforces the avoidance response, and in this way people's lives can become very restricted after a few painful experiences. The individual who has been shamed or scorned (or perceives this to be so, realistically or not) may develop such strong (over-generalized) habits of social withdrawal that no opportunity arises to test reality and discover the irrationality of the fears. Such individuals may be helped out of their loneliness, as indeed most fears can be deconditioned, by graded experience of success in increasingly lifelike settings (see desensitization, Chapter 12).

The muscular tension characteristic of anxiety can give rise directly to pain, particularly in the jaw (if clenched for long periods) and the neck and shoulders. Tension in the frontalis (forehead) muscle, a particularly difficult one to relax deliberately, is the source of non-migrainous headaches.

A complex relationship between anxiety, uncertainty and health can be seen in the studies of the variables affecting postoperative recovery. Egbert *et al.* (1964) found that surgical patients who were told what kind of postoperative pain to expect, and were reassured about its normality and given instructions about pain control, consumed half as much narcotic medication and left hospital an average of 2.7 days earlier, compared with controls. That some of this improvement may have been a placebo effect of getting special treatment is suggested by the results of Cohen and Lazarus (1973). In their study, more days in hospital and more minor complications were suffered by the 16 per cent of patients who were preoperatively assessed as *vigilant* (i.e. overly alert to the threatening aspects of surgery, well-informed about the reasons for it and the risks, and willing to talk about it), compared with the mixed (61 per cent) and *avoidant* (23 per cent) patients. They suggest that avoidance and denial can be an adaptive response to threat when the likely outcome is positive, and that the vigilant information-seekers' usual coping strategy fails them in the face of postoperative pain and dependence.

There are many psychological tests which purport to measure anxiety as a general personality trait, and as a current state, by getting the respondant to answer Yes/No or True/False to descriptive items such as 'I feel tense and jittery much of the time'. The usefulness and pitfalls of these measures will be discussed at greater length in Chapter 11. We may note here that pitfalls do exist and that such tests are not the complete answer in deciding how anxious a person may be and about what.

Asking the person straight out or listening to their own report is another possibility which is engagingly direct, and makes use of the special information available only to the person concerned. Of course, if for any reason people wish to conceal their true feelings, or, if by various defensive manoeuvres they successfully avoid all anxiety-provoking situations, their answers may mislead you. Observing non-verbal behaviours is another avenue of data-gathering. If a person cannot bring himself to look at, touch or approach nearer to a snake, you may correctly conclude the presence of snake-related anxiety. Behavioural methods of treatment often rely on that kind of behavioural measure of anxiety strength.

Finally, anxiety in another person can be recognized from smaller movements, especially of the hands, eyes and mouth. Waxer (1977) found that psychology students could rate the degree of anxiety of psychiatric patients quite successfully on the basis of one-minute silent videotaped samples of their behaviour. Anxiety was indicated by cues such as jittery but non-signalling gestures of the hands (twitches, tremors and self-touching), significantly shorter duration of eye contact, less smiling, and a tendency for the torso to be held rigidly still. In all such interpretations of non-verbal behaviour, we are frustrated by the fact that the clearest messages, coming from the face and most closely watched by the observer, are also subject to the greatest control and possible dissimulation by the sender. In many instances of doctor-patient interaction however it may be crucial for the doctor to receive these non-verbal messages sensitively, and the capacity to do this forms a large part of the usual training in interviewing skills (see Chapter 10).

ANGER

Like anxiety, anger is a mixed blessing. The inability to recognize and cope constructively with one's anger is an extremely frequent component of social and personal maladjustment of the 'neurotic' type. Such difficulties can be the source of severe anxieties, perhaps about the devastating imagined consequences of getting angry, as well as of resentment at the ill-treatment that an overly submissive attitude is likely to attract. Assertiveness training is now a well developed body of techniques to help people of this sort to communicate angry feelings clearly and appropriately. The generalization of these skills to the expression of other feelings helps to strengthen relationships, reduce isolation and improve self-esteem.

On the other hand there are people who are often a nuisance or hazard to others, rather than being a worry to themselves. They are deficient in ability to *inhibit* the expression of anger, and get into trouble for excesses of aggressive behaviour. From the over-officious authority figure to the vandal and on to the 'psychopath', who acts as though the infliction of suffering on others is a major reinforcer to him, runs a continuum of increasing deviance from our societal norms of aggressive impulse control.

Antecedents

The classical explanation for the arousal of anger is frustration. When a desired reinforcer is withdrawn or otherwise made unavailable, anger is the result. Machines which stop working or friends who break appointments at the last minute are good examples of anger-arousing situations familiar to most of us. This **frustration-aggression hypothesis** (Dollard *et al.* 1939) has been supported both experimentally and by naturalistic observations of correlations between, for example, falls in the price of cotton and increases in the frequency with which cotton farmers form lynching parties.

Biologists and ethologists have tended to stress a view of aggression as innate, a force like hunger or sexual tension which must be satisfied one way or another (Lorenz 1966). Working mainly with animals and extrapolating to humans, they have described the **dominance hierarchy** or 'peck order' which is established within any group by trials of strength amongst the males, and thereafter determines social and sexual relations quite rigidly. Psychoanalysts have similarly characterized aggression, with sex, as a primary instinctual drive (i.e. part of the id), and they see much of the process of healthy personality development as one of learning how to express these drives in ways gratifying to the self and yet acceptable to society (a major function of the ego). The universality of anger experiences in humans is not necessarily proof of an 'instinctive' basis: frustration is also a universal human experience.

Constitutional and genetic influences upon aggressiveness have been explored by many researchers. The usual difficulties of gene-environment interaction and of self-fulfilling prophecies obscure to what extent (although we may take for granted that it is to at least *some* extent) relative aggressiveness may be inherited. The XYY genotype discussed in Chapter 3 is evidently not a sufficient explanation in itself. Bigelow (1972) provides a balanced and comprehensive review of the evolution of human aggression, cooperation and self-control. Hormonal factors may act similarly to predispose individuals towards aggressive responses in frustrating situations. Production rates of the male sex hormone, testosterone, are correlated with measures of aggression, and 62 per cent of the (few) violent crimes committed by women occur during the premenstrual week. Electrical stimulation of, or tumours upon, the amygdala section of the brain induce aggressive responses, and stimulation of the septal area appears to inhibit them. The physiological control of violence by surgery or implanted electrodes raises many ethical questions which have not yet been fully resolved.

Other broad influences upon aggressive behaviour are known to be the ambient temperature (more murders, riots and revolutions during the summer), the degree of crowding if there is competition for resources within the affected population, and the phase of the moon (Moos and Insel 1974). Like the biological variables mentioned above, these environmental factors act non-specifically to raise or lower the aggression threshold of designated groups of people, but do not allow accurate predictions about individuals.

It is worth noting here that anger and aggression are not of course synonymous. Aggressive behaviour is a convenient clue to angry feelings, but it is as possible to behave in a way which injures another person without feeling angry towards them (e.g. through an accident, or through impersonally 'doing one's duty'), as it is to feel angry and not express it through overt aggression. Sometimes indeed, when anger is directed inwards, perhaps when the self rather than external agents is perceived to be the source of frustrations, people do behave aggressively towards themselves, demeaning themselves, denying themselves pleasure and even acting violently towards themselves. This form of self-hatred is regarded as a form of depression. There is another way in which anger and sadness are closely related. Grief over a significant personal loss, such as in bereavement, normally contains a component of anger; all kinds of positive reinforcers have been withdrawn. People need to recognize that hostility towards the dead is not some shocking aberration but a natural part of the mourning process (see Chapter 10).

Whatever may be the extent to which aggression is a natural response to frustration, or a natural expression of dominance, it would be foolish to overlook the important influence of learning, in determining both when and how it is expressed. The first point to make is that frustrations are inevitable in the course of infancy and childhood, and that there are many occasions for shaping how the child expresses the resultant aggression. The parent's response is likely to provide a model as well as a lesson in the consequences of, say, hitting versus 'telling on' the child who has commandeered your tricycle. A primitive response by the parent teaches that counter-aggression is acceptable, with the proviso that the target be chosen carefully. The bully, who ingratiates himself with those of higher status and torments those of lower, is nurtured this way. It must also be recognized that in our society, aggressiveness is regarded as normal, regrettably or even desirably so in males, and abnormal in females except perhaps in the defence of the young, or in protection of an exclusive relationship with a male (when it is expected but still condemned by men). Relative aggressiveness is one trait which tends to show intra-individual consistency from boyhood to manhood, just as dependency is a stereotypical female attribute and is relatively consistent from girlhood to womanhood (Kagan and Moss 1962).

For boys especially, there are considerable pressures to display exactly the right degree of aggression, neither effeminately little nor brutally too much. Apart from the same-sex parent, other potent models for aggressive behaviour are found in the entertainment media. Comics, books, movies and more recently television, with the vicarious lesson that violence is acceptable in heroes and contributes to their eminence, form a particularly significant influence on children whose parental identifications are weak. Eron (1963) found a significant relationship between preference for violent TV programmes at eight years of age, and delinquent behaviour *ten* years later in the same boys, and many studies have indicated that exposure to TV violence increases the incidence of subsequent aggressive behaviours (Murray 1973). Such findings have relevance not only for the kind of children's programmes which parents and others should demand to be made available, but also for the kind of therapy suitable for people with problems specific to anger expression.

Behavioural results

Anger inspires attack, which may consist of blows and shouting, or be restricted to intention movements such as glares, clenched fists, threatening gestures, a raised voice and bared teeth. As with anxiety there are numerous non-verbal signals of anger perceptible to the alert observer, which will sometimes represent leakage of an emotional state not openly acknowledged by the person concerned, and sometimes constitute a deliberate counterpoint to the spoken message. As pointed out before, anger against oneself may be inferred when self-injurious behaviours occur.

In people brought up to be 'over nice', the experience of anger can result in anxiety. The typical learning of avoidance responses which results may lead to denial of the anger. This may be covertly expressed through dreams and fantasies (e.g. of mutilation and calamity), or to over-compensatory defences such as an unrealistically protective and subservient attitude towards the source of the anger. Unexpressed anger in other words is a stressor, and it has the bad effect on health which can be expected from an understanding of how the body responds to stress – with sympathetic ANS arousal.

Expressed anger varies widely in its appropriateness, as noted previously. **Assertiveness** is the term for communications about angry feelings which are informative, without being seen as aggressive (and therefore inviting counter-attack). Being able thus to cope constructively with anger is an invaluable skill which tends to strengthen rather than weaken bonds with others (see Bach & Goldberg 1974).

Because aggression is (at least officially) negatively valued culturally, asking people about whether or not they feel angry, or getting them to fill out psychological test forms on the subject, is likely to have limited validity. An investigation of how the person behaves in specific frustrating situations is likely to be more helpful.

The military technology available today makes our facility for systematic aggression against large numbers of our conspecifics a serious social problem. At the same time there is agreement amongst psychiatrists and psychosomatic medicine specialists that how a given person handles anger is a vital consideration in that person's physical as well as emotional health.

SADNESS

While we all experience low moods occasionally, and some of us have more cheerful dispositions than others, chronic sadness constitutes the important and pervasive clinical syndrome of **depression,** which will be the main topic of this section.

Its characteristics are a conscious affect of sadness, hopelessness and emptiness, loss of interest and appetites, withdrawal from social situations, undue pessimism (about both the future and about one's current capabilities), and associated behavioural signs such as insomnia, lack of energy and crying easily. It may vary in intensity from dejection to profound despair. There is a continuing argument amongst workers in the area over questions such as how to differentiate normal from pathological sadness, whether depression can be categorized as *reactive* versus *endogenous* (not reactive to an external cause), and other technical matters. We will confine the description here to the most commonly agreed upon points.

Antecedents

Depression is usually found to follow upon a loss to the individual of some source of gratification. Depressive behaviours are expected in the course of normal mourning for the death of a loved one, and also after the loss of anything of psychological significance, whether it is a job, possession, hope, or view of oneself. The loss of physical wholeness, as with advancing age or after some accident or illness which leaves impairment in its wake, is a further example of such loss and can similarly be expected to result in some depression.

Another antecedent of depression which has gained much attention recently is the experience of helplessness. While feelings of helplessness have long been regarded as a characteristic part of established depression (Beck 1967), **learned helplessness** has recently been proposed (Abramson, Seligman and Teasdale 1978; Seligman 1975) to precipitate depressive episodes. Experiences of lack of control over the environment have been shown in both animals and humans to lead to a state (learned helplessness) where the victim seems to 'give up hope' that adaptive responses can be made, and will fail to try, even if such responses are objectively available. Passivity and hopelessness reflect the person's negative expectations about his ability to control important reinforcers.

Another contributing factor is likely to be the loss or withdrawal of social reinforcers for depressed persons. Coyne (1976) explored what happened when normal subjects spoke on the telephone for twenty minutes with depressed patients. He found that they felt significantly more depressed, anxious and hostile themselves than subjects who had conversed with non-depressed patients or with normal controls. The unrewardingness, or even aversiveness of interaction with a depressed person, from anyone else's point of view, probably lead to avoidance and denial of support which exacerbate the depression.

In considering possible physiological antecedents of depression we face the same sort of chicken-and-egg problems as with the motivational and behavioural explanations. Certainly depression can be induced by certain drugs such as reserpine (commonly used to treat hypertension), and successfully treated by drugs (tricyclic antidepressants and monoamine oxidase inhibitors) which *reverse* the characteristic biogenic amine depletion. Akiskal and McKinney (1973) have proposed, for all these diverse facts and theories about the origins of depression, an integrated model taking account of chemical, genetic, developmental and interpersonal determinants. They see depression as a psychobiological end-product of helplessness, involving hyperarousal, biogenic amine depletion, disturbances of the neurophysiological bases of reinforcement, and deteriorating coping skills.

Behavioural results

The main features of depression already described include affective (low spirits), cognitive (reduced expectations) and behavioural (passivity and lack of positive reinforcers) components. Irritability, weight loss, sexual disinterest and sleeplessness are also common. Sometimes agitation prevails, and sometimes, in the more severe cases, psychomotor retardation. Where feelings of guilt and worthlessness actually constitute a delusion, the person is out of contact with reality and may correspondingly be labelled as psychotic. In such cases there is occasionally an alternation between depression and the hyperactive, euphoric state with delusions of grandeur or omnipotence called mania. There are various paper and pencil measures o depression – again, non-verbal behaviour will also provide clear cues to the alert observer.

Depression has been found to accompany and to antecede a wide range of medical conditions. The difficulties of persuading people who are not sick to act as subjects in investigations, and the time and expense involved in following individual cases over the twenty or forty years which would be ideal, are obstacles to research. It means that we do not yet fully understand to what extent depression alone can precipitate illness. Certainly it is a frequent accompaniment or consequence of illness and physical disability, and may sometimes require separate treatment. But researchers who have worked on the problem for many years have concluded that depression may be causally connected with the onset of illnesses, ranging from infections to cancer (Schmale 1972). Remembering that a person is a whole, it makes sense that events which affect conscious experience should also affect not only the sympathetic ANS functions of which we may be or become aware, (such as heart rate, etc. discussed earlier), but also endocrinological and immunological systems beyond awareness but crucial to health.

Depression seems to be a common pathway through which events in a person's life may result in the onset of illness. The most heavily weighted items in the Schedule of Recent Experience, which correlates with illness onset (Holmes and Masuda 1974), involve psychological losses such as bereavement, divorce and job loss. If the response to such losses is one of hopelessness and helplessness, health changes are likely. Some people, however, undergo such stressful events without the depressive response, and do not demonstrate increased illness susceptibility (Birley and Connolly 1976; Dohrenwend and Dohrenwend 1978). Whether a person responds with depression or not will depend on all the developmental, biochemical and interpersonal predispositions discussed earlier. In particular, the availability of **social supports** in the form of trusted friends and confidants, who allow the stressed individual to express unhappy emotions and remain assured of personal worth, seems to be a major variable in mitigating the illness susceptibility results of psychological trauma (Cassel 1976; Cobb 1976).

Depression affects health and becomes the concern of the doctor in another obvious way through its common result of suicide (which is not, however, always related to depression). Always a possibility in cases of moderate or severe depression, suicide shows peaks of incidence in adolescence and after sixty. For each person who dies there are probably ten other people who attempt it, and many apparent accidents may in fact represent suicides or suicide attempts. There are ethnic and cultural variations in the prevalence, usual methods and precipitants, and also some differences in the characteristics of those who attempt it unsuccessfully compared with those who succeed.

HAPPINESS

The pleasant emotions have been relatively little studied by behavioural scientists, perhaps because they are assumed to represent an ideal with which anxiety, hostility and depression interfere.

Antecedents

Positive reinforcement, whether by presentation of a positive stimulus or removal of an aversive one, is the most usual source of good feelings. The arousal dimension is as usual a significant one, and provides experiences grading from contentment (satisfaction and perhaps mild satiation) to ecstasy. At the extremes of sexual or religious passion, or possibly altered forms of consciousness such as a drug trip, ecstasy shares cognitive and behavioural restrictedness with the other extreme emotional states (such as panic and fury).

In line with our analysis in Chapter 6 of the different kinds of reinforcer to which humans are responsive, we may distinguish different kinds of pleasurable emotional experience. Food, drink, warmth and other biological reinforcers result in feelings of satisfaction, but in each case a surfeit may be aversive. Much harder to satiate, and also more variable according to age and personality factors, are the positive feelings associated with physical contact (including sexual) with other people, and approval and attention from them. Attachment to a relatively small number of trusted intimates, as well as status and social stimulation from others, are included here. These social reinforcers are vital contributors to feelings of self-esteem, security and worth. They are relevant to one's estimation of oneself as loveable and capable, and therefore to one's expectations about being able to cope with life's difficulties. Conditioned reinforcers such as money, or familiar objects associated with happiness in the past, seem to be able to act as partial substitutes for these social reinforcers, by symbolizing the approval or affection of others.

Cognitive reinforcers result in yet other pleasures. Knowledge of results contributes to feelings of effectiveness and mastery (one aspect of self-esteem), while perceptual novelty can cause the sort of intellectual exhiliration or interest felt when, for example, listening to music or poetry. (Note, by the way, that over-arousal with cognitive stimulation may be aversive: the middle range of familiarity is probably the most reinforcing, and anything discrepant from established expectations may be experienced as incomprehensible and therefore unpleasant.)

Behavioural results

By definition, positive reinforcement strengthens the antecedent response. Thus people will tend to spend more time on, and feel more enthusiasm for, enjoyable activities compared with less rewarding ones. As usual, the relationship between response and reinforcement need not with humans be a simple temporal one. If you are sitting in the library reading a textbook and you receive news that you have won a lot of money in a lottery, ticket-buying rather than studying is likely to be strengthened. Holmes and his co-workers included positive events such as getting married or gaining new family members in the Schedule of Recent Experience. Although other workers have claimed that only negative events affect illness susceptibility, it is true that many happy events involve readjustments and possible losses as well as pleasure. Marriage clearly brings responsibilities and restrictions, as well as increased opportunities for sexual pleasure and attachment security. There are well documented instances in which sudden windfalls of money have had extremely bad consequences for health (such as heart attacks) and for personal adjustment (e.g. the pools winner may suffer ostracism or alienation from former friends, disruptions in lifestyle and so on). We may hypothesize that undesirable results of joy are due to a combination of excessive ANS arousal and helplessness. Non-contingent rewards (delivered independently of responses) produce some of the same passivity and withdrawal of effort as non-contingent punishment: Carder and Berkowitz (1970) found that rats preferred to work for food rather than have it given 'free'.

In the psychotherapy situation, Bandura (1969, see ref. Chapter 6) has pointed out that non-contingent social reinforcers may inadvertently strengthen undesirable behaviours. There appears to be a conflict here between a learning analysis of how to change behaviour, and those therapists of a Rogerian persuasion (see Chapter 12) who advocate 'unconditional positive regard' for the patient as a necessary precondition of therapy. The solution lies in distinguishing between the therapist's non-specific regard for and interest in the patient *as an individual,* and his or her arrangement of positive (and increasingly self-administered) reinforcers contingent upon desired *behaviours.* The former contributes towards a warm relationship between the two parties, which strengthens the therapist's power to succeed at the latter. The same considerations apply to child-rearing.

Happiness then is at least as complex an emotion as any other, and at least as important to medicine. While its sources vary according to developmental stage and personality patterns, there are regularities which derive from the classes of reinforcement to which we are innately predisposed to attend. The net result of many pleasant experiences, and possibly the most basic condition for happiness, is a symbolic, self-reinforcing condition of perceived ability to win reinforcers and cope with obstacles. It is such feelings of competence and security that are our best equipment for life's vicissitudes. Their inculcation is the ultimate goal of child-rearing practices and perhaps, too, of medical care. Pericles said in 500 BC, 'Health is that state of moral, mental and physical well being which enables a person to face any crisis in life with the utmost grace and facility'. If you accept such a definition you will see the need for medical practitioners to understand how feelings affect the body, and vice versa, as well as how people acquire their individual patterns of emotional response (Chapter 9), and how to modify them (Chapters 10 and 12).

SUMMARY

The ANS and endocrine system mediate physiological arousal in emotional states, which depends for its interpretation on cognitive factors. The optimum level of arousal for different tasks varies according to task complexity, but extremes of arousal tend to be aversive. Taking account of the individual variability of human reinforcement discussed in the last chapter, it is possible to list the usual precipitators and common behavioural results (at different levels of generality) for the most important emotional states. Anxiety is a response to threat which may be reduced or avoided by a variety of behaviours, some of which are maladaptively restricting. The appropriate expression of anger is a major interpersonal skill. Depression follows loss, whether of health, loved ones, or feelings of control of the environment. It seems to be related to illness onset, if adequate social supports are not available. Happiness is associated with positive experiences and expectations about one's ability to cope with and control the environment.

TERMS AND CONCEPTS

sympathetic ⎫
parasympathetic ⎭ branches of ANS
Yerkes-Dodson Law
frustration-aggression hypothesis
dominance hierarchy
assertiveness
depression
learned helplessness
social supports

FOR DISCUSSION

1. Keep a diary for a week or more, with careful regular entries concerning your feelings and moods. Try to relate your emotional states to the preceding events (e.g. of frustration, threatened loss, social approval, etc.) of your life. Also try to observe in yourself the physiological *and* the overt behavioural responses characteristic of your different states of feelings.
2. In a group, practise conveying and assessing emotional states non-verbally.
3. Think about (and if possible observe) the practice of medicine in terms of the likely sources of emotional arousal on the part of doctors. What sources of emotional support do or might doctors have?

SUGGESTED READING

Cobb; Schmale; Seligman: different but overlapping perspectives on the intriguing relationship between feelings and health.

REFERENCES

Abramson, L. Y., Seligman, M. E. P. and Teasdale, J. D. 1978. Learned helplessness in humans: Critique and reformulation. *J. Abnorm. Psych.* **87,** 49–74.

Akiskal, H. S. and McKinney, W. T. 1973. Depressive disorders: Toward a unified hypothesis. *Science* **182,** 20–9.

Bach, G. R. and Goldberg, H. 1974. *Creative Aggression.* New York: Double day.

Bauer, D. H. 1976. An exploratory study of developmental changes in children's fears. *J. Child Psychol. Psychiat.* **17,** 69–74.

Beck, A. T. 1967. *Depression: Causes and Treatment.* Philadelphia: Univ. Penn. Press.

Bigelow, R. 1972. The evolution of cooperation, aggression and self control. *Nebraska Symp. on Motivation* **20,** 1–57.

Birley, J. L. T. and Connolly, J. 1976. Life events and physical illness. *Mod. Trends in Psychosom. Res.* **3,** 154–65.

Carder, B. and Berkowitz, K. 1970. Rats' preference for earned in comparison with free food. *Science* **167,** 1273–4.

Cassel, J. 1976. The contribution of the social environment to host resistance. *Amer. J. Epidemiol.* **104,** 107–123.

Christie, M. J. 1976. Electrodermal activity. *Mod. Trends in Psychosom. Med.* **3,** 66–89.

Cobb, S. 1976. Social support as a moderator of life stress. *Psychosom. Med.* **38,** 300–14.

Cohen F. and Lazarus, R. S. 1973. Active coping processes, coping dispositions, and recovery from surgery. *Psychosom. Med.* **35,** 375–89.

Coyne, J. C. 1976. Depression and the response of others. *J. Abnorm. Psychol.* **85,** 186–93.

Dohrenwend, B. S. and Dohrenwend B. P. 1978. Some issues in research on stressful life events. *J. Nerv. Ment. Dis.* **166,** 7–15.

Dollard, J., Doob, L. W., Miller, N. W., Mowrer, O. H. and Sears, R. R. 1939. *Frustration and Aggression.* New Haven: Yale Univ. Press.

Egbert, L. D., Battit, G. E., Welch, C. E. and Bartlett, M. K. 1964. Reduction of postoperative pain by encouragement and instruction of patients. *New Engl. J. Med.* **270,** 825–7.

Eron, L. 1963. Relationship of TV viewing habits and aggressive behavior in children. *J. Abn. soc. Psychol.* **67,** 193–6.

Holmes, T. H. and Masuda, M. 1974. Life change and illness susceptibility. In B. S. Dohrenwend and B. P. Dohrenwend (eds) *Stressful Life Events: Their Nature and Effects* 45–72. New York: Wiley.

Kagan, J. and Moss, H. A. 1962. *Birth to Maturity: A Study in Psychological Development.* New York: Wiley.

Lorenz, K. 1966. *On Aggression.* London: Methuen.

Mandler, G. 1962. Emotion. In R. M. Brown, E. Galanter, E. H. Hess and G. Mandler (eds) *New Directions in Psychology* **1,** 267–343. New York: Holt Rinehart and Winston.

Moos, R. H. and Insel, P. M. (eds) 1974. *Issues in Social Ecology: Human Milieus.* Palo Alto: National Press Books.

Murray, J. P. 1973. Television and violence: Implications of the Surgeon General's research program. *Amer. Psychol.* **28,** 472–8.

Schachter, S. and Singer, J. 1962. Cognitive, social and physiological determinants of emotional state. *Psychol. Rev.* **69,** 379–99.

Schmale, A. H. 1972. Giving up as a final common pathway to changes in health. *Adv. Psychosom. Med.* **8,** 20–40.

Seligman, M. E. P. 1975. *Helplessness: On Depression, Development and Death.* San Francisco: Freeman.

Watson, J. B. and Rayner, R. 1920. Conditioned emotional reaction. *J. Exper. Psychol.* **3,** 1–14.

Waxer, P. H. 1977. Non-verbal cues for anxiety: An examination of emotional leakage. *J. Abnorm. Psychol.* **86,** 306–14.

Chapter 8

Individual Differences in Intelligence

Having explored in the preceding chapters the processes of psychological function common to all, we now turn to the determinants of inter-individual variation. Although it does some violence to the subject, there are advantages, mainly derived from the traditions of how to approach the topics, to separating out influences upon cognitive and motivational characteristics of the person. This chapter deals with the former and Chapters 9 and 11 with the latter.

An individual's intelligence is one of his or her most basic characteristics, and it colours many aspects of life other than school success. It is also one of the few human characteristics which are highly valued by nearly everyone. There is therefore considerable interest in how to foster intelligence in children and encourage its demonstration throughout life. This chapter first considers the question of what intelligence consists of, and then reviews the influences, both biological and psychosocial, which affect it.

DEFINITION OF INTELLIGENCE

It is rather tempting to regard 'intelligence' as some fixed characteristic and to forget that it is actually a descriptive abstraction distilled from observations of behaviour in a variety of situations. It is a **hypothetical construct** and can be inferred only from the evidence of intelligent *behaviour*. While most of us understand or think we understand what that implies, difficulties arise in pinning down the concept with sufficient specificity for measurement. For example, is a nomadic Australian aborigine who successfully survives the desert, but is illiterate, as intelligent as a suburb-dweller who works in a factory and spends the rest of the time watching television?

Comparisons across cultural groups are still impossible to make with any validity because of the origin and nature of the usual measuring instrument: the intelligence test.

Definitions of intelligence range from the defeatist operational one of 'what intelligence tests measure', to the carry-all by Wechsler (1958, p. 7), the originator of the best known measuring device: 'the global capacity of the individual to act purposefully, to think rationally and to deal effectively with his environment'. Common elements in many definitions are that intelligence has something to do with being able to grasp abstract and complex relationships, and something to do with problem-solving and learning from experience. For our purposes, intelligence can be summarized as the ability to think up effective solutions to problems. Note that artistic creativity is a separate psychological attribute altogether.

MEASUREMENT OF INTELLIGENCE

What intelligence tests measure is the ability to find solutions to a rather special kind of problem, namely those most related to academic success. The forerunner of modern instruments was devised in 1905 by the French psychologist, Alfred Binet, with the aim of deciding which schoolchildren were in need of special education due to subnormal ability. From the results of thousands of tests he developed a progressively-ordered scale of items, such that a child's performance could be compared with that of age-mates. The four-year-old who passes tests like an average six-year-old has a **Mental Age** of six, and thus an **Intelligent Quotient** of 150, using the relationship IQ= (Mental Age/Chronological Age) × 100. Similarly the four-year-old who can pass only two-year-old items will have an IQ of 50.

Binet's tests, updated and revised for American use, are still valuable for the clinical psychologist working with young children. One difficulty with such a formula, however, is the rather embarrassing finding that, because Mental Age usually shows little further increase after about 16, adult IQs would show progressive decline from then onwards, a most unpalatable conclusion to most adults. The solution devised by Wechsler was to calculate IQ on the basis of how a given person's score compares with a (hopefully) representative sample of others of the same age. His intelligence scales, one for adults and one for children, were constructed such that at each age the average IQ score is 100 and scores fall in a **normal distribution** about the mean (i.e. in a bell-shaped curve). This arrangement has the effect that a predetermined proportion of the population obtains scores within each category of IQ. (Actually there may be a preponderance of low scorers greater than expected.) Approximately two thirds of the population score between IQ 85–115, for example. Wechsler classed IQs of 120 or better as superior (9.9 per cent of the population), 70–79 as borderline (6.7 per cent), and 60–69 as mentally defective (2.2 per cent). Other intelligence tests can be administered to groups of people at a time and scored by machine; these are even more influenced by verbal facility.

The overall IQ represents a sampling of performance in many different areas. General knowledge, oral arithmetic and vocabulary are clearly influenced by educational opportunities, but other subtests such as copying a pattern with coloured blocks, or matching digits and symbols, are less obviously so. Other subtests require the display of social judgement and reasoning, and familiarity with common objects, which may be influenced by social class and cultural background. While age and sex biases have been eliminated from the tests during construction, the same is not true of social and ethnic differences.

One benefit of giving an IQ test, unrelated to IQ, is that the clinical psychologist gets a good impression of how cooperative the testee is, how he or she copes with stress and novelty, relative impulsivity versus reflectivity and quality of concentration, as well as specific indications of brain impairment (shown by difficulties with some subtests rather than others), and of speech or thought disorders characteristic of psychosis. The administration, scoring and inter- pretation of a W.A.I.S. (Wechsler Adult Intelligence Scale) takes up considerable time. In non-clinical situations therefore, group-adminis- tered machine-scored tests are more frequently used. These are necessarily limited to pencil and paper tests, and tend to be even more directly aimed at assessing scholastic aptitude. Particularly in America the educational system relies heavily on such measures to determine such opportunities as college entrance.

EVALUATION OF THE TESTS

A critical question concerning psychological tests is naturally that of how good they are, and this is usually evaluated in two parts. **Reliability** refers to the extent to which the same person will get the same score on different test occasions, other things being equal. A tape measure which gives different answers on different days is obviously no use. The problem with IQ scores is that we can never be absolutely sure that other things are equal. A person who is suffering from fatigue or a heavy cold, or who has just had an argument with somebody important, may perform less well that day (and may even be less capable of intelligent behaviour), than at another time. Familiarity with the whole concept of being tested and trying your hardest, as well as with the types of questions and tasks involved, may also influence relative performance on different occasions. If the examiner is different from one administration to another, or even treats you differently, a whole new set of sources of unreliability is introduced. Overall IQ differences between tests of ten points or so are not unusual. They probably reflect partly genuine fluctuations in individual performance (remember it is this and not capacity which is being measured), and partly inherent unreliability of the tests. One solid fact is that test reliability improves with the age of the testee, being relatively poor until 10 to 12 years of age.

Validity refers to whether a test measures what it purports to measure. An intelligence test therefore should measure ability to think up effective solutions to problems, not which school the testee attended or how long ago. The fact that many of the possible contaminating variables may themselves be correlated with IQ score is a complication which makes convincing validation extremely difficult. Remember from Chapter 2 that the fact that two variables are correlated does not necessarily mean that they are causally related; both may be influenced by a third factor. Social class, for example, correlating as it does with parent's belief in the value of education for their children, and also with the elaboratedness of the home language code, may affect both scholastic attainment and IQ test score. The famous long term studies of gifted children by Terman and his associates, which found that high-scoring eleven-year-olds grew up happier, healthier and more successful and productive than the rest of the population, have been contaminated by Terman's failure to control for such biases: his original group were socio-economically advantaged.

By and large intelligence test scores correlate reasonably well with academic achievement, especially if we take account of the whole and not a truncated range of both variables. Therefore knowledge of IQ score could be of assistance in advising someone about the likelihood of success in educational ventures. Even here, however, motivational and attitudinal variables may be at least equally good as predictors.

What relationship then exists between academic success and achievements in later life? Surprisingly little, according to the evidence. While a certain level of attainment opens doors to further opportunities, ordinal position within the class (or in America, the grade-point average) shows exceedingly little predictive validity. Doctors in the top and bottom thirds of their graduating class were found in one study to display only very slight differences in quality of practice thereafter, and even these disappeared after the first few years (Becker, Geer and Miller 1972). The use of IQ tests to exclude individuals from the opportunity to receive training can be seen, not as a valid method of directing teaching resources to those most likely to benefit, but as a self-protective manoeuvre by the power elite whose children are likely to benefit from such measures.

A fairer way to distribute opportunities and educational resources is the use of tests, not of 'general mental ability', but of competence at the *critical* components of the task concerned. McLelland (1973) suggested that test constructors should first find out what is involved in the skill concerned, and then find ways of sampling the adaptive behaviours relevant to success. The more directly criterion behaviours are sampled, the less need there is for secrecy about test 'answers', because faking becomes impossible. In addition, attention should be paid to non-intellectual activities critical for success, such as communication skills, patience, realistic goal-setting and personal maturity.

Non-intellectual factors of a social kind are equally as important in determining life adjustment and achievement (however we agree to measure that), at the 'below average' levels of intelligence. People with measured IQ of 50 to 70 form the largest group, and tend to show great diversity in achievements, some being confined to institutions and others managing their own affairs quite successfully in the community.

With all the reservations one needs to hold about the relationship between intelligence and IQ score, which we have been discussing so far, IQ tests remain the best indicator available of individual differences in cognitive ability (and indeed, the best measures yet developed for any complex psychological function). Let us now turn to an examination of factors known to influence IQ score. It would be misleading to conceptualize the operation of these biological, psychological and social variables as discrete. There is a continuous interaction between them which is very apparent in practice but equally difficult to describe in quantitative terms.

BIOLOGICAL INFLUENCES ON IQ

BRAIN CONDITION AND AGE

Compared with other species, the human brain has a large association area free from fixed sensory and motor responsibilities, and this is presumed to be the basis of our greater behavioural flexibility and capacity for learning and abstract thought. Within our own species, however, there are no clues in the intact brain as to the relative intelligence of its possessor. Brains damaged by accidents or alcohol can be expected to have belonged to people with cognitive limitations, depending on the extent and site of the damage and the age at which it occurred. Often brain damage is diagnosed by means of an assessment of the degree and type of cognitive impairment, and various psychological tests have been developed to explore such functions as memory, concept formation and so on. Any form of damage to the CNS is likely to be reflected in IQ performance, although sometimes only some component abilities may show deterioration. Severe mental disorder, such as in schizophrenia, is also likely to affect IQ performance adversely, but more through lack of concentration and cooperation than through loss of capacity, as is shown by normal test results of successfully treated sufferers.

Nutrition, particularly the amount of protein in the diet, is an important factor which affects the brain from conception onwards. Thus an under-nourished or poorly nourished mother may pass on disadvantage to her child in a transgenerational perpetuation of the culture of poverty. Malnourished children are less able to take advantage of the educational opportunities they receive.

Quality of obstetric care concerns not only the drugs or irradiation a mother may receive during pregnancy, and protection from diseases like rubella, all of which may damage the foetus, but also the sensitivity of the brain to damage during the birth process itself (see Chapter 3). As with nutrition, there is an uneven distribution of these resources through our societies.

Ageing, at the other end of the age spectrum, may also affect brain intactness in a way which influences IQ performance. Senility is a special case, where there is discernible atrophy of brain cells (especially in the vital frontal areas), but in the course of normal ageing the gradual thickening of arteries, loss of perceptual acuity, and reduced cardiovascular efficiency might be expected to affect mental function. The answers you get in looking at intelligence in old age depend very much on the particular tests you use, on which old people take them for you, and when.

A diverse IQ test like the W.A.I.S. usually shows differential decrement with age in performance on different subtests. Information and vocabulary do not decline with increasing years, whereas there is an absolute deterioration in the ability to solve new problems (such as posed by the Block Designs subtest), particularly where time is limited. (Remember that because of how the test is standardized, absolute decrements in performance will not necessarily be shown up in lower IQ for older people.) Any complication of the task, such as having to repeat digits in reverse order to that heard, also places older people at a disproportionate disadvantage. Cattell (1963) drew a distinction between the **fluid** and non-specialized type of intelligence relevant to new learning (e.g. of a computer language) and novel-problem solving, and the other **crystallized** type of intelligence which represents accumulated wisdom. It is fluid intelligence which is seen to decline with age from the early twenties onwards, and the crystallized which continues to increase, at least until late middle-age and possibly thereafter.

In practice, daily life does not very frequently demand the speedy solution of unfamiliar problems, or the mastery of a new complex cognitive skill. In many cases, a combination of judgement and knowledge derived from past learning, and a decision arrived at over several days, is perfectly adequate intellectual equipment. Although old people, like other disadvantaged groups in society, do not match the facility at mental gymnastics of the powerful middle-aged generation, they should not be dismissed as unintelligent. (At the time of writing, laws against compulsory retirement are in fact progressing through the American parliamentary system.) Always to be borne in mind is the increasing heterogeneity of the aged: individual differences get larger rather than smaller (see Chapter 9).

The second problem mentioned above, with regard to unravelling age effects on IQ, was the choice of aged subjects and of research design. Naturally participation in research must be voluntary, but we have evidence that elderly people who refuse to participate, or to continue to participate in a **longitudinal** study (one where the same people are retested at intervals), are not a random sample of those who are initially approached. In fact, they tend to be those who are less able to begin with, and their absence therefore gives an unrealistically rosy impression to the results of longitudinal studies. Comparison of groups of 40, 60 and 80-year-olds, for instance, in a

cross-sectional design, is also hazardous. Many of the differences may be due to non-age-related differences between generations, such as different educational opportunities and current socioeconomic status. It also appears that a relatively sudden decrement in IQ may occur up to five years before death (this is known as the **terminal drop** and has been described by Riegel and Riegel 1972). This may bias the results of cross-sectional studies, because more people undergoing terminal drop are included in the oldest group.

While debate continues about the best way to design research projects, it seems fairly safe to accept Botwinick's (1973) conclusions, which are: 1) People of high initial ability tend to retain high verbal ability, and show decline in relation to younger people but not to their peers, in non-verbal tests; 2) People of low initial ability decline in both sorts of ability in later life; 3) People with middling initial ability keep up verbally but not otherwise; and 4) *Health* strongly influences the age-sensitive, non-verbal, 'fluid intelligence' performance.

SEX

As with age, items which discriminate against members of one sex or the other have been eliminated from IQ tests used today. Males and females do show small but fairly consistent average differences in ability at tasks calling for different cognitive skills: the average for males is often higher where the test calls for mechanical under-standing, or spatial and quantitative reasoning, whereas the female average tends to be higher where perceptual discriminations, memory, computational or verbal skills are required. Aptitude tests commonly use sex-based norms in order to cancel out the superiority of women and men on verbal and quantitative sections respectively.

Whether sex differences in cognition are biologically or culturally determined is certainly too simple a question to ask. The findings discussed in Chapter 3, concerning specific patterns of deficit in IQ test performance for people with sex-linked genetic abnormalities, suggest that at least some of the observable sex differences have biological predispositions. The apparently greater variability within the male sex has also been cited as the reason for a preponderance of males over females at *both* extremes of the IQ distribution. For all practical purposes, the differences within each sex, which are far larger than the differences between the sexes, are more important.

GENETICS

Inherited mental defects due to chromosomal abnormality were discussed in Chapter 3. More controversial at present is the debate over whether different racial groups amongst members of the human species have different genetic endowments for intelligence. There are usually found to be several IQ points difference between the averages for groups with different skin colour and culture, which, over large numbers of people, reach statistical significance. There is, however, always a large degree of overlap in the distributions, so that knowing what an individual looks like is of no practical use in predicting the score. The thought of racially based IQ potential arouses more passion and alarm than that of racially based eye colour, because our society prizes achievements believed to be dependent on high IQ. Fears therefore arise that such a belief would worsen discrimination and prejudice against already disadvantaged minority group members. Jensen (1969) suggested that compensatory preschool education for poor black children is bound to be a waste of resources, due to their 'inferior' intellectual capacity.

Geneticists themselves have usually expressed a great deal of caution in discussion of heritability of IQ. Bodmer (1972), in an excellent review of the topic, has pointed out that complex quantitative characteristics such as height, weight and IQ are much more susceptible than polymorphisms, such as blood group, to environmental influences. (Blood group shows one of the most distinctively different patterns of distribution across different human groups.) After analysing the evidence and the arguments, Bodmer concluded that there is at present no way of answering the question of relative racial contribution to IQ. Even studies of the IQ of black children adopted early into white homes would not be fully satisfactory, as the children concerned would still suffer the effects of the prejudice against blacks in most white communities.

Some of the difficulties of disentangling genetic contributions to human intelligence were discussed in Chapter 3. To what extent either MZ or DZ twins have the 'same' environment, before birth, after birth, or even if raised in different adoptive families, is obviously a crucial question upon which little concrete evidence is available. Twins themselves may not be representative of the rest of the population; they are often born to older mothers for a start. While it is clear that IQ has some inherited characteristics, as seen by the fact that IQ correlations between relatives vary in size depending on the degree of genetic overlap, environmental factors such as nutrition, educational opportunities and others discussed more fully below also have a crucial influence. Being reared with a twin, or being the youngest child in a large family, are both agreed to result in lower IQ than other members of the same family, who presumably receive more concentrated parental attention. Children whose mothers had an average IQ of 85.5, and who were adopted before six months of age into relatively advantaged homes, had an average IQ at 13 to 14 years of 106, a much greater discrepancy than could be explained on the basis of regression towards the mean (Skodak and Skeels 1949). As Butcher (1968, p. 271) points out, environmental circumstances impose lower ceilings on intellectual achievement than do genetic factors, for the majority of people, and it is therefore at environmental factors that we should direct our efforts in order to realize the full potential of every member of society.

PSYCHOSOCIAL INFLUENCES ON IQ

Social influences affecting intellectual capacity can be expected to be those which affect cognitive development during the formative years. This is while the brain is still susceptible to the external environment (for example, a stimulus-enriched living space increases the myelination and the overall weight of rat brains), and while basic cognitive skills such as reading and writing are being acquired. It is fairly easy then to see which sorts of factors are likely to affect IQ performance beneficially.

Sensori-motor stimulation provides opportunities for learning through action in the way Piaget has shown us to be essential during early childhood. Such stimulation can be provided by colourful and interesting toys, not necessarily purchased as such but available playthings amongst the household objects. The best ones are those which allow an infant to manipulate and explore the object's response, and later to apply some creative imagination (rather than having the toy define all of its own necessarily limited possibilities). Freedom to explore involves, beyond a basic minimum of 'toys', permission to touch and experiment, to get dirty, and to investigate novel and diverse environments. All these depend on the presence of a suitably motivated caretaker without too many other demands upon her or his time and attention. As child care is unpaid or poorly paid work, such devotion of adult time and energy to the child's cognitive development is a luxury not available to all children.

Linguistic stimulation similarly depends upon the presence of adults or older children who provide learning experiences of graduated difficulty to stimulate language, and with it the complex repertoire of abstract cognitive skills discussed in Chapter 5. As vocabulary is the best single indicator of verbal IQ, and as school success is largely dependent upon verbal skills in the transmission and display of knowledge, it is not surprising that the quality of the linguistic environment during the early years is strongly related to later IQ. Thus story-telling, books, proper explanations and answers to the inevitable questions, and encouragement to express one's feelings and hypotheses verbally as precisely as possible (i.e. to use an elaborated language code), all equip the child with a crucial resource for which it may be inordinately difficult to provide a later substitute.

Encouragement to learn concerns, first, the child's identification with an attachment figure who provides basic security and thus willingness to explore the outside world. It also involves rewards for learning such as parental interest and approval for progress, helping the child to set attainable goals, treating school progress as important and making clear the long term benefits it conveys, and in similar ways creating an environment in which learning (both informal and scholastic) is strongly positively reinforced. Intellectual achievement is therefore likely to be discouraged by strong identification with parents and, later, peers who see no advantage in education, as well as by a failure to identify with very ambitious parents.

Socioeconomic class is a very molar variable (see Chapter 19) which relates to both income and attitudes. It is consistently found that IQ and social class are correlated, and there is an even stronger correlation between educational achievement and social class. The reasons for this relationship seem to be contained in variations between social classes in the three factors discussed above, which *frequently but not necessarily* vary according to social class. That is, a middle-class child is more likely than a working-class child to have an enriched physical and linguistic environment, and strong rewards for academic attainment. There are two other factors which should not be overlooked. One is the differential hazards according to social class of prematurity, birth damage, malnutrition, undetected sensory and other ailments (e.g. chronic ear infection), all of which reduce the child's capacity to benefit from what education is available. The second is that the quality of this education is likely to vary according to the parents' resources. This includes not only money but self-confidence in coping with 'the system', articulatedness, and sympathy with and belief in the value of the current educational system.

Expectations held by others, especially by teachers, are also likely to affect IQ performance, as was shown in an experiment by Rosenthal and Jacobson (1968). Children, whom teachers were led to believe would show an 'intellectual blooming' during the year, actually did perform better than controls eight months later, although the average differences were only a few points. Later studies explored exactly how this expectancy effect occurred. It seems that teachers, or supervisors, counsellors, and presumably anybody in such a role including parents and even medical advisors, actually create a different teaching environment for those whom they believe to have high potential to learn. The elements of this difference, which can be readily seen to amount to a substantial improvement in the educational process, include a) a warmer emotional climate, with more attention and friendliness, b) more and clearer feedback about the learner's progress, c) teaching of more material, and d) more opportunity for the student to respond (Rosenthal 1973).

Low expectations for poor or black children are thus likely to act as a self-fulfilling prophecy, with a cumulative effect over many years of schooling. In fact, all the psychosocial variables discussed here seem to have a cumulative effect. Although it is difficult and largely meaningless to speak of IQ in preverbal children – because all that tests can measure at this age is sensori-motor development and general alertness – disadvantaged babies do not appear to be significantly different from middle-class ones in cognitive capacities. By 3 to 4 years significant differences can be reliably found, and the relative deficit in performance of the disadvantaged child gets larger as time passes. Compensatory preschool education programmes are based on the logic of averting this **cumulative deficit.** They provide a concentrated experience of success-relevant skills (especially in language style and sophistication), to increase children's ability to make the most of educational opportunity. While the 1960s Headstart programme in America produced some very dramatic gains in educational attainment, these often faded out after children had spent a couple of years back in their overcrowded, poorly equipped slum schools.

Parental involvement in compensatory schemes is crucial for a long-lasting counter to the effects of poverty. First, parents control the day-to-day environment in a much more systematic way than the school, and of course for all the child's time during the critical pre-school developmental period. Secondly, involved parents provide a significant model of interest in and regard for educational achievement (as well as for a capacity to influence events, which may be just as important). Programmes which focus on improving the skills and understanding of the mother as a preschool tutor have achieved some encouraging results. The extent to which this is economically feasible on a large scale, acceptable to mothers without destroying their self-confidence, and able to achieve long term results by a short intervention, are all not known as yet.

So far, the psychosocial factors reviewed have been relatively enduring influences upon intellectual capacity, and expectancy effects can clearly be included here, insofar as they operate by means of the quality of the educational opportunities offered. However, expectancy can also be seen as a *short term* acting variable, affecting test performance independently of actual capacity. Expectancies on the part of both test administrators and test-takers, about the relative performances of old, young, black, white, poor and middle-class testees (all of whose characteristics are highly visible), may in fact influence the performance in question by altering the stressfulness of the testing session for the testee.

Bearing in mind the detrimental effects of excessive emotional arousal upon complex problem-solving (Chapter 7), it is clear that test performances may be adversely affected by chronically poor race relations. Anxiety and resentment could lower the scores of blacks tested by whites, and have been shown to do so (Watson 1972). Computerized testing was found by Johnson and Mihal (1973) to remove performance differences based on race, presumably because it eliminates face to face tester-testee interaction.

SUMMARY

Tests of intelligence measure skills related to academic success. Scores approximate to a normal distribution and are corrected for age and sex. Reliability and validity of the tests are not beyond question, and there is a tendency now to prefer for practical purposes, such as trainee selection, tests of critical components of the skills in question. Brain damage, malnutrition, poor antenatal and obstetric care, and old age can all affect IQ scores adversely in more or less specific ways. Inheritance and environmental factors both contribute to measured intelligence and it may be argued that the latter, being at least in principle modifiable, deserve close attention. Ideal conditions for intellectual development include pre-school language and sensorimotor stimulation, encouragement to learn, and positive expectations from others.

TERMS AND CONCEPTS

hypothetical construct
mental age
intelligence quotient
normal distribution
reliability
validity
fluid ⎫
crystallized ⎭ intelligence
longitudinal ⎫
cross-sectional ⎭ research designs
terminal drop
cumulative deficit

FOR DISCUSSION

1. What provisions are there in your area of residence for intellectual stimulation of young children? Question the directors of a kindergarten and of a day-care centre or nursery school. What facilities are available for children who do not attend these?
2. Discuss with an elderly person how he or she feels that age has affected cognitive functions. What compensations can or does the elderly person make for these changes?
3. Given the restrictions on admissions to medical schools, how do you think candidates could be selected who would make the best doctors?

SUGGESTED READING

Butcher; Richardson and Spears (see Bodmer reference): both give clear surveys of the issues of intelligence measurement.

REFERENCES

Becker, H. S., Geer, B. and Miller, S. J. 1972. Medical education. In H. E. Freeman, S. Levine and L. G. Reeder (eds) *Handbook of Medical Sociology* (2nd edn) 191–205. Englewood Cliffs, New Jersey: Prentice Hall.

Bodmer, W. F. 1972 Race and IQ: The genetic background. In K. Richardson and D. Spears (eds) *Race, Culture and Intelligence*. Middlesex: Penguin.

Botwinick, J. 1973. *Aging and Behavior*. New York: Springer.

Butcher, H. J. 1968. *Human Intelligence: Its Nature and Assessment*. London: Methuen.

Cattell, R. B. 1963. Theory of fluid and crystallized intelligence: A critical experiment. *J. Educ. Psychol.* **54,** 1–22.

Jensen, A. R. 1969. How much can we boost IQ and scholastic achievement? *Harvard Ed. Rev.* **39,** 1–123.

Johnson, D. F. and Mihal, W. L. 1973. Performance of blacks and whites in computerized versus manual testing environments. *Am. Psychol.* **28,** 694–9.

McLelland, D. C. 1973. Testing for competence rather than for 'intelligence'. *Amer. Psychol.* **28,** 1–14.

Riegel, K. R. and Riegel, R. M. 1972. Development, drop and death. *Devel. Psychol.* **6,** 306–19.

Rosenthal, R. 1973. The Pygmalion effect lives. *Psychol. Today* (Sept.) 56–63.

Rosenthal, R. and Jacobson, L. F. 1968. *Pygmalion in the Classroom: Teacher Expectations and Pupils' Intellectual Development*. New York: Holt, Rinehart and Winston.

Skodak, M. and Skeels, H. M. 1949. A final follow-up study of one hundred adopted children. *J. Genet. Psychol.* **75,** 85–125.

Watson, P. 1972. Can racial discrimination affect IQ? In K. Richardson and D. Spears (eds) *Race, Culture and Intelligence* 56–67. Middlesex: Penguin.

Wechsler, D. 1958. *The Measurement and Appraisal of Adult Intelligence* (4th edn). Baltimore: Williams & Wilkins.

Chapter 9

Personal Development through the Lifespan

An understanding of the sequences and hazards of emotional development is likely to help a doctor in several ways. First, it may allow the medical practitioner to communicate more effectively with patients of differing ages who are struggling with differing developmental tasks. Secondly, in consequence, it should alert doctors to the existence of periods of particular risk of the stressful experiences which have been implicated in illness onset. Thirdly, knowledge of the stages and variations within normal development is needed to recognize significant departures from normal and, it is to be hoped, to institute early corrective or preventive measures. Because of their privileged and long-lasting access to information about the emotional atmosphere within families, general practitioners are in a favoured position to monitor and collect data upon the cause-and-effect relationships between family events and individual health.

What follows is a survey by chronological age of the main stages and processes of individual personality development. As cognitive development has been outlined previously in Chapter 5, it will not be reiterated, but should nevertheless be borne in mind. The difficulties of obtaining scientifically valid data about human psychological development, let alone in finding a sufficiently comprehensive scientific theory to order such data, are due to the ethical constraints upon carrying out experimental research on one's hypotheses. They are also due to the unsatisfactory nature of retrospective rather than prospective studies. Apart from these obstacles, the sheer volume of relevant information has made it relatively easy for fragmentation to occur, with researchers concentrating on one mechanism, or one age-period, with consequent frustration for anyone trying to get an overall picture. The concepts described in this chapter are necessarily a composite from a variety of theoretical schemes, including ethological, psychodynamic, behavioural and experimental. The selection of material has been guided by medical relevance of the information, as hypothesized above.

GENERAL INFLUENCES ON DEVELOPMENT

It is clear that newborn babies differ from each other in ways, such as activity level, which are influential upon personality development. Adequate longitudinal information is, however, lacking about the durability of such apparently constitutional differences, and also about the results of different combinations of temperament and environment. The contributions of the prenatal environment also are known in mainly non-specific ways (see Chapter 3).

After birth environmental variation is extremely great, even within one city of one country. With different degrees of social status go not only differences in educational opportunity and the expectations of others, but nutritional and health differences which may one day be shown to affect personality through biochemistry. As yet, however, attempts to ground personality development in physiology are of little more practical utility than the dominant-humours system of the ancient Greeks. Birth order has proved to be a tantalizing variable, compounded as it is by the total number of children and by the numbers and spacing of children of each sex. Firstborns are the most distinctive group and may be predisposed, through heavy doses of parental attention, to being high achieving, conformist and responsible.

As a species, we are characterized by technical knowledge which has accumulated over many generations, and by corresponding physical and emotional dependency amongst the members of our social aggregate. We are adapted to social life, and most of the events which are thought to affect personality development are, congruently, social ones. Emotional relationships with others are, in the present state of knowledge, the most significant influence upon an individual's personality and its development.

INFANCY: ATTACHMENT

The first emotional relationship, and one which is mirrored in subsequent behaviour patterns, is that between the infant and whoever cares for her or him. Notice that 'caring' is meant to include affectionate and playful stimulation as well as the meeting of needs for nourishment, safety and comfort. The bond which forms between the infant and caregiver, in which the infant has an increasingly active role as time passes, is called **attachment,** and has been extensively studied by Bowlby (1971, 1977) and his colleagues. We will see that this concept is one of very comprehensive utility, and relevant to all later stages of life as well as to infancy.

During the first year of life there is a fairly consistent sequence in the infant's demonstration of attachment. By four months, infants seem able to discriminate perceptually between their attachment figure and others. The baby smiles at, vocalizes to, and visually follows the attachment figure, rather than strangers. By seven to eight months there is **stranger anxiety,** an active display of distress accompanied by clinging to the attachment figure, in the presence of strangers, especially if the environment is an unfamiliar one. At this age also, babies cry upon the caregiver's departure and approach with a greeting response upon reunion. As soon as babies can move independently they follow the caregiver about, and this proximity-maintaining behaviour is intensified by any stress, such as a novel environment, or times when the infant is tired, ill, jealous or frightened. There are variations amongst children in the speed at which they develop attachment behaviour, and to whom it is mainly shown. Bowlby's original proposition that attachment is *monotropic* (shown to only one person) has since been challenged. It may well be that most infants begin with one attachment figure (usually in our society the mother), but by eighteen months of age only 13 per cent of Scottish infants in one study (Schaffer 1971) did not show multiple attachments. The system of child care in Israeli kibbutzim, where multiple primary attachments were made within the peer group, does not appear to have had pathological personality effects, according to a recent survey by Beit-Hallahmi and Rabin (1977).

The choice of attachment figure is determined, as has been previously stressed, by who in the infant's environment provides tactual, social and perceptual stimulation in a way responsive to infant overtures. At the same time, the presence of attachment figures gives a security which allows the infant to explore and learn about the world. Parent education programmes aimed at recent parents, increasingly commonly offered by American mental health professionals as part of their preventive activity, tend to stress the importance of this early emotional bonding, and give information about how to strengthen it. Elsewhere this educational responsibility may fall upon the family doctor. The low birth rate and geographical mobility of our society mean that many adults have no idea of how to meet a baby's needs – and uncertain, frustrated or depressed people cannot do their best as parents. Advice about the proper course of attachment may be as vital to the infant's current and future health as is advice about feeding and immunizations.

Although infant behaviours demonstrative of attachment are being explored by researchers, and although it is acknowledged to be a reciprocal process, it is much more difficult to specify the course of attachment in the mother or other caregiver. The hypothesis that maternal attachment may be triggered by stimuli provided by the infant from birth has been responsible for recent changes in the organization and arrangements in obstetric and neonatal wards. These now aim at allowing maximum social interaction between the mother and her newborn. This is in contrast to the former routine separation of mother and child, and even more strictly of germladen father and child, in many maternity hospitals. In general mothers like to keep their babies close to them, and report feeling stronger ties and more confidence in handling these babies compared with those kept in the hospital nursery for most of the time. Whether or not it will eventually be shown that these first few hours and days have the irreversible significance sometimes attributed to them by enthusiasts, the changes have the extra value of communicating to the mother that the 'experts' (doctor and hospital staff) think that her relationship with the baby is important.

ATTACHMENT DEPRIVATION

Children who never had the chance to form an attachment during the first two to three years were found in an early study by Bowlby to suffer from what he called **affectionless psychopathy**. This consists of two very serious handicaps. As successful attachment is a prerequisite for socialization, attachment deprivation tends to destroy the reinforcement value of approval, subvert the identification process, and result in a person who has not learnt delay of gratification and impulse control. He will instead be impulsive, thoughtless of others' rights, and correspondingly likely to get into trouble with the law (e.g. lying, stealing, truanting, etc.). In the second place, as attachment is the foundation of intimacy, somebody who had never experienced a stable, trusting, reciprocally pleasurable relationship (as attachment should be, even in infancy), has only a superficial understanding of other people's feelings, and little real confidence in his or her own love-worthiness. There will be a reduced capacity for sustaining the kind of close bonds with peers which, apart from providing emotional support and a possible buffer against the effects of life's stresses, are also required for psychologically successful parenthood.

The extreme cases of attachment deprivation as seen by Bowlby have largely become unavailable for study, fortunately, due largely to the impact of his work on the staffing arrangements in children's orphanages and foster homes. A 'cottage' style of accommodation more nearly resembling a family, or at least special care in the rostering of staff to avoid an ever-changing succession of caretakers, is now more usual. Tizard and Rees (1975) found twenty-six children who had been reared continuously in institutions which were well provided with staff and cognitive stimulation, but which still had a high rate of staff turnover. They compared the behavioural problems and affectional relationships of these children with thirty-nine who had been adopted between two to four years of age, and also with thirty home-reared children matched for social class. While the latter had mainly disciplinary problems, both the first two groups showed a higher incidence of problems in interpersonal relations. Eighteen of the still institutionalized children were described as 'not caring deeply about anyone', and some, like some of the adopted children but none of the controls, as 'over-friendly' in an indiscriminate way to strangers.

The possibility of degrees of damage, perhaps varying according to constitutional factors in the child, and including that of a latent kind which might not become evident until adulthood, and perhaps even then only under conditions of special stress, makes the long-term effects of attachment deprivation difficult to specify. It may also be impossible to discover details of an ameliorating relationship with a gardener or cleaner, or other functional but unofficial attachment figure. The limits of human psychological resilience are just not known. Clear recommendations about such matters as the value of early adoption and stability of foster-care arrangements do, however, follow from what is known at present.

It may be helpful to mention the concept of **maternal deprivation**, which still appears in the literature here and there. The term was originally used to explain the severe retardation in every sphere of development (physical growth, visual-motor coordination, speech, IQ performance and emotional adjustment) often found in institutional children. As Rutter (1972) has pointed out, the term is outmoded and is best discarded now that we are in a better position to distinguish the effects of deprivations of attachment and of perceptual and linguistic stimulation.

Other hazards to attachment

Apart from total deprivation of attachment opportunities, various distortions of the process are possible even where the child is raised at home. Parents who derive no pleasure from their interactions with the child, or whose affection is untrustworthy (e.g. by being interspersed with episodes of indifference or cruelty), will prejudice psychosocial development accordingly. Naturally adults vary in their own capacity to act as a satisfactory attachment figure for a baby; it may be helpful in such cases to recall that the role can be taken over by others. If parents can recognize the baby's needs, yet feel unable to satisfy them alone (perhaps due to preoccupation with their own emotional difficulties, or with a demanding career), they should be encouraged to find an attachment supplement. This person, like a nanny or grandmother, needs to be emotionally available to the child for at least several years, so that a lasting reciprocal attachment may be formed. Ideally this person would share the parent's attitudes and values in a way which would enable her (or him) to socialize the child appropriately. For example, it is no good if the parents are sexually liberated and the supplementary caregiver believes that sex is disgusting.

Parents need to face at the outset that the close bond which should form between the child and such another needs to be respected and protected by them; i.e. that there is no place for parental jealousy and subversion of their child's attachment to the supplementary caregiver. In a variety of situations where parents are physically or emotionally absent, decisions about the welfare of young children should best be based on an understanding of the attachment process. In addition, the special case of day care arrangements appropriate for children of working mothers may be an important concern to parents, including doctors.

Maternal employment

Working mothers of preschool children now form a significant proportion of the population and often feel considerable stress over child-care arrangements. Early reports that children of working mothers were damaged by the experience tended to confuse the effects of substitute maternal care with those of poverty and marital discord. On the whole these were the children of financially desperate, or rejecting or depressed, mothers who defied the post-war fashion for female domesticity. More recent reviews (Hoffman 1974; Wallston 1973) suggest that if good quality care can be arranged, young children of working mothers show no ill effects. Indeed, they are more likely to benefit, from a) increased financial stability of the home, better educational opportunities, etc., b) (especially for girls) the model of a competent, 'achieving' female, and c) a mother who feels good about herself rather than depressed and resentful. Yarrow *et al.* (1962) found that it was women who stayed at home only out of a feeling of duty who reported the most problems in childrearing. In arranging day care for young children, parents will of course wish to be satisfied that safety, nutrition, exercise, and intellectual stimulation provisions are adequate, in addition to the availability of an appropriate attachment-supplementer as described earlier. Low child–staff ratios and low staff turnover are both desirable in a group where young children are cared for while parents work.

ATTACHMENT DISRUPTIONS

Once attachment bonds have been formed, their disruption elicits a *mourning* response which we can study in several settings relevant to medicine: child hospitalization, parental divorce, and bereavement.

Hospitalization
Whether the disruption is temporary or permanent makes little difference to a preoperational child, whose ideas of time are extremely vague. The characteristic egocentrism of this age may lead the child to imagine that hospitalization is necessitated by naughtiness, or that if the parents really loved him they could fix him up by magic. When hospitalized therefore, separated from attachment figures in a setting most conductive to eliciting strong attachment behaviour, the child between seven months and two to three years shows a similar sequence of mourning responses to that seen in victims of any permanent separation. Children younger than seven months seem affected mainly by perceptual deprivation, and are very alert upon returning home. For their mothers of course, separation during the first few months may have a devastating effect on bond-formation, which proceeds through the interaction between the two. Premature or sickly babies who are confined to special life-sustaining environ-

ments show a high incidence of emotional problems later in childhood, and it may be hypothesized that mothers who are both insecurely attached to, and overanxious about the child, are an important part of the reason.

The first stage of mourning is **protest.** Here the hospitalized infant actively expresses grief and anger by loud wailing, refusal to be comforted, and constant vigilance in case mother returns. This stage last one to eight days, the warmer the mother-infant attachment the longer the reaction. Next the child seems to pass into a stage of **despair.** Crying stops and the child seems socially withdrawn, apathetic, and may spend time in rocking back and forth or thumb-sucking. If the mother should now return, the child will at first ignore her, but the initial unresponsiveness is followed by a period of 'difficult' behaviour, which expresses both anger (by unusual naughtiness) and anxiety (by over-dependency and refusal to be parted for a moment). Parents may need to be warned to expect such trials, which may continue for several weeks, and to interpret them as evidence of the child's attachment strength rather than as provocation or rejection.

If the separation continues even longer, the third stage, of **detachment,** may be reached. Now the child no longer seems to care about anyone. Equal, shallow friendliness will be shown to everyone, mother, nurses and strangers, indiscriminately. Bowlby (1975) considers that the child who is allowed to reach this stage will thereafter be permanently vulnerable to over-reaction in response to future losses and disappointments.

There are two important factors other than age which affect the child's response to hospitalization. The first is the past experience of the child. It may seem paradoxical at first, but in fact children who are unhappy at home are even unhappier away from home. The reason is that where attachment is insecure, due to past separations or, what Bowlby finds a common although deplorable disciplinary measure – parental threats to desert, go mad, become ill or have the child sent away – such children are *more* disturbed by physical separation than those whose attachment is secure and trusting. The second moderating factor is, as might be expected, how the child is treated in hospital. Obvious recommendations about facilitating parental visiting, even if it appears to upset the child at the time, and allowing mothers to live at the hospital with their very young children, follow from Bowlby's work and are beginning to be implemented in children's hospitals (Robertson 1970).

In addition, the hospital staff can cushion the trauma somewhat by providing the child with information and a chance to express feelings. Often in young children the latter may be better achieved through imaginative play or drawings than through discussion. One study described in Wolff's (1973) excellent review of the whole area compared children in hospital for squint operations who received, or did not receive, special opportunities to clarify both their feelings and what was going to be done to them. The experimental group were found to be *more* disturbed than the controls during the hospital stay, but recovered faster from the experience upon going home. Six months after the operation three of the twenty experimental group and eleven of the twenty controls still showed signs of disturbance. However, in this and other studies, improvements in hospital and nursing care only seem able to benefit children over four years of age. There is obviously a strong case on psychological grounds for postponing elective surgery until after four wherever possible, and minimizing the duration of hospitalization where it is not. This is in addition to encouraging the mother's physical presence as much as possible, preparing the child beforehand as much as possible, and allowing substitute security objects such as favourite soft toys or blankets to remain at hand.

There remains the possibility that the correlation between hospitalization and emotional disturbance does not necessarily reflect a directly causal relationship. In some cases at least, and the proportion will vary according to your belief in the role of stress as a precipitant of illness and accidents, both hospitalization and disturbance may share a common cause, such as tension at home, whether it is focussed on the child or not.

Parental death

Bond disruption due to parental death predisposes children to later emotional difficulties, although again the child's age, and the prior relationships between the child and the parents are important moderating variables. It is particularly damaging to lose the same-sex parent before sexual identification has occurred at between two to three years, especially if there is no other model attachment figure. Multiple attachments within a closely-knit group, characteristic of preindustrial societies, are increasingly rare in our nuclear-family-centred society. Great distances between parents and their adult offspring are common and, due to frequent residential changes, many families are fairly isolated from others in their communities. In this respect working-class families may, through being less geographically mobile, be more able to draw on the resources of support and information of their relatives and neighbours. The anthropologist Margaret Mead (1962) has suggested that some modern evolution of the extended family of the past could do much to reduce the stresses of parenthood and childhood, as well perhaps as incorporating roles of greater usefulness and self-respect for our discarded elderly population.

With bereaved children, as with adults, the mourning process is likely to be more painful where the relationship was marked by mixed (ambivalent) feelings, and subsequent guilt. The response of the surviving parent is also important and requires a balanced avoidance of both denial and depressed withdrawal. As noted previously, young children differentiate poorly between temporary and permanent separations, and are likely to make egocentric attributions of causality. Adults in the first shock of grief also regress and may feel both anger at being deserted, and inappropriate self-blame. The normal course of adult mourning is described fully in Chapter 10.

Parental divorce or separation
Here the child frequently continues to have some contact with the 'lost' parent, and therefore may more easily perceive the departure as voluntary and a deliberate rejection. The emotional consequences to the child of this increasingly frequent event will once more depend on the child's age, sex and the intensity of attachment to the parent who leaves. The experience is not necessarily a more damaging one, however, than living in a loveless household filled with psychological or physical violence between the two most important people in one's life (also a very poor model of adult male/female relationships).

ATTACHMENT PAST INFANCY

Attachment, as a set of proximity-maintaining responses directed at a trusted other, especially in stressful situations, shows little reduction in intensity until about the third birthday. Children of this age are more prepared to widen their circle of acquaintances and begin to play in a truly cooperative fashion with their peers, as opposed to the parallel or coordinate play of earlier years (see later).

The wish for contact with attachment figures continues to manifest itself throughout life. Whenever the situation is strange or threatening, the presence of an attachment figure reduces anxiety (and therefore pain), and gives confidence to explore and cope. One application of this is the encouragement of husbands, mothers or close friends to accompany women in labour throughout the birth process. As described earlier, attachment fosters a capacity for trust and commitment essential for later intimacy. When attachment is threatened by involuntary separation, anxiety results. People who have experienced relatively less secure attachments early in life are more vulnerable to threatened and actual separations in adulthood, and frequently need psychotherapeutic help (Bowlby 1977).

CHILDHOOD: SOCIALIZATION

The end of the sensorimotor period, heralded by the first uses of language, the capacity for representational thought and therefore memory and imitation, and (if attachment has proceeded smoothly) a wish to please, is an appropriate moment for the infant to begin to learn the rudiments of 'civilized' behaviour. The process of **socialization,** of learning 'how to behave', has begun.

DISCIPLINARY STYLES AND THEIR EFFECTS

Even within a culture, prevailing fashions in views about the nature of children change. So too do ideas of what behaviour can reasonably be expected at what age. It should not be overlooked that technological advances such as the availability of washing machines, non-iron clothes, and disposable nappies affects attitudes towards, for example, letting children get dirty, and their toilet-training. Because incontinence is messy and smelly, bladder and bowel control are amongst the first tasks mothers set, and therefore provide something of a window on disciplinary and training techniques within the home. In addition, because of their originally involuntary operation, the sphincters provide an ideal way for infants and older children to express their feelings in disguised ways.

It is a pleasant relief to urinate or defaecate, and it is also pleasant to win control of bodily functions and to meet with social approval. The child therefore stands to gain self-esteem and autonomy from acquiring the skills of appropriate toilet usage. Learning to attend to the interoceptive and proprioceptive cues associated with bladder and bowel fullness, and to gain voluntary control such that elimination can be initiated and delayed purposively, is a relatively simple process once the relevant neuromuscular maturation has occurred. It is likely to be aided by social reinforcement for successive approximations to success, and by modelling. Such training, begun in the second half of the second year, will help the child to achieve something which he or she wants to learn anyway, and in this spirit accidents will probably be rare after about three years of age.

There are great variations in the age at which children achieve bowel, daytime bladder and night bladder control, and possibly an even wider range in family attitudes towards the age which continued enuresis and encopresis may be defined as a 'problem'. The mother who cares a lot about cleanliness, obedience and punctuality will be more upset by the child's lack of control than a mother with a contrasting personality. If the first mother is also prone to use punitive methods, in toilet training as in other areas such as feeding, masturbation, etc., the child's counter-aggression may well take the form of a refusal to be toilet-trained, simultaneously meeting needs for self-assertion and for attention. There are effective behavioural techniques for achieving sphincter control (see e.g. Bollard and Woodroffe 1977), but clearly they work best where the child is a willing learner, and sometimes prior attention to relationships within the family may be beneficial.

Although toilet-training has been used as an example of the socialization process, it must be recognized that values and attitudes are subject to just as much training (via conditioning and modelling), as are physical habits. Sex-typing is discussed later. Other important processes occurring at this stage are the inculcation of moral and philosophical values, and of illness behaviour.

Disciplinary styles amongst parents, that is *how* they train, as well as *what* they train their children to do, are influenced greatly by demographic variables such as social class and religious and ethnic background, as well as by the individual parent's personality. Methods which work with one child may not succeed with another of a different temperament or sex, or may be applied with different degrees of rigour and of underlying warmth to children born at different stages of the parent's life. A family is an organic whole, a complex force-field, in which it is unrealistic to consider the elements independently of the overall context. Research on the consequences for individual personality of parental methods has been proceeding for a long time; more recently there has been increased attention to the consequences for cognitive development of the techniques, as well as the context, of home learning. All such research is hampered by the difficulties of obtaining comprehensive, representative and quantifiable data about the techniques and their consequences.

SELF-ESTEEM

We have already discussed (Chapter 6) the process of identification whereby the child develops the super-ordinate goal of 'being like' an attachment figure, and how this facilitates the modelling of values, attitudes and expectations as well as of overt behaviours. The child's sense of his or her own worth and capability (both to achieve goals and to merit love) is summarized as **self-esteem.** This is another very useful concept with which to approach personality development. Self-esteem develops out of experiences of efficacy and competence, and is therefore at first dependent on the responses to one of the surrounding significant others. Parents who are confident, interested, resilient and effective foster high self-esteem. Those who feel inadequate, burdened by the child, and who are either autocratic or over-permissive in their handling of the child, have the opposite effect. One can begin to see how emotional impoverishment acts transgenerationally no less than nutritional deprivation.

By middle childhood, children high and low in self-esteem can be distinguished fairly readily. High self-esteem in childhood and later means faith in one's judgement and capability to influence the environment, and a readiness to express feelings openly and to place trust in others. On the other hand feelings of helplessness, isolation and unworthiness (low self-esteem) foster anxiety and depression, and thus further contribute to poor objective achievement and to physical and mental ill-health.

In order to behave in the ways described as productive of high self-esteem in their offspring, parents may need some help or support from the environment. Advice from or the example of the last generation of parents is often felt to be outdated and irrelevant to changed social conditions, or parents have unhappy memories of how the grandparents treated them in childhood. When difficulties and doubts arise about the child's emotional development, the family doctor is frequently the first professional person to be consulted, and therefore has an opportunity for preventive or treatment-oriented care. Sometimes parents may need only information about the normal milestones of development. Otherwise counselling, or referral to a specialist in the area, for example a clinical psychologist or psychiatrist, (preferably one identified with the local community rather than with a mental hospital, and one readily accessible in terms of waiting list length too) may be required.

THE MEANINGS OF PLAY

Play does not often cause family problems in itself, unless it is excessively noisy or destructive from the parent's point of view. Yet it is of interest in considering personality development, as being the major activity engaged in by preschool children, and remaining central at least until adolescence. Millar (1968) has provided a very good review of the meaning and types of play. In line with increasing cognitive capacity, play slowly becomes less egocentric and more bound by formal rules from toddlerhood to middle childhood. **Solitary** and then **parallel** play gradually give way to **associative** (where each member of the group concentrates on only his part in the group game), and then to truly **cooperative** play (where, for example individual interests are merged in a united game of schools, houses, etc.) Harlow and Harlow (1962) have shown how infant-infant contacts are prerequisite for successful peer relationships in monkeys. The peers gain in importance with the child's age, as socializing agents, and may be particularly influential where identification with parents is weak.

One way in which play has long been studied is as a kind of projective test response. The child is provided with doll-figures representing different ages and sexes, plus some representations of household furniture, and perhaps also some symbolic implements of aggression, and is asked to show something happening, or to arrange a scene. This provides the observer with the same sort of clues to expectancies and preoccupations as does an adult describing what is seen in inkblots (see Chapter 11), or possibly one asked to free associate in psychoanalysis. Better still, it is relatively easy for the observer, by commenting on, say, the emotions or relationships expressed in the child's production, to elicit information about the child's own family and possible sources of tension. The play therapist can then proceed to improve family communication or whatever else may seem to be needed. Children's drawings, especially of their family members, can also be used in this way to tune in directly to the child's perception of the social environment, and as a stimulus to verbal discussions about it. The style of play (and of free behaviour in general) may indicate the presence of depression, anxiety or impulsivity. Lastly, the play situation may be one in which symbolic desensitization, and behaviour rehearsal in a non-threatening situation, may appropriately occur.

SEX TYPING

Whether our stereotypes about appropriate masculine and feminine kinds of behaviour reflect biologically determined sex differences, or cultural traditions left over from an age where both muscles and lactation were more important to survival than they are today, most parents are concerned that their children should learn appropriate sex-typed behaviours in the course of socialization. From the age of three, children do in fact show the required preferences in toys and activities. Societies vary in the extent to which it is permissible for males and females to show opposite-sex characteristics, e.g. (in our case) for men to be sensitive and expressive and women to be self-reliant and aggressive. Philosophical and economic influences also contribute to changing views of what is 'normal' behaviour for men and women (Hoffman 1977). Undoubtedly in every social group and every historical period there is at least as much behavioural variation *within* the sexes as *between* them, and this fact needs to be accounted for in theories of how differences arise. Money and Tucker (1976) provide an excellent review of prenatal, hormonal and social influences upon sex-typed behaviours.

The question of how individuals come to regard themselves as masculine or feminine, i.e. how **sex-role identity** develops, has been researched from both biological and environmental starting points. Biological sex is usually apparent at birth, and by three months of age reliable differences in the amounts and kinds of stimulation given to girl and boy babies can be found. In the rare cases of mismatch between external and internal sex organs (hermaphroditism), the gender assigned to the baby by parents has a greater influence upon sexual identity than does the hormonal pattern (Hampson and Hampson 1961). While the same-sex parent is important as a model, and will be effective as such in proportion to the strength of the child's identification with her or him, *both* parents are important dispensers of reinforcement for sex-typed behaviours. Boys who lack a father during the preschool years are therefore less 'masculine' in their interests than others, although this does not necessarily mean that sexual identity as a male is weaker. The lack of a father has a more delayed effect for girls, whose difficulties arise not through lacking the relevant model but through lacking learning experiences of interacting with males. At adolescence, fatherless girls may therefore be awkward in their social interactions with boys and men.

The masculine role in our society appears to admit of less individuality of interpretation than does the feminine. The area of behaviour in which sex differences are most unanimously expected is that of aggression, particularly in physical rather than verbal modes of expression. Dependency, especially as passivity and need for affiliation, is the corresponding female sex-typed attribute. It is not surprising, therefore, that relative aggressiveness in males, and dependency in females, tend to be the most stable personality characteristics through time. Interestingly enough, mortality and morbidity figures show consistent trends in favour of women in all industrialized societies (Nathanson 1977). Women become ill and men die, and the differences seem to be related to sex-typed behaviours such as smoking, drinking and willingness to accept the sick role.

Being able to describe the 'typical' (i.e. stereotyped) male and female personality does not necessarily bind one to following such stereotypes slavishly in one's own life. It has been recognized for some time that relations between the sexes are injured by over-rigid adherence to such prejudices (including that men have innate sexual expertise, see Chapter 10). The emerging concept of **psychological androgyny** refers to the possibility that the same person may demonstrate both masculine and feminine attributes, rather than being confined to one category or the other. Psychologically androgynous individuals can be both assertive and compassionate, according to the demands of the situation. Their increased potential for flexibility in adaptive responses seems to result in high self-esteem and maturity (Bem 1977). Kelly and Worrell (1976) investigated the child-rearing antecedents of students categorized as masculine typed, feminine typed, androgynous, and indeterminate (i.e. those who endorse neither masculine nor feminine statements about themselves, who are typically found to be the least effective people). Modelling and reinforcement of opposite-sex behaviours by the same-sex parent was found to be critical. Thus androgynous males were more likely than the other groups to report affectionate relationships with their fathers, while androgyny in females was related to intellectual competence and self-reliance in the mother. Many writers have commented on the value to society of tapping the skills of nurturance and conservation traditional in women, and at the same time widening the freedom of women to realize their potential in all possible areas.

Extensive changes in socializing practices are implied by such goals, which if implemented could lead to exciting innovations in social customs and expectations during this century.

ADJUSTMENT DISORDERS IN CHILDREN

Although child psychiatry has lagged in development behind services for adults, Child Guidance Clinics first appeared in the 1920s and usually worked on the treatment *team* model (psychiatrist, psychologist and social worker). It is usually considered by mental health professionals that at any one time about 10 per cent of children will be suffering severe enough emotional disorder to need expert help. Only about one in ten of those children, however, receive it, and in some communities the proportion of unmet need is undoubtedly greater.

The unity of mental and physical functioning is particularly clear in children. Anxiety is likely to come to professional attention, not through the child's report of feeling anxious, but through the eating or sleeping difficulties, stomach aches or other somatic disorders for which no sufficient organic aetiology can be found. School progress, like relations with other children, frequently acts as a mirror to the child's level of anxiety (via ability to concentrate) and self-esteem. Extreme separation anxiety may prevent the child even from attending school, and complementarily, school difficulties feed back to reduce the child's confidence, and strengthen determination to evade the stress of school. As the educational establishment claims so much of the child's waking energies, and as middle-class parents, at least, care greatly about academic performance, 'under-achievement' at school is cause for concern to all involved. The educational and clinical psychologist can often help by analysing the child's cognitive equipment, and by making recommendations about the teaching methods or materials which would be most beneficial.

The literature on child psychotherapy gives many illustrations of children whose problems were solved by being given, in interaction with the therapist, a chance to gain insight and the strength to use it adaptively. On the whole, however, the results of individual child psychotherapy have proved to be disappointing in the long term (Anthony 1970; Mellsop 1972). In particular, antisocial behaviour in boys (stealing, lying, cruelty, disobedience, etc.) is frequently the forerunner of a similar pattern of delinquencies in adulthood, despite treatment. Perhaps these disorders represent behaviours learned in an environment which is highly resistive to the therapist's intervention.

The issue of how to decide whether therapy has been successful or not is discussed elsewhere in this book (Chapters 2 and 12). At present it is relevant to emphasize the obstacle peculiar to the treatment of children's behaviour disorders: that the 'patient' frequently has as little control over his environment and its social and cognitive demands, as over his referral for treatment. Effective behaviour change calls for management of the reinforcement contingencies which control and maintain behaviour. Therefore in the case of a child, the therapist is unlikely to produce generalized adaptive change, without ensuring that parents and teachers are cooperative to the point of taking over responsibility for contingency management. They are the natural agents of reinforcement for the child, and will themselves be reinforced in their new techniques by evidence of the child's better adjustment. The only problem is getting the information about how to cope with children to the people who need it. The role of a familiar community advisor like the local doctor is obviously full of potential usefulness here. As it is, 10 per cent of child patients are likely to present with an overt behaviour disorder. We may suspect that in many further cases, the physical problem presented is being caused or exacerbated by tensions originating at home or school.

Specifically medical preventive efforts currently include genetic counselling, reduction of birth hazards (prenatal and obstetric care to reduce prematurity, perinatal anoxia with resultant neurological defects from spasticity and mental retardation to hyperactivity), early detection and treatment of physical syndromes with psychological sequelae (such as PKU), and corrective attention to hospital arrangements which separate mothers and children from birth to four. The knowledge is also available, if doctors see its use as part of their responsibility, for further preventive efforts in the fields of parent and teacher education and special surveillance of children known to be at risk of disturbance through physical handicap or family disruption. The general practitioner has a unique vantage point from which to observe and guide, based on the opportunity of repeated contacts over many years. Cooperation between doctors and psychologists especially offers hope of considerable benefits for children's health.

ADOLESCENCE: IDENTITY

The physical changes associated with puberty constitute a sign to both the adolescent and others that new behavioural possibilities are opening up. Cognitively, entry into the stage of formal operations gives a capacity for intellectual analysis and detachment, and the systematic search for ideal answers to real and hypothetical questions. The readjustment implied by these changes, and the relatively prolonged and ambiguous status of the adolescent (neither child nor adult) in our society, have traditionally led to 'storm and stress' expectations of adolescent behaviour. In fact, the individual continues to show behaviours reinforced in the past, and to respond to environmental contingencies and cognitive representations of these, in an orderly manner. The discontinuities and unpredictability of adolescence can be greatly overemphasized. The several main developmental tasks of this period (roughly twelve to eighteen years) will now be briefly described in turn, although in practice they are all interrelated.

PEER AND SEXUAL RELATIONSHIPS

The adolescent talent for friendship, which is partly derived from rejection of too-obvious identification with adult models, can provide a very important source of support to the young person concerned. Friends made now may last forever in a way which later-made friendships may not. To establish independence from parents and their generation of authority figures, adolescents develop their own modes of dress, speech and entertainment. It is profitable for commercial interests to publicize and nurture the 'generation gap' by every possible means, as it is likely to stimulate sales, to the relatively affluent and financially-uncommitted adolescent, of whatever insignia are distinctive to the age-group. Although there remain differences between individuals in the extent of their conformity to the peer group, by and large social acceptability to peers is of paramount importance. This potentially provokes differences of opinion between adolescent and parent; in a psychologically healthy family, parents can encourage self-assertiveness as a prerequisite to the self-esteem necessary to cope with adult responsibilities.

Teenage boys have a capacity for frequent orgasms which will never be equalled in their later lives. Girls of the same age have many years to wait for their sexual peak, but often keenly desire romantic involvement. The task of meeting sexual and affiliative needs in a way which is mutually satisfying to the people concerned, and socially acceptable, is one which consumes much adolescent thought and energy. The situation is a) relatively unstructured: nobody really knows 'how far' it is usual or permissible to go in sexual experimentation, and b) very important to deal with adequately: peer group status is likely to be heavily influenced by reputation and performance in these matters, and fine discriminations need to be made to avoid being thought either backward or fast and loose.

ECONOMIC INDEPENDENCE

Growing realism compared with childhood in the area of vocational and occupational choice means that commitments are made to training and educational programmes, or to their avoidance, which will determine income and job satisfaction for many years ahead. Pressures involved in gaining the necessary qualifications, and then in finding the right job (increasingly difficult in these times of high youth unemployment), are another source of stress during adolescence. With economic independence from the parents comes the expectation of emotional independence (i.e. not isolation, but greater freedom to regulate the intensity and duration of interactions). What then of young people such as students or unemployed who do not become economically independent until much later?

IDENTITY

The end result of psychosocial development in adolescence is the individual's sense of personal identity. A strong sense of **identity** is related to perceiving oneself as unique, consistent and continuous, and as an integrated whole. Failure to develop this sense of identity has been extensively analysed as the source of emotional difficulties then and in later life. Erikson (1965, 1968) claims that it is only upon the basis of a firm sense of one's own identity that one can proceed with the subsequent attainment of intimacy and productivity (the latter expressed through parenthood or otherwise).

The antecedents of identity are found in earlier security of attachments and identification with effective, approving parents. Sometimes a period of experimentation in the context of relative freedom from responsibilities is needed for the adolescent to achieve this condition of knowing who he or she is, and what is wanted next.

Sexual and moral values, occupation, and social and political attitudes are all components of the final product. Activism, drugs, dropping-out and promiscuity are some of the avenues which may be chosen to express the search for identity. Alcoholism, drug abuse and venereal disease are therefore health hazards of the period for some. The medical care of adolescents will need to take into account their transitional and possibly conflict-ridden psychosocial stage, and their wish to be regarded as autonomous.

MATURITY: LOVE AND WORK

The equation of maturity with the ability to love and to work was made originally by Freud. Although the rate of personality development and change slows after adolescence, few adults are likely to agree that no further development occurs. There is increasing efficiency and perhaps predictability in a person's behaviour as judgement and wisdom (crystallized intelligence) begin to accumulate. However, even if job and residence stay the same for forty years, the passage of those years renders change inevitable in a person's body and relationships, and in those of the people that matter to that individual. Children are born, grow up and move away, friends die, marriages change, health and vigour may alter. More frequently of course, there will be additional changes, of job and residence, which themselves require readjustment. Through all these events people need to get satisfactions of their own out of being alive. Increasingly with time this includes a wish to be able to feel that one's life has mattered.

Generativity is Erikson's label for the psychosocial task which succeeds the attainment of intimacy, and it consists of the effort to pass something valuable on to the next generation. Elements of both creativity and productiveness are involved, and for many people these goals are most clearly attained through parenthood.

This stage-by-stage kind of descriptive analysis is helpful in understanding what are the challenges of each period of chronological development, and which concerns and achievements are important to persons of a given age. At a more theoretical level, however, it remains frustrating that we know relatively little of the determinants of psychosocial growth or of the relationships between stages. It is not clear, for example, whether the adolescent who fails to attain a sense of identity is likewise doomed to isolation (the converse of intimacy), and to stagnation and futility (the converse of generativity). The question of to what extent later healing influences can be effective is just not fully answerable. Certainly, these healing influences need not always consist of formal psychotherapy, which in any case is likely to remain relatively inaccessible to a large proportion of those who might benefit from it. The role of social supports as a buffer against illness has already been discussed (Chapter 7), and their value in psychological adjustment is even more obvious. Social skills training techniques (see Chapter 12) may prove to be one way to equip people to cope better with life, by increasing their access to naturally occurring sources of support.

NORMALITY

It is always much easier to study disorders of adjustment than to state explicitly what 'normality' or 'adjustment' might consist of, and this applies to physical and psychological parameters equally. Recent years have seen a tendency to relinquish definitions which depict an ideal freedom from problems, in favour of more realizable and functional assessments of coping ability. For the sake of the exercise let us now briefly review in what areas of function a psychologically normal/healthy/mature adult needs to display coping adequacy (Lazarus 1969).

Cognition: perception of the world and the internal bodily environment should be realistic.

Emotion: expression should be appropriate, neither over- nor under-controlled for the circumstances.

Social relationships: should be characterized by competence, intimacy and mutuality.

Work: should contribute to self-esteem as well as meeting economic needs for self and dependents.

Love and sex: cultural ideal is considerable fusion of these (see next chapter).

Self: positive self-regard, harmony between the private experience of self and its public manifestations.

Such a list is unsatisfying in that it is loaded with value judgements and generalizations, and gives no clear indication of what amount of deviation needs to occur before 'abnormality' is diagnosed, or how strengths in one area might counterbalance weaknesses in another. It leaves out dreams, creativity and nonconformity. The built-in biases reflect our culture and our times and are thus not immutable, much as fashions have altered in the medical significance attached to masturbation or constipation (Comfort 1968). With all its deficiencies, however, such a list does allow the assessment of relative areas of strength and of difficulty.

We have described elsewhere the disorders of emotion, cognition and overt behaviour which can be distinguished in people who are frankly maladjusted. In practice, inability to get on with other people is usually a prime reason for referral for help with psychological difficulties. The need for expert intervention is most likely to be recognized when capacities to love and to work are diminished. As for the psychological mechanisms which contribute to the happy state of adjustment, this chapter constitutes a review of several key concepts. Personal effectiveness ('self-efficacy'), both in winning love and in maintaining some control of the non-social environment, has recently been suggested by Bandura (1977) to determine whether and how successfully a person will keep trying. As was seen in Chapter 7, the opposite experiences from perceived self-efficacy, namely feelings of helplessness and hopelessness, do seem to be related to adjustment failures in both psychological and physical modes of health.

LIFE EVENTS OF ADULTHOOD

The 'mature' individual of roughly thirty to sixty years tends to be regarded unsympathetically by both the older and the younger generations. Both may resent their dependence (physical, financial and emotional) upon the middle-aged, and complain of being patronized, misunderstood and neglected. Although middle-aged people appear to be at the peak of their strength, power and capacity to cope, and are universally expected to assume responsibility and keep the wheels of society turning, they have challenges and psychological hazards to face which stress most and overwhelm some.

Marriage

Most people still get married, and re-married, or enter into relatively long term sexual relationships. The entry and exit choices, and the day-to-day coordination of two different personalities forced into constant propinquity, all provide many opportunities for stress. Early marriages, and those where partners have misperceived each other's needs or capacity for enduring intimacy, are all more vulnerable. Second marriages tend to work as well as first ones which endure.

Parenthood

More significant psychologically than marriage is parenthood, a state which cannot be reversed. The physical and emotional dependence of young children makes great demands on the energies and coping powers of parents, despite the correlated rewards. We have already considered from the child's point of view the benefits of having competent, loving parents; parents who feel they are failing in that role are likely to be depressed and frustrated in a way which clearly calls out for help – but who can provide it? Infertility may also be a source of distress, and in some cases appears to have emotional causes.

Post-parental stage

With smaller families and an earlier end to childbearing, many people will be relatively young when their children leave home, and probably within a few years make them grandparents. The 'post-parental' stage of marriage may therefore encompass many years, and if there has been dissatisfaction with the marriage and resignation to it for the sake of the children, separation is now likely. The independence of the children, often co-occurring with *menopause* (the end of reproductive capacity), is classically seen as representing a mid-life crisis for women, especially those who have based their identity on motherhood for many years. The menopausal symptoms with which doctors are frequently consulted can be particularly disturbing to women who fear that they signal the end of desirability and worth. Men in their late forties are similarly likely to become aware that their total achievements will never measure up to their youthful aspirations, and that competition from younger men may threaten their job satis-faction and security. **Involutional melancholia** is a form of depression characterized by insomnia, feelings of tension and somatic symptoms, which affects previously well adjusted middle-aged people of both sexes.

Awareness of mortality

The death rate from cardiovascular disease and cancer begins to rise in the late fifties, and many 'healthy' people suffer from chronic problems such as obesity, hypertension and arthritis. As vigour declines, contemporaries begin to die (from disease rather than in accidents, as earlier) and so will the individual's own parents; grief will be encountered. The increased awareness of mortality which is likely to result from these events spurs some middle-aged people to rethink their priorities. This may lead to new interests or lifestyles, possibly including new sexual partners, especially for men anxious about their virility, all of which demand readjustments.

Again, we know much more about adjustive failures at this age than about the determinants of success. Perhaps the subject is too close to home for largely middle-aged researchers. But the period should not be seen exclusively in terms of its demands and restrictions. Potentially, a new flowering of individuality and self-directedness may occur, as family responsibilities decline and the need to conform to get ahead is less pressing. It is time to re-allocate energies and concerns in preparation for the official rolelessness of old age.

OLD AGE: DISENGAGEMENT

The main psychosocial challenges of old age are retirement, widowhood and facing one's own death. Each of these represents loss; as before, the individual's ability to cope is influenced by self-esteem and by supportive attachments.

The concept of **disengagement** describes the average older person's gradual reduction in total range of activities. The diminution in social contacts, financial resources and authority actually increases the elderly person's freedom in some ways. Stripped of responsibilities and obligation, he or she can exercise options about both interpersonal and non-social activities (within the limits, commonly, of poverty). There is some evidence that sex-role stereotypes weaken in effect: old women become less submissive and old men more nurturant. As a relatively powerless minority group, old people suffer biased evaluations by the dominant middle-aged generation, and they resist labelling themselves as 'old' with great tenacity. Yet, continuing personal growth can make this stage of life satisfying. Erikson describes the psychosocial challenge as being that of coming to an integrated acceptance of one's life and its meaning, with despair as the result of failure to achieve that.

It is difficult to generalize validly about personality changes in old age. Contrary to the unthinking assumption of some younger people, individual differences are exaggerated, not diminished, in old age. There probably is a tendency for older people to be more cautious, and less achievement-oriented than before, and the characteristic cognitive changes discussed in Chapter 8 should be kept in mind.

Characteristic disorders

Dementia associated with irreversible brain dysfunction (due to cardiovascular disease, alcoholism, etc.) affects judgement and emotional state as well as memory and intellectual processes. Depression in response to the bereavements, failing health and loneliness of this age period may become pathologically severe, and is the most common psychological disorder (Botwinick 1973). Perhaps as one expression of this, a hypochondriacal preoccupation with bodily functions may occur: it is more socially acceptable to be sick than to be unhappy.

PREPARATION FOR OLD AGE

The heterogeneity of the aged, and their freedom from many of the social demands affecting others, make it unrealistic to prescribe a psychologically ideal environment for them. Some old people will be happy to disengage themselves from the wider world and others, probably fewer, will remain actively engaged until the last. Some will prefer the company of their peers, and others that of younger people and grandchildren. As at other ages, a feeling of helplessness and lack of control of the environment may be very damaging. Also, the presence of a confidant continues to act as a buffer against depression and associated ills. Apart from remaining alert to the close interaction between physical and emotional adjustment in the elderly, and checking that nutrition and housing conditions are adequate, perhaps the best health care a doctor can offer to geriatric patients is respect. The provision of a range of home-nursing and household services (e.g. help with shopping, cleaning and cooking), plus assistance with welfare and pension arrangements, can obviously do much to enable frail but healthy old people to retain their autonomy. Preparation for old age and retirement should ideally be begun well beforehand: prior information-seeking and rehearsal of the ideas can cushion the shock as it does with surgery.

In a similar way, people can prepare themselves for their own death; reaching a stage of acceptance can ease the process of dying for the elderly person and also the grief of those who are left. Psychological preparation for death cannot consist of gathering information, as this last journey must be made alone. Rather, courage can be gained from making whatever arrangements seem appropriate (e.g. wills, reconciliations, funeral wishes), and from the recognition of a worthwhile and meaningful life. The doctor's role will be one of facilitating the former by providing what information is needed about the approach of death, and of helping the living to adjust and cope. Relatives and others close to a dying person are at special risk of illness themselves, particularly after the death if mourning is not complete. Mortality was found to be 40 per cent higher than expected in the first six months of widowhood by Parkes *et al.* (1969), and depression from unresolved grief may in turn constitute a stress for those, such as children, who are psychologically dependent upon the depressed (and therefore withdrawn and cold) individual.

However actively doctors choose to undertake bereavement counselling, a knowledge of the recognized stages of grief will assist the doctor's ability, not only to be of support and use to the living, a form of preventive medicine, but will also enable him or her to feel less personal distress and discomfort when patients die, despite all efforts, and as all eventually must. The doctor who cannot cope appropriately with the death of patients risks his or her own health. The next chapter treats death more fully.

SUMMARY

This necessarily condensed review of human emotional development from birth to death has attempted to focus on concepts of central utility for understanding and predicting interpersonal behaviours relevant to health and disease. Much of our knowledge in the area unfortunately remains descriptive and fragmentary. Attachment in infancy, which proceeds from a stable and mutually enjoyable relationship with a caregiver and stimulator, is seen as a foundation for the socialization tasks of childhood and the intimacy of young adulthood. Children learn the habits and values of their society; adolescents need to discover themselves. Development in adulthood encompasses demands to love, work, face mortality, and eventually, achieve serenity.

TERMS AND CONCEPTS

attachment
stranger anxiety
affectionless psychopathy
maternal deprivation
protest ⎫ stages of
despair ⎭ mourning
detachment
socialization
self-esteem
solitary ⎫
parallel ⎪ stages of
associative ⎬ play
cooperative ⎭
sex-role identity
psychological androgyny
identity
generativity
involutional melancholia
disengagement

FOR DISCUSSION

1. Observe or question new mothers with regard to their first minutes, hours and days of interaction with the baby. Try to find out something about the attachment process in the mother, how it is affected by different variables such as drugs administered during labour, and how and where the newborn and mother are allowed to spend time together.

2. From observations, questions and memory, gather information about how children are socialized into patterns of illness behaviour. How do they learn the significance of different bodily sensations, and appropriate responses to them? What influences do ethnic background, social class and parental health have upon the process?

3. Many textbooks give an impression that all significant personal development ceases after adolescence. Discuss the validity of this view with adults of varying ages.

SUGGESTED READINGS

Hoffman; Wolff; Erikson: well-written reviews of specialist areas of particular interest.

REFERENCES

Anthony, E. J. 1970. The behavior disorders of childhood. In P. H. Mussen (ed.) *Carmichael's Manual of Child Psychology*. (3rd edn) *II.* New York: Wiley.

Bandura, A. 1977. Self-efficacy: Toward a unifying theory of behavioral change. *Psychol. Rev.* **84,** 191–215.

Beit-Hallahmi, B. and Rabin, A. I. 1977. The kibbutz as a social experiment and as a child-rearing laboratory. *Amer. Psychol.* **32,** 532–41.

Bem, S. L. 1977. On the utility of alternative procedures for assessing psychological androgyny. *J. Cons. Clin. Psychol.* **45,** 196–205.

Bollard, R. J. and Woodroffe, P. 1977. The effect of parent-administered dry-bed training on nocturnal enuresis in children. *Behav. Res. Therapy* **15,** 159–65.

Botwinick, J. 1973. *Aging and Behavior: A Comprehensive Integration of Research Findings.* New York: Springer.

Bowlby, J. 1971. *Attachment and Loss I. Attachment.* Middlesex: Penguin.

Bowlby 1975. *Attachment and Loss II. Separation: Anxiety and Anger.* Middlesex: Penguin.

Bowlby, J. 1977. The making and breaking of affectional bonds. I. Aetiology and psychopathology in the light of attachment theory. *Brit. J. Psychiat.* **130,** 201–10.

Comfort, A. 1968. *The Anxiety Makers.* London: Panther.

Erikson, E. H. 1965. *Childhood and Society.* Middlesex: Penguin.

Erikson, E. H. 1968. *Identity: Youth and Crisis.* London: Faber & Faber.

Hampson, J. L. and Hampson, J. G. 1961. The ontogenesis of sexual behavior in man. In W. C. Young (ed.) *Sex and Internal Secretions.* (3rd edn) Baltimore: Williams & Wilkins.

Harlow, H. F. and Harlow, M. K. 1962. Social deprivation in monkeys. *Scientific Amer.* **207,** 136–46.

Hoffman, L. W. 1974. Effects of maternal employment on the child – A review of the research. *Devel. Psychol.* **10,** 204–28.

Hoffman, L. W. 1977. Changes in family roles, socialization and sex differences. *Amer. Psychol.* **32,** 644–57.

Kelly, J. A. and Worrell, L. 1976. Parent behaviors related to masculine, feminine and androgynous sex role orientations. *J. Cons. Clin. Psychol.* **44,** 843–51.

Lazarus, R. J. 1969. *Patterns of Adjustment and Human Effectiveness.* New York: McGraw-Hill.

Mead, M. 1962. A cultural anthropologist's approach to maternal deprivation. In *Deprivation of Maternal Care: A Reassessment of its Effects.* Geneva: World Health Organization.

Mellsop, G. W. 1972. Psychiatric patients seen as children and adults: Childhood predictors of adult illness. *J. Child Psychol. Psychiat.* **13**, 91–101.

Millar, S. 1968. *The Psychology of Play.* Middlesex: Penguin.

Money, J. and Tucker, P. 1976. *Sexual Signatures: On Being a Man or a Woman.* London: Harrap.

Nathanson, C. A. 1977. Sex, illness and medical care: A review of data, theory and method. *Soc. Sci. and Med.* **11**, 13–25.

Parkes, C. M., Benjamin, B. and Fitzgerald, R. G. 1969. Broken heart: A statistical study of increased mortality among widowers. *Brit. Med. J.* **1**, 740–3.

Robertson, J. 1970. *Young Children in Hospital.* (2nd edn) London: Tavistock Publications.

Rutter, M. 1972. *Maternal Deprivation Reassessed.* Middlesex: Penguin.

Schaffer, H. R. 1971. *The Growth of Sociability.* Middlesex: Penguin.

Tizard, B. and Rees, J. 1975. The effect of early institutional rearing on the behaviour problems and affectional relationships of four-year-old children. *J. Child Psychol. Psychiat.* **16**, 61–73.

Wallston, B. 1973. The effects of maternal employment on children. *J. Child Psychol. Psychiat.* **14**, 81–95.

Wolff, S. 1973. *Children under Stress.* Middlesex: Penguin.

Yarrow, M. R., Scott, P., De Leeuw, L. and Heinig, C. 1962. Child-rearing in families of working and non-working mothers. *Sociometry* **20**, 122–40.

Chapter 10

Sex, Death and Communication

Are not sex and death antithetical? In fact they share several
characteristics which occasion their conjunction in this chapter. Most
obviously, both are subjects which many people feel considerable
anxiety in contemplating, and embarrassment at discussing. Even the
sophisticated, who can speak in all the right generalities, find it hard
to face their own sexual difficulties and their own death. While there
is much greater public attention to matters of sexuality than formerly,
such that those patients who regard themselves as 'modern' may not
suffer from reticence in raising the topic with a doctor, in the matter
of death and dying our society seems to be more fearful and denying
than were the Victorians.

The doctor is a natural resource for help in both cases. What
human functions could be more biological? However, the social taboos
surrounding sex and death affect the doctor as well as the patient
which is why, in order that the doctor should be able to function most
effectively in these areas, preparation in the form of information and
attitudinal desensitization is necessary. This is the goal of this
chapter. Unless communication is good between the doctor and
patient and their relationship trusting, questions may remain unasked
on both sides in a way unsatisfying to both and detrimental to the
patient's health. We shall therefore use the opportunity of these
sensitive topics to begin an exploration of doctor-patient communication.

Lastly, sex and death can be seen as linked, in that both are
irreversibly and enormously important to the way people feel about
themselves, and both are potentially great sweeteners of life.

HUMAN SEXUALITY

Facts about human sexual behaviour have provided a basis for scientific enquiries in only the last thirty years. Alfred Kinsey was the pioneer, an expert on the gall wasp, who began to interview people about their sexual habits and experiences when, at forty-two years of age, he discovered no reference sources for a course he had to teach on marriage. He questioned 18,000 Americans (Kinsey 1948, 1953) and produced an unprecedented amount of data about what was being done sexually, and by whom. One of his innovatory concepts was that of **total outlet,** the number of orgasms per week achieved by any means (i.e. including intercourse, wet dreams, masturbation, petting and bestiality). Although his sample was somewhat biased, Kinsey's data on how sexual behaviour and attitudes varied according to age, sex, social class, level of education and so on have proved immensely valuable. Masters and Johnson (1966, 1970) made the next milestone: their approach involved detailed laboratory studies of the physiological processes involved and their emotional correlates. Numerous surveys and investigations of lesser scope (e.g. Schofield 1968) have added their contributions to the remarkably rapid accumulation of knowledge, such that today the problem is one of dissemination of the facts rather than primarily one of collection. Also, liberated from hearsay and conjecture by the availability of facts, we can now reconsider the psychosocial aspects of sex and how it relates for the individual to love and happiness.

PHYSIOLOGY OF SEX

The stages of response to sexual stimulation, according to the detailed investigations of Masters and Johnson, are as follows: 1) **excitement:** penile erection in the man and vaginal lubrication and clitoral engorgement in the woman. 2) **plateau:** a shorter period of more intense arousal which occurs if effective stimulation is continued. Further thickening of the penis, elevation of the testes, and vasocongestion of the outer third of the vaginal barrel proceed along with other changes in breasts and nipples, internal sex organs, skin colour, muscular tension and finally, retraction of the clitoris. 3) **orgasm:** the 'seizure-like ... summit of physical and emotional gratification in sexual activity' (McCary 1973, p. 192). There is a rapid discharge of neuromuscular tension accompanied by ejaculation of semen by the man, involuntary vaginal contractions in the woman, hyperventilation and greatly increased blood pressure in both. The experience lasts only seconds, is more variable in women than in men, and is superlatively pleasurable. 4) **resolution:** gradual return to pre-excitement bodily state, often with sweating and drowsiness. Duration is in direct proportion to the duration of the excitement phase.

Effective stimulation may derive from a wide variety of sources including cognitive (thoughts and fantasies), tactual (particularly of the sensitive erogenous zones), visual (possibly more important to man than to woman) and olfactory. Individual preference show enormous diversity, and are strongly influenced by learning.

Sexual pleasure can result from many activities other than intercourse, and need not always culminate in orgasm. In fact, regarding orgasm as a 'performance' to be 'achieved' and counted, can, by making it seem like work, remove all the fun from sex. Yet for the majority of people orgasm is the ultimate sexual goal. Women find it more elusive than do men, yet women are capable of multiple orgasms if effectively stimulated, while men suffer a post-orgasmic refractory period which increases with age. While men reach their peak of orgasmic frequency at about eighteen, and gradually decline thereafter, women increase in sexual responsiveness until their early thirties, and remain at a plateau thereafter if circumstances permit. Both sexes can experience orgasms in the absence of emotional ties to the partner, or by impersonal means. However because anxiety disrupts, and sensitivity and communication facilitate sexual pleasure, the best experiences are likely to occur within an affectionate, mutually giving relationship.

The sympathetic part of the autonomic nervous system, which is activated in situations of emotional threat and anxiety, inhibits erection and speeds ejaculation in men, and inhibits excitement in women. The disruptive effects of stress on sexuality are therefore obvious.

COMMON SEXUAL PROBLEMS

The majority of sexual problems are due to ignorance, and medical students often are worse rather than better off than their peers in this area (Lief 1973). It is a prime necessity therefore for you to equip yourself with the basic facts of human sexuality, as set forth in books, for example by Cauthery and Cole (1971), McCary (1973) and Stenchever and Stickley (1970). Not only is sexuality not restricted to reproduction, as is so frequently implied by sex education material for adolescents, but other informal sources of 'information' (such as schoolyard gossip and also pornography) often perpetuate myths and misunderstandings to an appalling extent. The facts are that masturbation is *not* physically harmful, penis size is *not* particularly important (flaccid length is no guide anyway), the source of female orgasm is the *clitoris*, and sexual needs *do* continue into old age. In many cases the mere provision of information, in the context of the doctor's concern and freedom from embarrassment, has great therapeutic potential.

As pointed out by Lief (1973, p. 444) 'human sexuality is an area where there is an exquisite conjunction of the biological and behavioral sciences'. At the individual level this 'exquisite conjunction' is shown by an interdependence of emotional and genital behaviours. Anxiety, guilt or anger interfere with sexual pleasure just as affection or novelty facilitate it. In turn the quality of the sexual experience is taken as evidence of the feelings concerned, and of the individual's adequacy as a man or woman and as a person. A sexual relationship therefore both reflects and contributes to the individual's emotional adjustment. Complaints of sexual difficulty are accordingly likely to indicate some dissatisfactions with non-sexual aspects of the relationship between two people, or with the confidence and self-esteem of the person concerned. Apart from the intense physical pleasure of orgasm, the 'meaning' of sexuality to the individual will be determined by their stage of psychosocial development. Thus for teenagers sex is part of their search for identity, for young adults intimacy is the goal, and later sex strengthens the pair-bonds essential for child-rearing. At all ages attachment needs may be expressed through sexual behaviour.

In our society, men in particular feel extreme reluctance to admit to sexual difficulties. Our emphasis on sexual performance as a mark of masculinity, and on the male role as one of competence and expertise, make it more likely that the wife will be sent to the doctor for 'frigidity' or 'orgasmic dysfunction', than the husband for premature ejaculation (see below). Even where sexual ignorance in general is not a problem, ignorance of the partner's unique sexual response may be so. Frequently women are ignorant of their own sexual response pattern, and may need encouragement to explore it. Many of the sexual therapy programmes developed by Masters and Johnson (1970) and others (e.g. Bancroft 1975; Sollod 1975) can be conceptualized as training in communication, as well as more specific techniques. This may require fostering a greater degree of self assertiveness on the part of either or both of the partners, and it is difficult to imagine how the therapeutic gains could fail to generalize to other areas of the couple's relationship.

Organic disease, diabetes, drug effects (especially antihypertension drugs), and ageing can all interfere with orgasmic capacity, but psychological causes are relatively far more common. Maladaptive learning experiences, especially associating sexual excitement with anxiety (as in a repressive, anti-sensual childhood, or early experiences which were humiliating or frightening), can be reversed by techniques of behaviour modification (as in Chapter 12). Relaxation, desensitization and successive approximations are of particular value in helping people to be able to abandon themselves to pleasure.

Premature ejaculation refers to a pattern of very rapid sexual release by the man before the woman has been stimulated adequately to reach satisfaction. Thus it is defined in relation to partner requirements rather than as meeting certain time criteria, such as number of seconds between intromission and ejaculation.

Impotence is if anything even more distressing to a man, and can be classified as either *primary* (where erection sufficient for intercourse has never been achieved), or *secondary* (where incapability occurs after many experiences of success). Occasional erectile failures should be expected by all men, and can be associated with alcohol ingestion or negative feelings. However once fear of failure becomes established it becomes self-fulfilling, and enough to set off a downward spiral of anxiety and further failure. Refocussing attention on the enjoyment rather than the performance aspects of sexual encounter, in a programme of cooperative 'pleasuring' or **sensate focus** between the partners where at first intercourse is specifically forbidden, achieves success in about three-quarters of secondary cases and 60 per cent of primary, over a five year follow-up (Masters and Johnson 1970).

Orgasmic dysfunction in women is failure to get past the initial stages of sexual excitement to climax: this phrase has replaced the former evaluative and vague term 'frigidity'. As with male impotence, the condition has sometimes been a lifelong problem *(primary)* and is sometimes a later development *(situational)*. Also, as with men's problems, self-critical 'spectatoring' during sex inhibits a spontaneous response. Other common related female sexual problems are **vaginismus** (involuntary contraction of the vaginal muscles so that penetration by the penis is difficult or impossible) and painful intercourse (**dyspareunia**). Once again, treatments involving graded practice and desensitization of negative attitudes have been found to give considerable success. Attention to the overall relationship may remove the inhibiting effects of unexpressed resentments. Each of these difficulties illustrates anew the subtle interweaving of psychological and physiological in human bodily function, even under the influence of what is popularly regarded as one of our most compelling biological 'drives'.

SOCIOSEXUAL PROBLEMS

Failure to use contraception, and the contamination of sex with power-game aspects, are amongst many expressions of personal psychological difficulties *via* sex. Similarly, minority sexual preferences are often problems not of achieving sexual satisfaction *per se*, but of doing so in a socially acceptable way.

Perhaps because of the extreme sexual arousability of young males, and the correspondingly many opportunities for classical and operant conditioning to occur, all the variations in sexual preference to be described in this section occur much more frequently in men than in women. Social values regarding these variations from the statistical norm change according to time and fashion, as do attitudes towards the ethical aspects of sexual expression such as premarital sex, adultery, birth control and so on. It is particularly important for doctors to be aware of their own attitudes, as acquired during particular socialization experiences, and sensitive to different values in others.

Homosexuality is preference for sexual contact with members of one's own sex, and is a dominant preference in 5 to 10 per cent of men and about a third as many women. At least a third of American men were found by Kinsey to have had a homosexual experience leading to orgasm by the age of forty-five, and rates increase in settings of isolation from women, such as prisons. Although homosexuality was removed in 1973 from the list of mental disorders by the American Psychiatric Association, it remains true that many men continue to respond with terror or rage to imputations of homosexuality in themselves. Controversy persists about the causes. There is no clear support for genetic or hormonal explanations, but some evidence for disturbances of normal gender identification in childhood, due to lack of warmth from the same-sex parent and lack of trust in the opposite-sex parent (see Bieber 1976). It is probably more realistic to regard sexual preference as a continuum, with exclusive hetero- and homosexuality at the extremes, than as two discrete categories. The effects of early labelling, including by oneself, also need further study.

Paedophiliacs are sexually attracted to children, some for their own sake (where there may be fondling but no wish to hurt), and some because of the child's helplessness to avoid exploitation (as in sexual assaults on children and molestations of adolescent girls). Such encounters, especially the milder, non-violent forms, do not necessarily have a long-term damaging effect on the child victims.

Many other sexual habits, often involving impersonal stimuli, fall within a grey area between 'normal' variation and real pathology. Sexual partners often show considerable tolerance for the other's tastes. Voyeurism ('peeping'), fetishism (which ranges from strong preferences for certain hairstyles or types of clothing, to abandonment of the real partner in favour of the fetish object) and sado-masochism (where sexual arousal is a result of giving or receiving pain) are some 'deviant' patterns. Their harmfulness needs to be assessed in terms of effects on interpersonal relationships rather than of moral absolutes. In other words, attention needs to be directed to issues such as the amount of suffering being caused to the person concerned and to the sexual partner (e.g. via guilt, anxiety, discomfort, interference with sexual satisfaction by the deviant habit), risk of conflict with the law, and degree of interference with other areas of life, such as interpersonal relationships and work. As with other sexual difficulties, the doctor clearly needs information, tact and no false modesty, in order to provide a setting conducive to frankness about the problem, and subsequent treatment either personally or by referral.

DEATH AND DYING

Our society and other developed countries distance the dying and dead both perceptually and socially. The great majority of people die in hospital. There the dying person has access to life-prolonging instruments, but is frequently isolated from relatives and friends. Frequently too, the dying person is isolated both physically and emotionally from medical staff. Doctors and nurses may stay near as briefly as possible and experience various blocks to communication, caused by anxieties about how much the patient comprehends of the situation, and how all the participants feel about it. Medical professionals are trained to combat death, and therefore may feel even more threatened and discomforted by the subject than does everyone else. Kastenbaum and Aisenberg (1976) have described the numerous conflicts surrounding a doctor in relation to death (p. 171): 'He should be objective and scientific. He should be warm and personal. He must exert himself with equal vigor to save all lives. He is free to be selective, favor the "more valuable" lives over the "less valuable". He is responsible only to himself and his professional code of ethics. He is responsible to the community. He is responsible to the patient. He is a sage and all-round authority on life. He is a technician, a repairman.' We may add that the doctor is also a mortal human member of a particular socio-cultural group.

Although the current trend is for a decrease in formal mourning rituals (the tolling bell, black clothing and prescribed curtailment of social activities of our forebears), the bereaved individual must nevertheless carry out a definite mourning process in order to come to terms with the loss. As seen in Chapter 9, unresolved grief is a health hazard. Bereavement may occur not only in people who have suffered the death of a close relative or friend, but also in those who have reason to anticipate their own imminent death. In addition, it will be apparent that this mourning process is similar in kind, if not always in intensity, to the psychological response to other forms of loss, such as divorce, retirement, independence of children, chronic illness or physical disability, or even the loss of illusions and false expectations. Note too the parallel in the young child's response to separation from attachment figures (Chapter 9).

STAGES OF NORMAL MOURNING

Shock and disbelief are the first response to an unexpected loss, whether hearing of a death or of a fatal diagnosis for oneself or somebody one loves. This is the stage of *denial,* which cushions the individual from full awareness of reality. People may feel numbed and carry out all their usual or necessary duties, including perhaps comforting others. Gradually full realization of the loss begins to occur, in flashes at first, and heralds the second stage of response, which is one of *despair.*

The emotional pain and sorrow experienced may now be of overwhelming intensity, even such as to be frightening. The depression may be experienced partly as physical distress, feelings of emptiness, epigastric pain, or symptoms like those of the dead person's last illness. There may be hallucinations of hearing the voice or glimpsing the face. A preoccupation with the dead person is expressed through constant reminiscence and search for mementoes, in order to form a coherent, although at first idealized, mental image of the dead. It is not unusual for a feeling of anger, really a kind of diffuse rage at being deserted, to be directed towards those seen as responsible (by commission or omission, the latter possibly including medical staff) for the death. Guilt and regret is another common response, where the person unrealistically blames himself or herself for not having done enough or been kinder while life lasted. Finally, with full realization of the loss, there may be anxieties about how one can cope without the departed, with many practical readjustments to be made. It is during this stage, which lasts for several months after the funeral and constitutes a psychological crisis, that emotional support from others is most valuable. Partly this support should take the form of allowing the person to grieve. Admonitions not to feel sad, or angry, or guilty, or at least not to show it, have no useful place at all. A single confidant, who can accept and support the mourner's expressions of feeling and attempts to integrate the experience, is of greater value to the mourner than a host of superficial acquaintances who cannot. For some elderly or socially isolated people, the doctor may fill this confidant role.

As time passes the third stage of mourning, that of *acceptance*, begins to emerge and finally to predominate. The more unexpected the death was, and the more dependent the survivor was upon the deceased, the longer this will take. This successful endpoint of the mourning process is characterized by decreasing preoccupation with the loss, and corresponding ability to invest energies in new relationships and new roles, and in the ability to speak comfortably and realistically of the deceased. Identification with the dead may mean that the mourner takes over behavioural attributes such as some characteristic mannerism, or set of ideals.

These basic stages of 'grief work' apply also to the **anticipatory grief** undergone by a person facing impending death in himself or a loved one. The dying person faces losses of relationships and of identity. Kubler-Ross (1969) describes the successive denial, anger, bargaining, depression and final acceptance: the 'optimal death'. She and others (e.g. Cassem and Stewart 1975; Engel 1966) have many practical suggestions about how this desirable outcome may be facilitated by the doctors and nurses concerned. Dying children cause particular distress to all around them and, as they cannot be shielded from understanding the seriousness of their condition, the challenge of emotional support as well as physical care must be met (Binger *et al.* 1969; Spinetta *et al.* 1973).

Grief in children
In the case where a child suffers bereavement, egocentric preoperational notions of time and causality need to be taken into account (Chapter 5). Young children may fear that their own aggressive impulses are responsible for the death, or that it is a deliberate abandonment of them due to their 'badness'. Remaining family members, also grieving, may need help to provide the support needed by the child at this time. Unresolved grief in children, whose needs may be overlooked partly because of their different way of expressing grief, can show up in a variety of somatic complaints. There may also be schoolwork difficulties, behaviour regressions such as soiling or over-eating, and in the long term an increased vulnerability to respond to stress with helplessness, depression and illness.

Doctors and death
In order to fulfill the professional role of sensitively and compassionately providing information and support for the bereaved, while maintaining self-esteem and avoiding feelings of helplessness, the doctors and others concerned need emotional supports themselves. In clinical situations this will be facilitated by good communications within the caring team. At the preclinical level, a good beginning can perhaps be made if one can learn to contemplate death. As pointed out by Feifel (1959) and many others since, to gain awareness of death marvellously sharpens awareness of life.

DOCTOR-PATIENT COMMUNICATION

Constantly in this chapter and elsewhere through this book we have stressed the importance, for proper health care in the widest sense, of an open, collaborative relationship between doctor and patient. Patient cooperation will be enhanced above its usually rather low level (see Chapter 1), when patients are satisfied by the medical interaction. Even more basically, many aspects of behaviour relevant to health can only be asked about and told about where communication between the two participants to the consultation is good. The history of medicine and the study of healing in non-industrialized cultures (Chapter 20) both show how therapeutic a good doctor-patient relationship can be.

The doctor expresses general attitudes towards the patient in many non-verbal ways, such as the physical environment of the consulting room, the payment arrangements, the doctor's dress, manner and so on. Patients have similar channels of communication open to them, and both sides can form impressions on this sort of basis, with more or less deliberate accompanying attempts at manipulating the impression received by the other (see Chapter 16). For the present, however, let us give some attention to the verbal interactions between the two, since these provide the most complex and detailed information. We will also consider interaction primarily from the doctor's point of view, as a diagnostic and potentially therapeutic instrument.

The doctor's goals in the interview include both diagnosis and treatment, and can be summarized as: a) *to elicit information* about the nature and timing of the patient's past and current symptoms, which is accurate and detailed enough for hypotheses about diagnosis to be developed and refined, and also about lifestyle, drug intake, etc. which may be relevant to treatment prescriptions; and b) *to motivate the patient* to cooperate with whatever further diagnostic, treatment or preventive measures may be necessary. This in particular distinguishes the clinical from the research interview described in Chapter 2. The deservedly famous 'doctor-patient relationship' upon which so much of the success of treatment hinges (through placebo effects as well as patient motivation), is in effect a matter of clear communication of respect and caring for the patient.

Different proportions of attention may be given to these two goals in different circumstances. For example, the second becomes more vital in the mutual participation or guidance-cooperation models of doctor-patient relationship than in the active-passive model (see Chapters 1 and 17, Szasz and Hollender ref.). In all cases where behavioural and emotional factors are suspected to be important, such as the sexuality and grief problems discussed in this chapter, but also including many other consequences of stress or maladaptive habits, it becomes essential for the doctor to discover how the patient *feels* about things. Feelings about personal matters are not a usual topic of conversation between other than close friends, so the doctor needs skills beyond those of social conversation.

Clinical interviewing skills are not mysterious, and can readily be learned, but more efficiently by modelling and informational feedback for your efforts, especially in a group setting, rather than by reading about them. Role playing and video-recordings of interviews, with prompt supervisory feedback, are helpful training methods. Here we will briefly review some of the principles involved, as a foundation for practical training and also in order to guide your observations of others. Froelich and Bishop (1977) provide an excellent training manual. Common difficulties in beginners revolve around ignorance of how to cope with one's own emotional responses, for example to weeping, hostile, seductive, mutilated, terminally ill or socially or culturally 'different' patients (Pollack and Manning 1967).

Anybody who wishes to communicate effectively must acquire certain basic skills. Sharpening sensitivity to non-verbal expression of feelings (particularly of negative feelings such as anger, anxiety and depression), both in others and in oneself, involves learning what cues to attend to and their significance. For example not only facial expression but body position, breathing pattern, voice modulation and gestures can all give valuable information. Congruence between verbal and non-verbal behaviour is an important part of an impression of sincerity, thus a doctor wishing to convey interest in a patient's narration will not be cleaning his fingernails, tapping his feet, or leaning back in his chair gazing out of the window. Techniques for facilitating the other's flow of information, changing the direction of the conversation, expressing understanding, and for checking that the message received was the one that was sent, can be easily mastered with practice. Perhaps an attitude of respect for the patient as a person, with fears and failings but also with talents and aspirations, is one element of successful communication which will need no teaching. This will be the case if the doctor is sufficiently comfortable in the interview situation not to have to protect himself or herself against the anxieties which patients will evoke, by using defences (such as emotional isolation of the patient) which have a dehumanizing effect.

ELICITING INFORMATION: ASKING AND LISTENING

Open-ended rather than leading questions, especially in the early stages of enquiry, allow the patient to contribute more of his or her private knowledge, as well as to feel less like a suspect being interrogated. Thus it is better to ask 'What were your parents like?', than 'What was your mother like?' or 'Was your mother domineering?' It is better not to provide any opportunity for yes/no answers when exploring habits such as alcohol consumption, mastur-bation, or other areas such as marital conflict or child-rearing difficulties, about which the patient may feel ashamed or guilty. 'Why' questions are often unproductive, as are questions implying disapproval or criticisms of the patient's actions.

Where possible, try to find out exactly how (in terms of physiological response as well as affect) and when (social and behavioural antecedents) feelings of sadness, anxiety or anger were experienced. Tying vague terms down to concrete examples expressed in terms of the patient's daily life is helpful, both in investigating the scope of disability and in giving instructions or information. Remember too that more patients than you might expect have either an incorrect or even no understanding of the anatomical and technical terms with which doctors necessarily become familiar (Boyle 1970, ref. Chapter 5; Korsch and Negrete 1972).

A patient falling silent may need encouragement to go on, or time to formulate thoughts, or may have finished what needed saying, and naturally each of these possibilities needs a different response from the doctor. The use of silence by the interviewer is a difficult but rewarding technique to master. **Confrontation** of a patient implies making an interpretive remark based on non-verbal cues ('You're looking awfully sad as you tell me about this') or on inconsistencies in the story, and similarly requires sensitivity and timing.

BUILDING A POSITIVE RELATIONSHIP

How the doctor responds to patient disclosures and questions will strongly influence the patient's trust, and thus motivation to accept advice. Many kinds of response unwittingly demean the patient: false reassurance (which dismisses the validity of his concerns), judgemental remarks (especially hostile ones which stimulate counter-hostility), or endless further questions. The communication of **empathy** (an objective understanding of feelings which may be distinguished from the subjective *sharing,* of sympathy) on the other hand, builds patients' confidence that the doctor is interested in their problems and is concerned to grasp them clearly, and that he has confidence in their own capacity for growth and responsible action. Action advised on this basis is likely to seem more relevant (and thus produce more compliance) than advice based on what is perceived by the patient as an inadequate understanding or desire to understand by the doctor. Bernstein, Bernstein and Dana (1974) and Enelow and Swisher (1972) see the prime components of the understanding or emphathetic response as: a) *reflection of the feelings* implied by the patient's words (e.g. 'You seem to be saying that you feel some anxiety about the operation tomorrow'); and b) *acceptance* of and respect for the patient as an individual human being (which does not need to mean agreement with or approval of his or her actions). You will notice similarities between these recommendations and the principles of Rogerian counselling described in Chapter 12.

SUMMARY

Sexuality and death exemplify the socially sensitive yet medically highly relevant areas of human concern for which doctors need special preparation, in order to function most effectively. This chapter outlines (and provides references to more complete sources) the human sexual response and its common difficulties, and also the grief response. Communication between doctor and patient where feelings are important requires empathy, and training in how to communicate it, on the doctor's part.

TERMS AND CONCEPTS

total outlet
excitement ⎫
plateau   ⎪ stages of
orgasm   ⎬ sexual
resolution ⎭ response
premature ejaculation
impotence
sensate focus
orgasmic dysfunction
vaginismus
dyspareunia
anticipatory grief
confrontation
empathy

FOR DISCUSSION

1. What characteristics (both of knowledge and of attitudes) are needed by doctors to facilitate
    a) sexual happiness in themselves,
    b) treatment of common sexual difficulties in patients,
    c) counselling of patients about sex-related questions such as birth control, abortion, sex education of children, VD, etc.
2. On the basis of your experience, observations and readings, discuss the meaning of a) sex, b) death,
    to i) a preschool child,
    ii) a teenager,
    iii) a middle-aged person,
    iv) an elderly person,
    v) a doctor.

SUGGESTED READING

McCary (sex); Kubler-Ross (death); Enelow and Swisher (interviewing): basic texts.

REFERENCES

Bancroft, J. 1975. The behavioural approach to marital problems. *Brit. J. Med. Psychol.* **48,** 147–52.

Bernstein, L., Bernstein, R. S. and Dana, R. H. 1974. *Interviewing: A Guide for Health Professionals* (2nd edn). New York: Appleton-Century-Crofts.

Bieber, I. 1976. A discussion of 'Homosexuality: The ethical challenge'. *J. Cons. Clin. Psychol.* **44,** 163–6.

Binger, C. M., Ablin, A. R., Feuerstein, R. C., Kushner, J. H., Zoger, S. and Mikklesen, C. 1969. Childhood leukemia: Emotional impact on patient and family. *New Eng. J. Med.* **280,** 414–18.

Cassem, N. H. and Stewart, R. S. 1975. Management and care of the dying patient. *Int. J. Psychiat. Med.* **6,** 293–340.

Cauthery, P. and Cole, M. 1971. *The Fundamentals of Sex.* London: W. H. Allen.

Enelow, A. J. and Swisher, S. N. 1972. *Interviewing and Patient Care.* New York: Oxford Univ. Press.

Engel, G. 1966. Grief and grieving. In J. R. Folta and E. S. Deck (eds) *A Sociological Framework for Patient Care* 279–88. New York: Wiley.

Feifel, H. 1959. *The Meaning of Death.* New York: McGraw-Hill.

Froelich, R. E. and Bishop, F. M. 1977. *Clinical Interviewing Skills: A programmed manual for data gathering, evaluation, and patient management* (3rd edn). St Louis: C. V. Mosby.

Kastenbaum, R. and Aisenberg, R. 1976. *The Psychology of Death* (Concise edition). New York: Springer.

Kinsey, A., Pomeroy, W. B. and Martin, C. E. 1948. *Sexual Behavior in the Human Male.* Philadelphia: Saunders.

Kinsey, A., Pomeroy, W. B., Martin, C. E. and Gebhard, P. H. 1953. *Sexual Behavior in the Human Female.* Philadelphia: Saunders.

Korsch, B. M. and Negrete, V. F. 1972. Doctor-patient communication. *Sci. Amer.* (August), 66–74.

Kubler-Ross, E. 1969. *On Death and Dying.* New York: Macmillan.

Lief, H. I. 1973. Obstacles to the ideal and complete sex education of the medical student and physician. In J. Zubin and J. Money (eds) *Contemporary Sexual Behavior: Critical Issues in the 1970s* 441–53. Baltimore: Johns Hopkins Univ. Press.

Masters, W. H. and Johnson, V. E. 1966. *Human Sexual Response.* Boston: Little, Brown.

Masters, W. H. and Johnson, V. E. 1970. *Human Sexual Inadequacy.* Boston: Little, Brown.

McCary, J. L. 1973. *Human Sexuality* (2nd edn). New York: Van Nostrand.

Pollock, S. and Manning, P. R. 1967. An experience in teaching the doctor-patient relationship to first-year medical students. *J. Med. Educ.* **42,** 770–4.

Schofield, M. 1968. *The Sexual Behaviour of Young People.* Middlesex: Penguin.

Sollod, R. N. 1975. Behavioural and psychodynamic dimensions of the new sex therapy. *J. Sex & Marital Ther.* **1,** 335–40.

Spinetta, J. J., Rigler, D. and Karon, M. 1973. Anxiety in the dying child. *Pediatrics* **52,** 841–5.

Stenchever, M. A. and Stickley, W. T. 1970. *Human Sexual Behavior: A Workbook in Reproductive Biology.* Chicago: Case Western Reserve Univ. Press.

Chapter 11

Individual Differences in Personality

The consistent predispositions to behave in one way rather than another, which make people distinctive, have been a source of continuing fascination and a diversity of theories. What are the sources of these differences, and how can they be most economically described? How well can future behaviour be predicted on the basis of the descriptions available to us? Such questions about the aetiology and measurement of personality lie at the heart of psychology in both its scientific and clinical branches, and are also of central importance to anybody, including doctors, who is interested in understanding and predicting the behaviour of others. In Chapter 9 we made a broad composite survey of the main stages of personal development, but here more specific questions of measurement, and prediction of the end-result of these developmental processes in the *individual* case, are our main concern. What sort of patient responds best to drug X, or is prone to migraines? Such questions call for some quantification of personality.

It is possible to fuss a lot over the definition of personality, but for our purposes the one in the first sentence of this chapter will be adequate. Seeing personality in terms of distinctive behavioural predispositions is a usefully pragmatic perspective to maintain, amid the speculation and conflict which characterize this area of study. Theoretical dogmatism is not justified in the face of the weaknesses of the measuring instruments. People choose a pet theory of personality for the same reasons they do anything else – it leads to reinforcement, in this case probably in the forms of a) reduction of uncertainty and provision of conceptual tools to organize complex information, b) rewards from admired models for adopting it, and c) rewards of success when using it as a basis for clinical therapeutic practice.

In this chapter we first tackle the question of personality

measurement, and then sketch the theories about dynamics, which prepares the ground for a detailed consideration of treatment approaches in the next chapter.

MEASUREMENT

The development of reliable and valid measuring instruments which capture personality, in such a way that accurate inferences about future behaviour can be made, is a venerable human ambition. There is great charm in the idea of psychologists being able to quantify individual temperament as accurately as chemists analyse a compound or engineers specify what load a bridge can bear. Unfortunately, many attempts to achieve this level of quantification have proved to be premature excursions into the unknown with severely limited equipment. The main problem is that unlike a chemical compound or a bridge, the processes requiring measurement are subject to constant dynamic interaction with intrinsic and external forces, and have not in addition been clearly distinguished from other aspects of the owner's psychological functioning. Thus, although it is clear that personality factors such as motivation affect performance on an IQ test, the effect of intelligence upon personality test performance is even more complex. Clinical psychologists (the sort most likely to be working in the health care team, and with a long history of association with the medical profession, particularly psychiatrists), show some disillusionment with personality testing as a professional activity today, compared with the time of high hopes and enthusiasm about the usefulness of such measures twenty years ago.

PROJECTIVE TESTS

There are two main varieties of personality test. The projective tests (see Chapter 4) present the testee with an ambiguous visual stimulus and ask for an interpretation. The rationale is that, just as we know that perception is influenced by needs and expectations, it may be assumed that what someone 'projects' into the unstructured test stimulus will likewise reflect dominant needs, preoccupations, and learned methods of organizing and making sense of the world. The Rorschach inkblots are the best known example (and probably represent psychology and psychiatry to many viewers of soap opera) others include the Thematic Appreciation Test (TAT), in which testees are asked to describe the events, emotions and outcome of a pictured scene, and the Sentence Completion Test, where the stimulus is the beginning of a sentence, such as, 'My father ...'. The great advantage of projective tests is that it is very difficult, for anyone not intimately acquainted with the tests, to manipulate the impression their answers give. What for instance is a 'safe' or 'healthy' answer to the question of what you perceive in an inkblot? (Saying little will reveal little, but your defensiveness and lack of cooperation become obvious.)

The disadvantages of projective tests are, however, considerable. Because every testee gives a unique response, standardization of scoring is difficult and interpretation even more so. Reliability (even between different judges of the same protocol) tends to be fairly low, especially for indirect higher-order inferences about personality. Validity is difficult to assess accurately, because the scorer can base judgements on aspects of the protocol unrelated to content, such as the verbal fluency shown, which obscure the relationship between that specific test and the correctness of decisions about the testee's personality. As usual, validity can be gauged by a number of methods, including the extent to which the test results agree with the results of 'accepted' tests (difficult in a contentious area like personality assessment), or the extent to which test results enable accurate predictions to be made about future behaviour (**predictive validity**). On this criterion, projective tests have not been found adequate in the large body of research devoted to the subject (Mischel 1971, Chap. 9).

SELF REPORT OR 'PSYCHOMETRIC' TESTS

The alternative variety of personality measurement consists of pencil and paper tests in which the testee responds 'Yes' or 'No', or 'True' or 'False', to a large number of carefully selected items, or ticks off on a checklist the adjectives which are felt to describe him or her. The test is standardized in form and scoring, although subjectivity may still enter into its interpretation, and produces scores on usually several preordained dimensions of personality. The traits measured in this way have often been derived from, and gain their claim to importance from, prior factor analytic studies. **Factor analysis** is a statistical technique which tells you about intercorrelations amongst large numbers of test responses, and allows 'factors' or clumps of related items to be distinguished. Cattell's Sixteen Personality Factor (16 PF) test, for example, provides a profile of characteristics in the sixteen areas of personality found to be major in Cattell's (1965) previous work. Eysenck and Eysenck (1975) describe tests based upon their classification of people along the three dimensions of introversion/ extraversion, neuroticism/stability, and psychoticism/normality. While people who gain extreme scores may be fairly adequately characterized by such trait approaches, the great majority who score somewhere in the middle can only be described, by default, as 'normal'.

Many descriptions of personality are in fact so widely true of the human species that large numbers of people will agree with their accuracy, as applied to themselves, if led to believe that these 'conclusions' are based on psychological tests, or perhaps astrological divinations, or any other method in which the subject has some faith. Illustrative statements of this 'Barnum effect', named after the circus which provided a little something for everybody, are 'You have a great deal of unused capacity which you have not turned to your advantage ... While you have some personality weaknesses, you are generally able to compensate for them ... Your sexual adjustment has presented problems for you ... At times you have serious doubts as to whether you have made the right decision or done the right thing ... You pride yourself as being an independent thinker and do not accept other's statements without satisfactory proof.' (Snyder, Stenkel and Lowery 1977.)

Another very widely used self-report personality test is the Minnesota Multiphasic Personality Inventory (MMPI). Answers here are keyed to those of diagnosed psychiatric patients, and the profile obtained shows the extent to which the testee's reponses resemble those provided by the original standardization groups of hysterics, paranoids, schizophrenics, depressives and so on. Many questions can be raised about the adequacy of this rationale for the original norms; the fact remains that the MMPI now has a life of its own such that, regardless of whether for example it is reasonable to regard schizophrenia as one disease entity, and institutionalized sufferers in the 1940s as good examples of its manifestation, a high score on the relevant MMPI scale has a certain independent meaning, established through several decades of research. Handbooks (or 'cookbooks') exist which give personality sketches of individuals obtaining specified scale-score profiles. MMPI items have also been extensively used to develop more specific scales, particularly for anxiety, depression, and somatic preoccupation (hypochondriasis).

USES OF CURRENT TESTS

It is useful and even essential for researchers to be able to quantify personality in a more or less objective way, for instance when evaluating responses to different therapy techniques, or exploring in what ways specifiable groups of people may be psychologically similar. The pencil and paper tests, being administerable in groups and scorable by machine, are obviously much more convenient for these purposes, as well as constituting a more standardized stimulus, than the projective tests. The growing literature on psychosocial aspects of various illnesses is replete with personality test scores. Philips (1976) used the Eysenck scales to establish that headache sufferers who seek medical attention are high-scorers on neuroticism, but that in this regard they differ from the majority of headache sufferers who do not seek medical help, and who are indistinguishable from the rest of the population (i.e. 'normal') on the Eysenck tests. Blumberg, West, and Ellis (1954) found different MMPI profiles in individuals with fast- versus slow-growing cancers, but Watson and Schuld (1977) have recently failed to find MMPI difference between individuals who later develop benign versus malignant neoplasms.

PROBLEMS WITH STANDARDIZED TESTS

The study of relationships between personality, life change, psychophysiological strain and health status of first-year university students by Garrity, Somes and Marx (1977) exemplifies an important problem associated with reliance on self-report measures, which is that of **response bias.** In their case, it was 'propensity to report personal problems' which could not be ruled out as a source of all the interesting correlations found – an example of (a) below. Forms of response bias or response set which may contaminate personality test scores have been found to include a) social desirability, concerning people's relative readiness to admit to thoughts and actions which are strange or 'unacceptable' (see Chapter 2), b) acquiescence (or yea-saying), even to opposing statements, and c) avoidance of, or preference for, extreme responses (where graded responses or ratings of agreement are available).

The only way to overcome such problems is to have some unarguable external criterion for the person's behavioural predisposition, such as actual observations of the behaviour in question. You may recognize here the same dissatisfaction with efforts at quantifying global traits, and approval for criterion-referenced testing, which is apparent in our discussion of intelligence measurement. There is always a certain degree of conflict between seeking a direct behavioural observation, which is likely to be very specific to the situation in which the observation is made (e.g. influenced by who was present, explained purpose, physical and emotional state of the subject, etc.), and seeking to discover more generalized behavioural trends by asking general questions (and risking sampling only verbal, self-descriptive behaviour).

OTHER MEASURES OF PERSONALITY

Rating scales depend on the conclusions reached by trained or experienced judges, after interaction with or observations of the subject. Assessment may be based on a variety of clues both verbal and non-verbal, but is likely to be coloured by the **halo effect**: the judge's tendency to overgeneralize on the basis of a limited subsection of the information, and see people as all good (or likeable, or healthy) or all bad (or unpleasant, or disturbed). The judge's expectations, and also the subject's emotional response to the judge, are additional sources of bias.

Content analysis refers to the fine-grained analysis of verbal material for cues to emotional and personality characteristics. Gottschalk (1974) has described how traits such as hostility and anxiety can be evaluated from responses to the instruction 'speak for five minutes about any interesting or dramatic personal life experiences you have had.' McClelland (1961) and his associates have used TAT cards to stimulate speech which was then analysed for the presence of themes related to need for achievement (*n* Ach).

ASSESSING PERSONALITY INFORMALLY

There is considerable argument about how many and which personality traits are primary, what they should be called, and such questions. However, when people rate each other's personality, the main dimensions which recur again and again as important can be summarized as follows: a) warmhearted, frank, easygoing versus cold, reserved, obstructive, b) stable and mature versus impulsive and undependable, and c) active, dominant, ambitious versus passive, submissive, lazy (Mischel 1971). 'Warmth' in particular is such an important dimension to us in our assessments of other people's personality, that all sorts of related traits tend to be inferred along with it. Wishner (1960) found that people attribute generosity, wisdom and sociability to someone described as 'warm', and meanness, humourlessness and irritability to someone described as 'cold'. We also tend to hold certain stereotyped expectations about the personalities of individuals of different age, sex, and ethnic background (and these stereotypes may actually influence what we perceive about them, as discussed in Chapter 4).

Facial and physical characteristics may also imply certain personality traits: some of us evidently believe along with the ancients that people share the behavioural traits of the animals they most resemble (e.g. think what behaviour you would expect of persons described as rabbity, bovine, waspish or bear-like). The phrenologists, a very influential and popular movement during the early nineteenth century, believed that bumps on the skull revealed personality through relative brain allocation to different traits. Sheldon (1942) found high correlations between physique and temperament: soft round 'endomorphs' were relaxed food-lovers, hard muscular 'mesomorphs' were energetic and courageous, and long, thin 'ectomorphs' were timid and sensitive introverts. Later researchers have found more modest correlations, which, it must be remembered, do not necessarily imply a direct causality between body type and personality (in either direction). Being fat, thin or brawny in childhood might change both the expectations of the social environment and the opportunities to develop skills, which might both influence personality development. Or a certain kind of family (or other third factor) might encourage both fatness and sociability for example. Or adult physique might be independent of personality, and the small correlations a reflection of the raters' stereotypes.

Facial characteristics are notoriously unreliable as indications of personality, but probably provide us with first hypotheses about which we collect further evidence. Expressive movements of the face, hands or whole body are also regarded as indicative of enduring traits (e.g. to a graphologist), or at least of present emotion (see Chapter 7). It is somewhat disturbing to learn how little better 'experts' are at personality judgement than the rest of us. Mischel however (1971, pp. 168–76) has surveyed considerable evidence that untrained individuals, and experienced clinicians with or without the help of tests, are quite similar in the accuracy of their personality assessments of others. The processes by which we form an impression of what somebody else is like, and try to manipulate the impression we make ourselves, will be discussed in more detail in Chapter 16.

Mischel (1977) has recently called for more attention to functional analyses not of how people differ from each other, but of how they alter in response to alterations in the conditions of their lives. This person-centred **idiographic** approach is one with which therapists of all theoretical persuasions feel sympathy, while those behavioural scientists whose main interests are less applied continue to search, using the **nomothetic** approach, for valid ways to describe the consistent similarities and differences between individuals. Clearly, both approaches are necessary. The clinician trying to modify behaviour therapeutically may need to be able to describe the sorts of people for whom a particular technique works best, just as the researcher into individual differences may want to understand their sources, for example when relating personality traits to biochemistry or to health.

THREE THEORIES OF PERSONALITY

We turn now to the major theoretical systems which have attempted to explain the structure and foundations of personality. There are many more theories on the subject than three; the ones below have been chosen as the most comprehensive and currently influential orientations. In particular, each has practical implications for the treatment and prevention of emotional and possibly the corresponding physical disorders.

PSYCHODYNAMIC APPROACHES

Sigmund Freud (1856–1939) founded the system of psychoanalysis to treat disorders of adjustment and, from his observations of people in this plight, developed a personality theory which has had a profound influence upon Western culture in general, as well as upon the behavioural sciences and medicine. It also stimulated and inspired many followers, who have added their own elaborations and refor-mulations to Freud's original thesis.

The psychic structure is conceived of as a three-part iceberg, most of which remains unconscious. The **id,** unconscious source of all energy particularly through the biological drives of sex and aggression, seeks immediate satisfaction and is guided only by the pleasure principle. Derived from this in the course of development is the mainly conscious **ego,** which mediates between the id and the demands of both society and of conscience. It operates on the reality principle, is rational, can delay gratification, and seeks safety. The **superego** or conscience, partly conscious and partly unconscious, is a watchful and critical moralist which strives for perfection. The necessary conflict between these elements of personality, and how it is resolved, is seen as the source of personality. In Freud's time attention was focussed on the id and especially upon his contention of sexuality present from babyhood, manifesting itself in oral, anal and phallic stages, fixation at which, by blocking of the instinctual release, causes adult psychological disorder before the mature genital form is attained. Currently, and under the influence of major neo-Freudian theorists such as Adler, Erikson, Sullivan, Fromm and Horney, there is an increasing interest in the structure and functions of the ego. To cope with the anxiety engendered by the hazards of life (especially threats to self-esteem), and by the need to control one's impulses, the ego develops various helpful coping mechanisms such as memory, judgement, logical analysis, concentration, empathy and tolerance of ambiguity. Each of these if used immoderately can come to have a harmful rather than beneficial result (Kroeber 1963). Objective rationality, for example, if expressed in extreme forms such as **intellectualization** or **rationalization,** may cut a person off from real emotions to an artificial and damaging extent. **Denial** is the usually short-lived capacity to be selectively inattentive to external threats. Anxiety-provoking impulses or memories may be pushed into the unconscious by **repression,** which spares the ego from guilt and threat. Usually, however, some clues to the repressed material appear in the disguised symbols of dreams, slips of the tongue, and associations between ideas; these are the data from which the psychoanalyst draws conclusions about the nature of the conflict. Other defence mechanisms are **projection** (unrealistic attribution of our feelings to somebody else: a form of empathy gone wild), and **displacement** (choosing an inappropriate rather than an appropriate substitute expression for an unacceptable impulse).

The list of defence mechanisms can be considerably extended. It has met with great interest and acceptance by many people interested in mental life, not all of whom necessarily agree with other parts of Freud's model. Experimentalists have tended to have trouble in establishing a convincing body of evidence for the operation of these mechanisms, partly because they are not readily subjected to study in laboratory conditions; more seriously, because the predictions derived from the theory are often not specific enough to be disprovable. Kline (1972) concluded, after a balanced review of the area, that there is some support for some of the empirically testable propositions, although 'much of the metapsychology of psychoanalytic theory ... is unscientific in that it cannot be subjected to any kind of empirical test and so be refuted' (p. 358). In addition, he felt that where Freudian and non-Freudian concepts had been experimentally validated, it tended to be where they had concerned the reinforcers operating to produce and maintain maladaptive behaviour; with the implication that behavioural methods of treatment would be more efficient than the 'slow desensitization by talking' (p. 359) of psychoanalytic therapy.

Although it may eventually be recognized that many psychoanalytic concepts are vivid descriptions rather than scientific explanations, we are all indebted to Freud and his followers for making explicit the following characteristics of human mental life: a) personality is the result of past experiences (rather than predominantly of chance or inheritance), b) behaviour is not always rational in the face of anxiety, except insofar as defending against the anxiety becomes a major need, and c) the mechanisms by which we protect ourselves from anxiety can buy time and permit the development of better solutions (i.e. can help us to cope). Or they can, if allowed to dominate behaviour, lead to maladaptive patterns which may need expert help in the unlearning.

SOCIAL LEARNING THEORY

Rather than explaining personality as the expression of a set of traits or underlying motives, we have in this chapter adopted a definition more congruent with a behaviourist view. That is, there is relatively greater interest in what people *do*, in what circumstances, than in what they *are like*. That people behave differently in different settings is unarguable: the surgeon who is an autocrat in the operating theatre may give quite a different impression of his personality if encountered in the squash courts or at a party. In each case his behaviour is shaped by the prevailing reinforcement conditions, (this is not to deny that he may manifest some well-established predispositions across a variety of new situations).

The reinforcers which shape behaviour may be direct, vicarious or self-administered, as discussed more fully in Chapter 6 (also see

Bandura 1974). The 'situation' therefore to which behaviour is specific includes the person's perception and interpretation of it, as well as the raw physical setting. In the course of maturation, and increasing ability to process more complex and abstract information (Chapter 5), children learn a great deal about the consequences of different behaviours during the sensitive preschool years, largely from their parents and later, from teachers, peers and others. By this process of socialization each develops habits, values and attitudes in harmony with (and therefore rewarded by) the main identification figures available (Chapter 9). Adult 'personality' is thus a complex product of the current environment and of an individual with certain biological characteristics who represents an accumulation of learning interactions with past environments. In principle, if all of these could be accurately specified, and the effects of innate constitutional factors properly understood at the same time, the probability of future behaviour in specific circumstances could be accurately determined. More practically, it could be influenced.

The social learning approach to understanding personality (Bandura and Walters 1963; Mischel 1971), by means of analysing the antecedents and consequences of the behaviours in question, has proved to be a very fruitful one for clinical attempts at treatment for the sorts of 'personality disorders' which restrict human functioning. As indicated at the beginning of this chapter, personality theories often arise from and are validated in clinical practice, rather than the reverse. These applications, or rather natural examples, of the personality theories described here will be discussed in detail in Chapter 12.

One kind of behavioural predisposition which varies amongst individuals, and which is of particular relevance to medicine, is the one concerned with illness behaviour. Mechanic (1966, see ref. Chapter 1) described illness behaviour as the ways in which people evaluate and respond to awareness of physical malfunction or discomfort. It is not surprising, in view of the conditionability of physical functions (Chapter 6), to find that in different cultures, and in different social class and religious groups within a culture, there are differences in the patterns of pain perception (Chapter 4) and of symptomatology (Zola 1966). What people *do* about an experienced symptom also varies greatly within the population. Only about one in every three of those people aware of some physical symptom, i.e. reporting it to an interviewer when asked, seek a doctor's help, and help-seeking is not determined primarily by severity of symptom.

There is some evidence from sick adults undergoing psychotherapy that illness behaviour training occurs in childhood, like other sorts of socialization. The exact mechanics of this process, and even the distribution of illness behaviour predispositions in a given population, are only just beginning to be investigated. Pilowsky (1978; Pilowsky and Spence 1975) has developed a measure of illness behaviour patterns with which he is studying people who exhibit **abnormal illness behaviour** (in whom there is a discrepancy between the somatic pathology present, and the person's response to it).

HUMANIST APPROACHES

While both psychodynamic and learning theory approaches to personality regard the subject as part ultimately of the biological sciences, the humanistic stress is a more philosophical one, and more concerned with the human characteristics which set us apart from (or cannot be studied in) animals. Thus reflective self-consciousness, the experience of free will, and the foreknowledge of death with its correlated ethical and metaphysical concerns, are central concepts in this view of personality (Kinget 1975).

In contrast to the psychodynamic view of underlying motives which are obliquely expressed in observable behaviour, and the learning view that behaviour is shaped by its consequences, the humanists take perceived current reality as their major datum. Explanations of behaviour are therefore in terms of the subjective experience of the behaver. 'Experiential' is in fact another label, along with phenomenological, existential and self-theory, for this theoretical orientation which, like the others previously discussed, is over-simplified and made to appear unreally monolithic in this brief description. The most important force directing behaviour for the humanists is not sex and aggression, not reinforcement, but **self-actualization** (Maslow 1968; Rogers 1963). To achieve this state of fulfillment and growth, people need to be self-aware and self-accepting. Anxiety and maladjustments arise when there is incongruence between experienced reality and the expectations and values of the self-concept. Discrepancies between a person's description of his 'self' and his 'ideal self', or between the descriptions given by the person and by others of his 'self', indicate a need for assistance. Rogerians see the best therapist as one who cares for and values the person, and thus facilitates self-discovery.

It is easy to imagine the clashes which have occurred between exponents of this and the radical behaviourist views. Rogers and Skinner respectively have engaged in spirited public debate since the publication of Skinner's provocative 1971 book *Beyond Freedom and Dignity*. (As a fashion, this controversy seems to have replaced its outworn psychodynamics versus behaviourism forerunner.) The 'self' is exactly the kind of unobservable construct against which strict behaviourists have been arguing for years (Skinner 1975). The stress on immediate experience leaves unexplained exactly how the self's attitudes and values arose, and precisely how they influence behaviour. In some cases in fact it is clear that such cognitions change in order to fit changed behaviour, not vice versa.

There are currently indications of an amalgamation of the best elements of the behaviourist and humanist views, stimulated, as most theoretical changes are, by the practical demands of the therapeutic endeavour. The 'social learning' approach described earlier, with its attention to self-reinforcement, is already a modification of the strict behaviourist exclusion of all but overt behaviour. **Cognitive behaviourism** (Mahoney 1977) is emerging as a further development of the original paradigm. It consists of a) acknowledging that the individual's *perception* of reality is the crucial variable determining subsequent behaviour, b) treating those cognitive representations as behaviour to which the principles of learning can legitimately be applied, and c) exploring and refining therapeutic techniques which take account of the continuing interaction between thoughts, feelings and behaviours (see Chapter 12, also Ellis 1962).

SUMMARY

Projective tests of personality are hard to fake but lack validity, while self-report techniques, although much more standardized in scoring and interpretation, are subject to the distorting effects of various sorts of response bias. Body type and expressive movements may provide informal clues to correlated personality characteristics. There is a necessary reciprocity between the descriptive nomothetic approach to the study of personality differences, and the idiographic one.

Three dominant schools of personality theory are the psychodynamic (founded by Freud), social learning (Bandura) and humanist (Rogers). While the first sees the mainsprings of adult personality as the resolution of the conflict between id, ego and superego, the second emphasizes reinforcement in the context of past learning history, and the third current cognitions. Cognitive behaviourism extends social learning theory to take the individual's inner life into account as crucial.

TERMS AND CONCEPTS

predictive validity
factor analysis
response bias
halo effect
content analysis
idiographic
nomothetic
id
ego
superego
intellectualization ⎫
rationalization   ⎪
denial   ⎬ defence
repression   ⎪ mechanisms
projection   ⎪
displacement   ⎭
abnormal illness behaviour
self-actualization
cognitive behaviourism

FOR DISCUSSION

1. Popular magazines frequently publish 'personality' tests and quizzes. How would you evaluate such measuring instruments, and what kinds of information would you need to be able to decide how much faith to put in their results?

2. From your readings, of original sources if possible, construct a table showing the similarities and differences between the main schools of personality theory. Some areas you should consider include

personality structure
dominant motivation(s)
role of learning versus heredity
development: stages versus continuity

role of interpersonal and social influences
importance of a concept of 'self'.

SUGGESTED READING

Mischel 1971: good basic introduction to both measurements
and theory.
Pilowsky 1978: abnormal illness behaviour described and
classified.

REFERENCES

Bandura, A. and Walters, R. H. 1963. *Social Learning and Personality Development.* New York: Holt, Rinehart and Winston.

Bandura, A. 1974. Behavior theory and the models of man. *Amer. Psychol.* **29,** 859–69.

Blumberg, E. M., West, P. M. and Ellis, F. W. 1954. A possible relationship between psychological factors and human cancer. *Psychosom. Med.* **16,** 227–86.

Cattell, R. B. 1965. *The Scientific Analysis of Personality.* Baltimore: Penguin Books.

Ellis, A. 1962. *Reason and Emotion in Psychotherapy.* New York: Lyle Stuart.

Eysenck H. J. and Eysenck, S. B. G. 1975. *Manual of the Eysenck Personality Questionnaire.* London: Hodder and Stoughton.

Garrity, T. F., Somes, G. W. and Marx, M. B. 1977. The relationship of personality, life change, psychophysiological strain and health status in a college population. *Soc. Sci. and Med.* **11,** 257–63.

Gottschalk, L. A. 1974. Quantification and psychological indicators of emotions: The content analysis of speech and other objective measures of pyschological states. *Int. J. Psychiat. Med.* **5,** 587–610.

Kinget, G. M. 1975. *On Being Human: A Systematic View.* New York: Harcourt Brace Jovanovich.

Kline, P. 1972. *Fact and Fantasy in Freudian Theory.* London: Methuen.

Kroeber, T. C. 1963. The coping functions of the ego mechanisms. In R. W. White (ed.) *The Study of Lives* 178–98. New York: Atherton Press.

Mahoney, M. J. 1977. Reflections on the cognitive–learning trend in psychotherapy. *Amer. Psychol.* **33,** 5–13.

Maslow, A. H. 1968. *Toward a Psychology of Being* (2nd edn). New York: Van Nostrand.

McClelland, D. C. 1961. *The Achieving Society.* Princeton: Van Nostrand.

Mischel, W. 1971. *Introduction to Personality.* New York: Holt, Rinehart and Winston.

Mischel, W. 1977. On the future of personality measurement. *Amer. Psychol.* **32,** 246–54.

Philips, C. 1976. Headache and personality. *J. Psychosom. Res.* **20,** 535–42.

Pilowsky, I. 1978. A general classification of abnormal illness behaviours. *Brit. J. Med. Psychol.* **51,** 131–37.

Pilowsky, I. and Spence, N. D. 1975. Patterns of illness behaviour in patients with intractable pain. *J. Psychosom. Res.* **19,** 279–87.

Rogers, C. R. 1963. The actualizing tendency in relation to 'motives' and to consciousness. In M. R. Jones (ed.) *Nebraska Symposium on Motivation* 1–24. Lincoln: Univ. of Nebraska Press.

Sheldon, W. H. 1942. *The Varieties of Temperament: A Psychology of Constitutional Differences* (with the collaboration of S. S. Stevens). New York: Harper.

Skinner, B. F. 1971. *Beyond Freedom and Dignity.* New York: Knopf.

Skinner, B. F. 1975. The steep and thorny way to a science of behaviour. *Amer. Psychol.* **30,** 42–9.

Snyder, C. R., Shenkel, R. J. and Lowery, C. R. 1977. Acceptance of personality interpretations: The 'Barnum effect' and beyond. *J. Cons. Clin. Psychol.* **45,** 104–14.

Watson, C. G. and Schuld, D. 1977. Psychosomatic factors in the etiology of neoplasms. *J. Cons. Clin. Psychol.* **45,** 455–61.

Wishner, J. 1960. Reanalysis of 'impressions of personality'. *Psychol. Rev.* **67,** 96–112.

Zola, I. K. 1966. Culture and symptoms – An analysis of patients' presenting complaints. *Amer. Sociol. Rev.* **31,** 615–30.

Chapter 12

Therapeutic Behavioural Change

Behavioural change, broadly conceived, is the ultimate goal of all forms of therapy for psychological and psycho-physiological disorders. The different theories of personality described in Chapter 11 lead to different ways of describing the goals of therapy, as well as to different methods of achieving them. Here we review these therapeutic principles, devoting the bulk of the chapter to descriptions of behaviourally oriented techniques and their applications to medically relevant human difficulties.

A general understanding of the principles of various therapies will enable you to make specialist referrals intelligently. But in addition, because doctors control pain and anxiety, and because of their 'expert' status, they are powerful natural agents of reinforcement and behaviour change, and had best know what they are doing.

PRINCIPLES OF TREATMENT

WHO BEST PROVIDES TREATMENT?

The 'therapist' may be a specialist professional such as a psychiatrist or psychologist, or other socially recognized healer endowed with religious or medical authority. *De facto* therapy is also provided by respected and trusted friends and contacts who have no official healing qualifications. Some elements appear to be universal: the 'patient's' desire to change or to effect change in the behaviour of significant others, the shared belief system of patient and therapist (e.g. regarding the causes of psychological problems), the expertise attributed to the therapist and the placebo power of this authority, and the patient's heightened suggestibility and dependency. The relationship between the two is always of major importance. Added to that, as mentioned above, the therapist will usually have learned certain concepts about the sources of maladaptive behaviour, and certain techniques for curing it.

WHICH THEORY IS BEST?

It is quite easy to re-cast the competing theoretical approaches in terms of the one you happen to favour, for instance to analyse psychoanalysis as a learning process. At present an apparently increasing proportion of psychotherapists describe their theoretical orientation as **eclectic** (Garfield and Kurtz 1977). In other words, there is a readiness to draw from several approaches in the search for concepts and techniques which make sense for the particular patient, rather than insisting that all patients and their problems are interpreted within the confines of one theoretical system.

LIMITS OF TREATMENT

The development and diffusion of the discipline of sociology has also increased awareness in the last couple of decades that the source of many personal difficulties lies, not in the deficiencies or family traumas of the individual, but in injustices of the social hierarchy. Thus poverty, racial prejudice, sexism and related ills are seen by some as more pervasive problems, and more worthy of our therapeutic efforts, than individual unhappiness. Psychiatrists and by implication other mental health workers have been labelled by radicals (e.g. Szasz 1961), as minions of the *status quo* who perpetuate social inequities by seeking to make people 'adjusted' to them. This argument sometimes seems analogous to the rejection on principle of policemen, as enforcers of the conservative establishment view. When you are mugged or burgled, or a relative becomes psychotic or makes a suicide attempt, you see the need for a specialist helper (perhaps in addition to social revolution!).

A serious charge faced by all modes of psychotherapy is that of availability. There is a selection process on financial grounds regarding people who can pay for protracted individual treatment, and miss the necessary worktime without becoming unemployed. This is not a problem exclusive to mental health care delivery. The paucity of professional workers, their tendency to avoid rural areas, and their relative preference for patients with a good prognosis, all reduce accessibility of services to those who arguably stand in greatest need.

All therapeutic systems score a higher success rate with anxious 'neurotic' disorders than with psychotic disorders. In addition, all tend to do better with patients who are young, intelligent, and highly motivated to change (Schofield, 1964).

WHICH THERAPY IS BEST? (AND HOW TO TELL)

There are many obstacles to estimating success rates across different kinds of therapy. (If the task were easy, presumably the 'best' kind would have been recognized long ago.) One difficulty lies in the definition of success. If the therapist decides when success has occurred, it may mean only that the patient had learned to talk about the problem in ways that match the therapist's ideas. For example; the goal of psychoanalysis is the gaining of insight, yet possibly this could occur if the patient's verbal behaviour has been subtly shaped to approximate that of the therapist. Perhaps the patient should decide whether or not treatment has been a success. However, it is predictable from cognitive dissonance theory (Chapter 15) that patients, at the end of an experience which has possibly been expensive and harrowing, may overestimate the benefits. The **hello-goodbye effect** refers to this tendency by patients to dwell on their disabilities at the start of treatment and their strengths at the end, thus drawing an exaggerated picture of its efficacy. Some 'successes' in terms of statistical significance may not be so in clinical terms (e.g. small changes in weight or blood pressure).

How long must 'success' last in order to be convincing? This question becomes particularly pertinent where the natural environment of the patient's daily life tends to reinforce submissiveness, delinquency, low level of aspiration, or whatever the original problem was. It is one reason for an increasing interest amongst behaviourists and family therapists in working with the natural agents of rein-forcement, rather than only with the designated 'patient', especially where the latter is a child, institutionalized, or otherwise lacking autonomy for environmental choices.

How the goals of therapy are defined also affects evaluations of efficacy. On the one hand, very general aims such as 'psychological adjustment' are virtually meaningless without further refinement, and on the other, very specific behaviourally-defined goals such as 'being able to leave the house for a day without anxiety' (for an agoraphobic), may seem trivial and shallow. If success is estimated on more specific 'objective' grounds such as improved relations with others, avoiding hospitalization or legal hassles, or better vocational performance, biasing influences still operate and comparisons between patients become more difficult.

What if a cured snake phobic develops sexual difficulties two years later? **Symptom substitution** was predicted by early opponents of behavioural treatment methods, who believed that underlying mental disturbance would manifest itself in new ways as each behavioural disturbance was eliminated. As pointed out in Bandura's excellent review (1969), the concept is a muddled one incapable of proof: even if we could agree what constitutes a 'symptom' behaviourally, its appearance at some unspecified time after the end of treatment could show persistence of old maladaptive habits hitherto unnoticed, or could show learning of a new maladaptive response altogether (much as a new illness afterwards does not prove that a drug is ineffective).

The selection of controls for assessment of therapeutic efficacy is even more fraught with hazards where problems are behavioural and emotional, than where they are clearly somatic. Ethical considerations prevent treatments from being withheld where there is a reasonable hope of effectiveness, and treatments for which there is little hope of effectiveness from being administered. The matching of subjects who receive and do not receive Treatment X is made harder by the high natural wastage in all forms of psychotherapy, caused by people dropping out after too few sessions. Comparisons can also be subverted if certain types of patients are only interested in certain types of treatment (non-random selection of subjects), and also by personality or procedural variations amongst therapists who ostensibly share the 'same' theory.

Some subjects who are officially untreated controls get informal therapy from priests, doctors or friends. The **spontaneous remission** (untreated recovery) rate was loudly claimed by Eysenck (1965) to be about two-thirds anyway, and few treatments seemed able to better that.

Recent and on the whole more sophisticated and detailed studies have been rather more cheerful about the positive results of therapy. Smith and Glass (1977) analysed all the studies they could find where there was any attempt at a control group, and arrived at a much larger population of studies than had previously been gathered together. They concluded that the typical recipient of psychotherapy is better off afterwards than 75 per cent of untreated controls. Interestingly, they report insignificant variation in effectiveness between different schools of therapy. Perhaps the lesson to be drawn from that is a re-affirmation of the importance of the relationship between the participants, rather than the particular belief system of the official treater.

METHODS OF TREATMENT

Serious depressive and psychotic states have always been recognized as deviant, a danger to both victims and social group, and have been treated by whatever methods seemed appropriate in the light of explanations current at the time. That is, when deviant behaviour was seen as a sign of demonic possession, exorcism of evil spirits was the treatment of choice, for example by making the body of the sufferer an uncomfortable home by spinning it violently. A great advance was the reconceptualization of deviant behaviour in terms of illness, which led to nursing rather than punitive treatments for the afflicted.

PHYSICAL METHODS OF TREATMENT

Today, treatment methods based on a strictly illness model of psychological disturbance are usually combined with or even replaced by those based on a 'maladjustment' model, as will be described hereafter. Hospitalization ensures custodial care and removes the seriously disturbed individual from the community. It may of course also remove the person from social and community supports, although modern psychiatric hospitals make every effort to counteract that possibility. The hospital can be used as an opportunity for intensive daylong therapy, for example by exploiting the potential of patients' groups and specially trained nurses. A hazard of poorly funded mental hospitals of the past was that patients would be forgotten by society, and through a process of adapting over-well to the demands of institutional life, become progressively less able to cope with independent life outside the walls.

Drug therapy is an extremely valuable part of the treatment of depressive and psychotic disorders, *if* the patients can be persuaded to keep taking their medication as required. The reasons for the efficacy of antidepressants and major tranquillizers used as anti-psychosis agents are not really understood yet, but provide clues to the biochemical aetiology or concomitants of these conditions. Like hospitalization, drug therapy may be seen as a holding measure which gives the physician sufficient control over symptoms for the patient to be reached and possibly re-educated. Drugs have lesser utility in treating the milder neurotic disorders; doctors tend to have more faith in them than do psychologists, who cannot prescribe them anyway. **Electroconculsive therapy** (ECT) is for unknown reasons helpful in the treatment of some depressive illnesses.

PSYCHODYNAMIC THERAPY

As may be expected, there are as many variations in psychoanalytically oriented therapy as there are in the theory. Common assumptions include the unconscious nature of intrapsychic conflicts and their source in childhood experiences. The goal of therapy is conceptualized as **insight** (conscious awareness) into one's problems, which has an emotional as well as an intellectual impact. The expectation is that behaviour (including feelings and attitudes as well as overt actions) will alter in response to the patient's new self-understanding.

Analysis is seen as a miniature of the patient's life (Fine 1973). Therapy proceeds by a series of individual interviews, which in orthodox psychoanalysis may occur several times weekly over several years. An intense **transference** relationship develops on the part of the patient, who replicates towards the therapist feelings and actions reminiscent of other intense relationships earlier in life. By analysing the patient's transference feelings therefore, the therapist gets much information about how parents, siblings, the marital partner and others have been perceived and responded to, and the sources of the patient's current psychological debilitation. The therapist develops counter-transference feelings for the patient too, but through having undergone a personal analysis previously, is able to remain detached and to provide a supportive but emotionally neutral atmosphere, in which the patient is free to explore and resolve his or her problems. It is also taken for granted that at some level there will be *resistance* to therapeutic change, which needs to be overcome.

Techniques for investigating the unconscious conflicts involve the analysis of dreams and of verbal slips, and **free association** (an uncensored report of the patient's sequence of thoughts and images). Sometimes projective tests may be used to stimulate analyzable verbal behaviours. Jung initiated a somewhat similar form of therapy emphasizing the symbolic nature of expressions of the unconscious such as dreams, and relying heavily upon them for clues to assist the therapeutic process of making the unconscious conscious. Adler believed in the primacy of the need for mastery. As described in

Chapter 11, neo-Freudians including Freud's daughter Anna, Erikson and others, are more interested in the ego than the id. They tend to interact more actively with the patient, aim to strengthen the conscious, reality-oriented skills, and speak of needs for mastery and competence as well as for sex and aggression.

CLIENT-CENTRED THERAPY

Psychotherapy in the Rogerian model lays very great emphasis upon the relationship between client (note the change of designation of the one helped) and the therapist, as it is directly experienced by both. Explanation of past sources of the problem is minimized in favour of the 'here and now'. The necessary and sufficient conditions for client improvement are seen as being attitudes within the therapist of genuineness, empathy, and unconditional positive regard. In the unusual interpersonal setting of being thoroughly understood by an open, caring, optimistic other, the client's potential for self-actualization is freed from restrictions, and can promote change and growth. Meador and Rogers (1973) describe the goals of client-centred therapy as being able to a) admit to and express feelings, not remain out of touch with inner experience, b) rely on one's inner experience as a guide to behaviour rather than look to others, c) construe (interpret) experiences in a flexible, self-relevant, non-absolutist way, d) communicate about oneself rather than avoid it, e) act in a way which is congruent with the newly experienced inner self rather than playing roles which deny or hide it, f) admit to having problems, and avoid blaming others for them, and g) express feelings about other people to them as they occur, rather than fearing close relationships.

The therapist's role is seen as a *facilitative* rather than prescriptive or interpretative one. Clients are to be helped to help themselves. One natural area for learning to acknowledge and express feelings towards others as they arise, is in a group. The encounter or personal growth group movement of recent years provides an opportunity for over-controlled, emotionally inhibited people (a typical result of social pressures in our culture), to learn how to relate more warmly and openly to others, and gain greater understanding of themselves. Other kinds of difficulty, and more severe ones, indicate a more extensive and individual form of therapy.

Another application of the approach, apart from individual and group counselling, has been in the training of those whose occupations demand effective interpersonal relationships, for example teachers, health workers, ministers and executives. The focus on the relationship between participants makes this approach a particularly useful and versatile one for interactions, where, although 'therapy' is not the main acknowledged goal, one person is in a position to influence the behaviour of the other. Guidelines for medical interviewing, such as those summarized in Chapter 10, tend to incorporate findings from the extensive research stimulated by Rogers' ideas. Related therapeutic methods which have been developed include Gestalt therapy (Perls 1969), reality therapy (Glasser 1965) and Transactional Analysis (Berne 1964), the latter two also showing psychoanalytic influences.

BEHAVIOURAL THERAPY

Behaviour change techniques based on the principles of learning (Chapter 6), and on the related view of personality (Chapter 11), are similar to the previously described Rogerian approach in being useful to practitioners in a variety of influence situations. For cases where specialized therapy training is needed, clinical psychologists are beginning to work in health care teams.

Behavioural approaches rest upon a set of general principles, and include a number of specific techniques which have been developed in the last thirty years or so and which are undergoing constant research and refinement at present. In line with the orientation throughout this book, greater detail will be provided about this method than about the others described. First let us briefly recapitulate the principles which guide the behaviour therapist.

Principles

Maladaptive behaviour (i.e. that which requires alteration) is learned by association, reinforcement or modelling, as is any other behaviour, within fairly broad limits determined by species-specific and genetic predispositions. Therefore treatment can be seen as a relearning process. A training approach can also be applied where the problem is one of behavioural *deficit* rather than disorder, where skills are absent for reasons such as physiological trauma (e.g. aphasia) or lack of opportunity to learn (e.g. academic achievement).

As behaviour is the problem, it is necessary to collect detailed information about its frequency, situational antecedents, and the reinforcers which are maintaining it, who dispenses them, and so on.

The 'same' behaviour may have quite a different reinforcement context, and therefore require different treatment, in different individuals. For example some child molesters may be orgasmically conditioned to children, while others may use children as a substitute for women, whom they desire but fear to approach. Individual tailoring of therapy is essential, and can only be based on a detailed **behavioural analysis**. Outcome measurement and monitoring of progress also become simpler when the problem is defined as precisely as possible.

Generalization of the behaviour change over time and setting needs to be specifically programmed for. Thus control of reinforcements needs to be passed from the therapist to the client or those in the client's environment who control reinforcers, or to both of these. Only with the active cooperation of the client therefore (and often, of associates), will treatment be successful.

Techniques

All the principles of learning discussed in Chapter 6 can be applied therapeutically.

Successive approximations to desired behaviours are an effective way to shape behaviour. By starting at the level of someone's current performance, and with careful attention to the reinforcement schedule and the size of the steps required, new skills can be gradually added on to the behavioural repertoire. Group settings may often provide a useful non-threatening but informative environment in which, for example, assertiveness and communication skills may be rehearsed. *Extinction* of undesired behaviours by withdrawal of reinforcers, like punishment, needs to be set in a context of teaching alternative and more acceptable methods of gaining the same reinforcers. *Modelling and vicarious reinforcement* are helpful in both desensitizing fears and teaching new responses. *Autonomic conditioning* has been successfully tried with some psycho-physiological complaints such as hypertension and headache. The development of increasingly sophisticated and portable technological equipment, by increasing the availability of constant biofeedback to the person, holds further promise. *Nonspecific treatment aids* such as placebo power, suggestion, and the therapist-client relationship are as important in behaviourally oriented change procedures as in the explicit relationship psychotherapies such as Freudian and Rogerian. The behaviourist may make particular efforts to model clear communicatory behaviours and to reinforce evidence of progress on the patient's part by extra attention and approval. Compatibility of expectations and background between therapist and client also appears to help, and undoubtedly many treatments are prematurely terminated when some conflict occurs in these personal areas of the interaction.

Progressive muscular relaxation is taught by successive contraction and relaxation of muscle groups, as a state incompatible with anxiety. Along with the ability to relax deeply and voluntarily, goes greater awareness of the sources and location of contrasting psycho-physiological tensions. **Systematic desensitization** of anxieties occurs by pairing examples of the feared situation in a graded way with the experience of relaxation. A hierarchy of anxiety-provoking scenes is constructed first. For example, for a dental phobia it might range from hearing a radio talk on the need for regular dental checkups at the lowest extreme, to sitting in the dentist's chair and hearing the drill at the top. By starting at the bottom and imagining each scene on the hierarchy in turn while relaxed, anxiety is progressively extinguished. Desensitization may also be carried out in *actual* situations rather than by imagery if a graded series of experiences can be arranged. Royce and Arkowitz (1978) used this technique in their successful treatment of social isolation in college students.

Aversion therapy consists of learning to associate the stimulus relevant to the undesired behaviour with an aversive stimulus (e.g. taste of alcohol with electric shock or nausea). **Massed practice** or repetition of behaviours such as tics and nervous mannerisms (smoking) is also aversive, and stopping is therefore rewarded. **Tokens** of future reinforcement are intrinsically worthless objects such as poker chips, stamps, ticks or coloured stars, which act to bridge the time lag between correct response and backup reinforcer, and also help to solve problems of satiation. They have been particularly useful in institutions such as psychiatric hospitals, classrooms, and re-formatories where a token economy set up by the authorities can act to reinforce desired behaviours in a very systematic and com-prehensive way.

Thought stopping is a technique for modifying cognitive behaviours such as intrusive obsessional thoughts, a tendency to see life in terms of extremes and apply excessively high standards to one's own efforts, or to be influenced by implicit catastrophic conclusions (e.g. if I speak up and am wrong *everybody will think I'm stupid* and then *nobody will ever like me again*). Rimm and Masters (1974) provide a more detailed description of this and other aspects of behaviour therapy. As discussed previously (Chapter 11), cognitive behaviour therapy draws from both the humanist and behavioural approaches, such that the distinctions between them become irrelevant.

Self reward for accomplishment of therapeutic goals may need to be strengthened. **Social skills training** usually emphasizes increasing the ability to communicate clearly and effectively with others (including to be appropriately assertive), while decreasing anxieties associated with social interaction (such as of rejection and criticism). Behaviours which facilitate dyadic communication include checking that messages have been understood, taking advantage of non-verbal channels, creating a receptive, non-judgemental atmosphere, and congruence between words, facial expression and feelings. Nervous habits such as giggling, loss of eye contact and blustering, which may be reinforced by anxiety reduction, and failure to express positive feelings definitely, are further blocks to communication which may need work. A group of learners may again provide a good chance to rehearse new behaviours acquired through shaping and modelling (see Piaget 1972).

BEHAVIOURAL CHANGE RELEVANT TO HEALTH

The following examples of behaviourally-oriented treatment for a variety of health-related problems give some of the flavour of what is at present an extremely active and fast-growing area of research. By the time preclinical student readers of this book begin to practise medicine, it can be expected that there will have been significant advances in our knowledge. The doctor educated in the behavioural sciences is, as we have commented earlier, in a uniquely favourable position to gather extensive and long term information about human behaviour in relation to health, illness and medical intervention. It is to be hoped that the opportunity will be seized upon, to the mutual benefit of medicine and social science.

The studies which are described below are representative of recent work. The criteria for evaluating research efforts given in Chapter 2 should be kept in mind when you read the originals.

PAIN

Fordyce (1976) bases his treatment of chronic pain, for which there is no or insufficient organic cause, on the following principles (p. 123): 1) The proper question is not whether the pain is real or not, but what are the factors which control it; 2) Pain can be influenced by conditioning (like most other bodily processes); 3) Conditioning is not a voluntary process; and 4) Where there is a significant amount of conditioned pain, it can be relieved by 'unlearning' procedures. He provides details of how to analyse the operant and respondent components of pain and how to reduce pain behaviours where the former are important. The main ways in which pain may be reinforced are a) by direct positive reinforcers contingent upon pain expression, such as increased attention, solicitude or submissiveness on the part of others, b) by indirect positive reinforcers consisting of time-out from aversive consequences (for example pain allowing the individual to avoid disliked work or avoid admitting to incompetence, etc.), and c) non-reward or punishment of 'well' behaviour and recovery, e.g. where an impotent husband prefers a wife banned from sexual activity, or where employability has been ruined by a long illness. Each of these three processes has its own implications for treatment, and Fordyce gives many examples of shaping non-pain behaviours with careful use of baselines, reinforcement schedules, and reinforcers such as rest and attention.

Headache afflicts nearly everyone at some times, and is a serious problem for some people. Migraine is associated with constriction and then dilatation of the arteries of the head, mediated by an unstable or over-responsive ANS (Bakal 1975). The more common muscle contraction or 'tension' headaches tend to be diagnosed by exclusion, lacking both an organic cause and the classic migraine symptoms of unilaterality, nausea and visual prodromata (precursors, in the form of disturbances of vision such as flashing lights, etc.). Frontalis (forehead) muscle relaxation by biofeedback has been used to treat tension headaches (Budzynski, Stoyva and Mullaney 1973), while migraine has responded to assertiveness training and to digital-temperature-control training (Sargent, Green and Walters 1973).

SEXUAL DIFFICULTIES

Annon (1974, 1975) has reviewed and described in considerable detail the behavioural treatments for all the common sexual difficulties and deviations discussed in Chapter 10. He provides a conceptual model for increasingly intense forms of therapy, which is claimed to guide the therapist as to the depth and treatment required by different problems. Each descending level of treatment requires of the clinician more time, knowledge, experience and skill. The first level is one of permission-giving and applies to the relatively non-serious difficulties where people are concerned about their sexual behaviours, and wish to hear from an expert whether their actions, including dreams, fantasies and feelings, are 'normal' or not.

The next level of treatment (only necessary for problems which persist after the first), is that of limited information. Here the client is given specific factual information relevant to the problem. Frequently it will involve dispelling the common myths, and therefore the associated anxieties, concerning penis size, masturbation effects, menstruation, oral-genital contact and so on. The third level of treatment consists of specific suggestions for overcoming difficulties such as premature ejaculation, impotence, female orgasmic dysfunction and vaginismus. A detailed history of the sexual problem is needed before the therapist can offer focussed advice, and at this level brief interviews of ten to thirty minutes are expected to suffice.

For problems resistant to all of the above, the fourth level, of intensive therapy, is required. Fetishes, sado-masochism, transvestism, paedophilia and similar problems need the more extensive and more individualized treatments which are now available. After an initial assessment, changes in behaviour, including attitudes and emotional responses, are programmed. Frequently it will be necessary to teach new skills, some of which are not specifically sexual, (e.g. of social interaction with members of the opposite sex), as well as to remove undesirable old behaviours. Communication and assertiveness techniques will therefore be needed along with desensitization (both covert and overt), relaxation, counter-conditioning and cognitive control. Brownell, Hayes and Barlow (1977) have found that decreasing arousal to deviant stimuli did not necessarily increase heterosexual arousal by itself; separate training was required for this.

EATING DISORDERS

Obesity is a common cause and complication of illness, and also a source of negative evaluations of the sufferer by that individual (low self-esteem) or by others (prejudice). Many behavioural approaches including aversion therapy, covert sensitization, therapist reinforcement for weight loss, and self-control procedures have been tried. Abramson (1977) concludes that the last-named of these is the most consistently successful, especially in terms of maintenance of weight loss after treatment finishes. Self-monitoring (daily recording of weight and food intake) is effective particularly if combined with self-reinforcement (reward more than punishment, and for changed eating habits more than for weight loss *per se*, see Mahoney 1974). At present the treatment of choice for obesity appears to be a behavioural one consisting of a battery of self-control measures. Kingsley and Wilson (1977) found group treatment superior to individual over a six month follow up, and support the idea that once specific weight-reduction skills have been acquired, which is best done via explicit instruction and practice, their continued usage depends on motivational factors influenced by the social reinforcers operating.

Anorexia nervosa is a potentially fatal eating disorder consisting of excessive dieting. Leitenberg, Agras and Thompson (1968) described a successful operant treatment programme where access to all reinforcers was made contingent upon weight gain. Hospitalization is usually a prerequisite for this therapy, although post-treatment generalization depends on environmental supports, frequently requiring family involvement in behavioural change. Successful results have been reported by a number of researchers since (e.g. Halmi, Powers and Cunningham 1975), although the disappointing outcome described by Williams (1976) indicates that further questions still require study.

SMOKING

Lando (1977) discussed the short-lived abstinence from nicotine which has been frequently achieved by 'one shot' methods. His use of a broad spectrum treatment including aversion, contractual management, booster sessions and group support techniques, resulted in experimental subjects maintaining an 81 per cent reduction in smoking six months post-treatment, compared with 44 per cent for controls. This very encouraging result is now being further explored by researchers.

ALCOHOLISM

Many early behavioural therapies for alcoholism used aversion therapy whereby nausea-inducing drugs, electric shock or even paralysis were associated to the sight, smell and taste of alcohol (Yates 1970). High relapse rates, as well as the aversiveness of these methods for the therapist, have led to their decreasing use. Current interests centre upon the use of rewards rather than punishments, involvement of the natural contingency managers such as employers and the pursuit of controlled social drinking rather than total abstinence as a therapy goal (Hamburg 1975; Schaefer 1972; Vogler, Weissbach and Compton 1977).

COMPLIANCE

Zifferblatt (1975) has described the use of stimulus control (cue) techniques, behavioural contracts and teaching of self-management, whereby physicians can increase patient compliance with medication regimens. Reasons for non-compliance are frequently analysed in terms of cognitions (beliefs and attitudes) counter to the doctor's recommendations (Berkanovic 1976). The same sort of behavioural influence is required in preventive efforts, for example to reduce cardiovascular disease. Although few reports of success have yet been published, Pomerleau, Bass and Crown (1975, p. 1277) believe that 'the successful application of behavioural principles to problems in preventive medicine may prove to be as important a contribution to medical practice as the development of effective antibacterial agents was in the first half of the century'. Kegeles *et al.* (1978) have recently reported increased rates of compliance by children in a twenty week mouthrinse programme using material rewards.

INSOMNIA

Findings that mild to moderate insomnia responded equally well to active and placebo treatments led Lick and Heffler (1977) to choose severe insomniacs for their comparison of progressive relaxation measures with a plausible placebo, which consisted of fake biofeed-back of autonomic arousal. The former led to a halving of the average time needed to fall asleep and of the percentage of days on which sleep-inducing drugs were taken, but the placebo was ineffective. It did not make a significant difference however whether relaxation lessons were supplemented with a take-home tape of instructions or not. Ribordy and Denney (1977) criticize the use of drugs to treat insomnia, because of their undesirable side-effects on the sleep cycle, and review the state of knowledge about behavioural methods.

ANXIETY

Relaxation and desensitization techniques for the treatment of anxiety were some of the first behavioural therapies to be widely accepted. In recent years, interest has turned from the monosymptomatic phobias, which although very convenient for research purposes are relatively rare in the general population (with the possible exception of the fear of flying), towards more complex and pervasive anxiety states. Effective treatment must, as always, take into account the reinforcement contingencies of the natural environment: coping skills may need to be specifically taught, or other members of the patient's family counselled about how to maintain, or in some cases how to come to terms with, the patient's behavioural improvement.

Stress-innoculation training (Meichenbaum and Turk 1976) is an example of one comprehensive approach. It combines training in physical relaxation and in cognitive strategies including a) rehearsal in imagination of future stress situations, b) recognition and monitoring of the person's usual anxiety-provoking thoughts in a situation of stress, and c) rehearsal of more realistic and controlled 'self-statements', and of self rewards for coping successfully with a stressor. Transfer and durability of training are facilitated, because the anticipation of stress comes to trigger off the coping techniques practised during therapy.

DEPRESSION

Behavioural theories about the origins of depression have been reviewed by Blaney (1977), who made clear the problems remaining whether one adopts a cognitive, learned helplessness, or low rate of reinforcement explanation. Much of the experimental research on the problem of depression at present suffers from lack of follow-up and use of student rather than clinical populations of subjects. McLean (1976) has described a comprehensive treatment programme aimed to teach skills in the six areas commonly deficient in depressed people: interpersonal communication, behavioural productivity, social interaction, assertiveness, decision-making and problem-solving, and cognitive self-control. His interesting and detailed paper is a model of a broad spectrum approach to this debilitating condition.

CHILDHOOD BEHAVIOUR DISORDERS

Bedwetting training, another early success for behaviour therapy, has always required parental involvement (e.g. Bollard and Woodroffe 1977, see Chapter 9). Operant techniques to control a very wide range of behavioural disorders in children, from autism to hyperaggressiveness, have been taught to parents (and teachers) in recent years. Large-scale **parent effectiveness training** schemes currently available aim to give parents insight into and experience of the relationship between their management techniques and the consequences in the child's behaviour (see review by O'Dell 1974). Observational and reinforcement methods are explained to parents (e.g. see Patterson and Gullion 1971) in a way which, if mastered, should result not only in reduction of aversive or maladaptive child behaviours, but in greater parental self-esteem and improved emotional relationships within the family. Motor and cognitive skills have also been taught by parents of retarded children following similar principles.

SUMMARY

Behavioural change by somebody is needed in the treatment and prevention of many physical, psychological and psycho-physiological disorders. Difficulties in evaluating different theoretical approaches to therapeutic behaviour change include how to define success, what permanence can reasonably be expected of it, and both ethical and research design problems.

Physical methods of treatment sometimes increase the patient's accessibility for behavioural change. Psychodynamic therapy aims at insight on the patient's part; client-centred therapy approaches at self-actualization via self-knowledge and acceptance. Behaviour change techniques based on the principles of human learning include progressive relaxation, desensitization, aversion, thought stopping and social skills training. A sample is presented of recent research work dealing with behavioural change in pain, sexual difficulties, eating disorders, smoking, alcoholism, compliance, insomnia, anxiety, depression and childhood behaviour disorders.

TERMS AND CONCEPTS

eclectic
hello-goodbye effect
symptom substitution
spontaneous remission
electroconvulsive therapy
insight
transference

    free association
    behavioural analysis
    progressive muscular relaxation
    systematic desensitization
    aversion therapy
    massed practice
    tokens
    thought stopping
    social skills training
    anorexia nervosa
    stress-innoculation training
    parent effectiveness training

FOR DISCUSSION

1. Select a paper reporting an attempt at therapeutic behaviour change (either one of the examples used in this chapter or another paper from a journal mentioned in the Reference list). Now evaluate it methodologically using the criteria discussed in this and Chapter 2. Would you feel inclined to use the method described? What else would you like to know about the reported results?

2. Read case histories (e.g. in Corsini, see Fine reference), and observe video-taped or filmed examples of psychotherapy. Then discuss your personal preferences amongst the different approaches. What style of help would you feel most comfortable at receiving yourself?

SUGGESTED READING

    Pomerleau *et al.*: the general medical relevance of behaviour
        modification.
    Rimm and Masters: comprehensive survey of behavioural
        techniques.
    Patterson and Gullion: behavioural child-rearing advice
        addressed to parents.

REFERENCES

Abramson, E. A. 1977. Behavioral approaches to weight control: An updated review. *Behav. Res. Ther.* **15**, 355–63.

Annon, J. S. 1974. *The Behavioral Treatment of Sexual Problems. I Brief therapy.* Honolulu: Enabling Systems.

Annon, J. S. 1975. *The Behavioral Treatment of Sexual Problems. II. Intensive therapy.* Honolulu: Enabling Systems.

Bakal, D. A. 1975. Headache: A biopsychological perspective. *Psych. Bull.* **82,** 369–82.

Bandura, A. 1969. *Principles of Behavior Modification.* New York: Holt Rinehart & Winston.

Berkanovic, E. 1976. Behavioral science and prevention. *Prev. Med.* **5,** 92–105.

Berne, E. *Games People Play.* New York: Grove.

Blaney, P. H. 1977. Contemporary theories of depression: Critique and comparison. *J. Abnorm. Psychol.* **86,** 203–23.

Brownell, K. D., Hayes, S. C. and Barlow, D. H. 1977. Patterns of appropriate and deviant sexual arousal: the behavioural treatment of multiple sexual deviations. *J. Cons. Clin. Psychol.* **45,** 114–55.

Budzynski, T. H., Stoyva, J. M. and Mullaney, D. J. 1973. EMG biofeedback and tension headache: A controlled outcome study. *Psychosom. Med.* **35,** 484–96.

Eysenck, H. J. 1965. The effects of psychotherapy. *J. Psychol.* **1,** 97–118.

Fine, R. 1973. Psychoanalysis. In R. Corsini (ed.) *Current Psychotherapies* 1–33. Itasca, Illinois: Peacock.

Fordyce, W. E. 1976. *Behavioral Methods for Chronic Pain and Illness.* St. Louis: Mosby.

Garfield, S. L. and Kurtz, R. 1977. A study of eclectic views. *J. Cons. Clin. Psychol.* **45,** 78–83.

Glasser, W. 1965. *Reality Therapy: A New Approach to Psychiatry.* New York: Harper & Row.

Halmi, K. A., Powers, P. and Cunningham, S. 1975. Treatment of anorexia nervosa with behavior modification. *Arch. Gen. Psychiat.* **32,** 93–6.

Hamburg, S. 1975. Behavior therapy in alcoholism: A critical review of broad-spectrum approaches. *J. Studies Alcohol* **36,** 69–87.

Kegeles, S. S., Lund, A. K. and Weisenberg, M. 1978. Acceptance by children of a daily home mouthrinse program. *Soc. Sci. and Med.* **12,** 199–210.

Kingsley, R. G. and Wilson, G. T. 1977. Behavior therapy for obesity: A comparative investigation of long-term efficacy. *J. Cons. Clin. Psychol.* **45,** 288–98.

Lando, H. A. 1977. Successful treatment of smokers with a broad-spectrum behavioral approach. *J. Cons. Clin. Psychol.* **45,** 361–6.

Leitenberg, H., Agras, W. S. and Thomson, L. E. 1968. A sequential analysis of the effect of selective positive reinforcement in modifying anorexia nervosa. *Behav. Res. Ther.* **6,** 211–18.

Lick, J. R. and Heffler, D. 1977. Relaxation training and attention placebo in the treatment of severe insomnia. *J. Cons. Clin. Psychol.* **45**, 153–61.

Mahoney, M. J. 1974. Self-reward and self-monitoring techniques for weight control. *Behav. Ther.* **5**, 48–57.

McLean, P. 1976. Therapeutic decision-making in the behavioral treatment of depression. In P. O. Davidson (ed.) *The Behavioral Management of Anxiety, Depression and Pain* 54–89. New York: Brunner-Mazel.

Meador, B. D. and Rogers, C. R. 1973. Client-centred therapy. In R. Corsini (ed.) *Current Psychotherapies* 119–65. Itasca, Illinois: Peacock.

Meichenbaum, D. and Turk, D. 1976. The cognitive-behavioral management of anxiety, anger and pain. In P. O. Davidson (ed.) *The Behavioral Management of Anxiety, Depression and Pain* 1–34. New York: Brunner-Mazel.

O'Dell, S. 1974. Training parents in behavior modification: A review. *Psych. Bull.* **81**, 418–33.

Patterson, G. R. and Gullion, M. E. 1971. *Living with Children: New Methods for Parents and Teachers.* (Revised Edn) Champaign, Illinois: Research Press.

Perls, F. 1969. *Gestalt Therapy Verbatim.* Lafayette, Calif: Real People Press.

Piaget, G. W. 1972. Training patients to communicate. In A. A. Lazarus (ed.) *Clinical Behavior Therapy* 155–73. New York: Brunner-Mazel.

Pomerleau, O., Bass, F. and Crown, V. 1975. Role of behavior modification in preventive medicine. *New Eng. J. Med.* **292**, 1277–82.

Ribordy, S. C. and Denney, D. R. 1977. The behavioral treatment of insomnia: An alternative to drug therapy. *Behav. Res. Ther.* **15**, 39–50.

Rimm, D. C. and Masters, J. C. 1974. *Behavior Therapy: Techniques and Empirical Findings.* New York: Academic Press.

Royce, W. S. and Arkowitz, H. 1978. Multimodal evaluation of practice interactions as treatment for social isolation. *J. Cons. Clin. Psychol.* **46**, 239–45.

Sargent, J. D., Green, E. E. and Walters, E. D. 1973. Preliminary report on the use of autogenic feedback training in the treatment of migraine and tension headaches. *Psychosom. Med.* **35**, 129–35.

Schaefer, H. H. 1972. Twelve-month follow-up of behaviorally trained ex-alcoholic social drinkers. *Behav. Ther.* **3**, 286–9.

Schofield, W. 1964. *Psychotherapy: The Purchase of Friendship.* Englewood Cliffs, N.J.: Prentice-Hall.

Smith, M. L. and Glass, G. V. 1977. Meta-analysis of psychotherapy outcome studies. *Amer. Psychol.* **32**, 752–60.

Szasz, T. S. 1961. *The Myth of Mental Illness.* New York: Hoeber.

Vogler, R. E. Weissbach, T. A. and Compton, J. V. 1977. Learning techniques for alcohol abuse. *Behav. Res. Ther.* **15**, 31–8.

Williams, W. 1976. A comprehensive behaviour modification programme for the treatment of anorexia nervosa: Results in six cases. *Aust. N.Z. J. Psychiat.* **10,** 321–30.

Yates, A. J. 1970. *Behavior Therapy.* New York: Wiley.

Zifferblatt, S. M. 1975. Increasing patient compliance through the applied analysis of behavior. *Prev. Med.* **4,** 173–82.

Chapter 13

The Individual in the Social Environment

With this chapter, we begin our consideration of social behaviour. An understanding of social behaviour is extremely important to medical practice because so much of health-related behaviour, both in medical settings such as doctor-patient interaction and outside of medical settings such as patient compliance with doctor's orders, is influenced by social factors. First we look at some of our reactions to the presence of others, including affiliation, the effects of crowding, social facilitation and attraction. Then we proceed to some examples of social behaviour, specifically cooperation and competition, and helping behaviour, a topic that is particularly relevant to the practice of medicine.

THE PRESENCE OF OTHERS

We all know that being in a room with only one other person is a qualitatively different experience from being in a room by ourselves. The mere presence of another person, apart from any communication or interaction with that person, usually has some subtle (and some not so subtle) effects on our own behaviour.

CONSTANT CONTACT, ISOLATION AND AFFILIATION

Sometimes one feels a strong need for contact with other people, perhaps after being alone for a period of time. Conversely, at other times one feels the need to get away from other people, to be alone. Although most of us spend much of our waking day with other people, clearly there is some optimal balance between time spent alone and time spent with others. In fact both constant contact and isolation have been found to have detrimental effects on human behaviour.

In a three-man space capsule on the way to the moon, in a prison cell shared with another person, on a submarine, or less dramatically, on a long car journey, constant contact with others is experienced over a period of time. After a while the presence of others may become irritating and oppressive. Studies of constant contact in which men were confined with each other for a number of days have indicated that such situations have a number of negative effects on human beings. For example, Altman, Taylor and Wheeler (1971) found that the men progressively withdrew from social contact; they spent about 50 per cent of their time engaged in social activity during the first four days of an eight day confinement period, but only about 25 per cent during the last four days. Other researchers have reported that 'subjective stress' and 'state anxiety' were higher during the experiment than either before or after (Altman and Haythorn 1967), and that men confined together experienced more conflict than controls who were not (Haythorn and Altman 1967).

Examples of total isolation are not frequent, but some individuals such as explorers and individuals in solitary confinement have experienced this state. From written accounts of this experience, it is apparent that isolation is an anxiety producing state which can be accompanied by hallucinations.

It is clear that we need to **affiliate** (but not excessively) with others. Right from the start of human life, social relationships are essential as evidenced by the detrimental effects of their lack (see attachment disruptions and deprivation, Chapter 9). Throughout life, others are a powerful source of rewards (Chapter 6); not only do they help us to satisfy our biological needs, but our social needs as well, such as our needs for attention, approval and sex. Others are also an important source of information, both about the world around us (see Chapter 14) and about ourselves (see Chapter 16).

In addition, people generally have a greater need to affiliate when they are afraid. Schachter (1959), in a well-known experiment, manipulated fear in his subjects by leading them to anticipate either painful electric shocks or mild shocks. Subjects were then asked whether they would like to spend a ten minute waiting period before they would actually receive the shocks with others, alone, or had no preference. Of those who anticipated painful shocks, 63 per cent preferred to wait with others compared with 33 per cent of those who anticipated mild shock. Generally, this relationship between fear arousal and desire to affiliate has been supported. However, one study (Sarnoff and Zimbardo 1961) reported that high anxiety arousal (as opposed to high fear arousal) actually resulted in less (rather than greater) desire to affiliate.

Both birth order and sex tend to be related to affiliation needs; in general, first-born and only-born individuals tend to have a greater need to affiliate, and so do females. However, as the traditional sex role stereotypes become less prevalent, we can speculate that this latter relationship may disappear.

THE EFFECTS OF DENSITY AND CROWDING

Many studies of animal populations have reported that normal social behaviour is disrupted in high density conditions. Some researchers, in an effort to demonstrate negative effects of high density on human behaviour, have cited correlations between human population density and various types of social pathology, such as crime rates, juvenile delinquency, mental health, and so forth. However, these relationships tend to disappear when the effects of other variables, such as socioeconomic status, are taken into account, casting doubt on the belief that high density *per se* causes such ills.

Only recently have researchers begun to investigate the effects of density on human behaviour, in controlled laboratory and field experiments. However, these experiments have yielded inconsistent results. Freedman (1975), in his review of the experimental work, stated that 'There is no evidence from this body of work that crowding causes either stress or arousal. It does not affect task performance, it does not make people more anxious or nervous, and it certainly does not make the experience more unpleasant.' (p. 104). But not all of the experiments have supported this conclusion. Schettino and Borden (1976), using university classroom settings which varied in both density and class size, found that females reported feeling more nervous and crowded, and males, more aggressive in high density than in low density conditions. Langer and Saegert (1977) found that in a real world setting (i.e., New York grocery stores) density did have a negative effect on task performance (the selection of the most economic product for each of a number of items).

One explanation for these confusing results may be that the effects of density are more complex than we thought. High density may have different effects, depending upon the situation in which it is found; it may be pleasant at a cocktail party or football game but not during a final examination. Saegert (1973) contends that specific effects of high density, attentional overload and behavioural constraint should be considered. Needless to say, not all highly dense situations will produce these effects to the same degree. Furthermore, Stokels (1972) has distinguished between '... the physical condition, density, involving spatial limitation, and the experiential state, crowding, in which the restrictive aspects of limited space are perceived by the individuals exposed to them.' (p. 275). He views **density** as a necessary but not a sufficient condition for **crowding**, an experience which is mediated by personal and social variables. Different individuals will have different reactions to high density levels and these reactions will also be determined by aspects of the situation itself, such as the type of activity in which the individuals are engaged.

SOCIAL FACILITATION

How does the mere presence of others affect our performance of various tasks? Does their presence help us or hinder us in our own activities? Numerous studies have shown that we perform familiar tasks better in the presence of others than we do alone. This effect, known as **social facilitation**, has been obtained when the others are competitors, when they are merely an audience, and when they perform the same task without competition. But there are some cases in which task performance has been found to be worse in the presence of others than when alone. This interference effect typically occurs when subjects are required to perform unfamiliar tasks or learn new material in front of others. Zajonc (1965) contends that these differential effects can be understood by distinguishing tasks which require learning from those which require the performance of a response that has already been learned. Social facilitation is likely in the latter, and interference in the former. Why? Zajonc (1965) argues that the presence of others increases our level of motivation. Increasing motivation level increases the likelihood that the dominant response will be emitted. When tasks have already been learned, the correct response is the dominant one, but with new, unfamiliar tasks, the dominant response is not likely to be correct.

ATTRACTION

Our reactions to those around us are seldom neutral; they arouse in us feelings of attraction or hostility in varying degrees. This evaluative response to others is related to a number of variables.

Berscheid and Walster (1978) claim that much of our attraction (or hostility) toward others can be explained by the principles of reinforcement (see Chapter 6). Basically, those who provide rewards, or are even merely associated with pleasant experiences, are liked, while those who provide punishments or are associated with unpleasant experiences are not. However, this effect is reduced if the rewards, for instance compliments, come from someone who has something to gain by our positive reaction or who seems to be extravagant. Not surprisingly, we like those who appear to like us.

Many studies have also found that attractiveness is related to similarity, particularly when it comes to attitudes, although we do tend to assume that those we like are more similar to us than they actually are. Newcomb (1961) studied the formation of friendship patterns in a men's university residence where the students were previously unacquainted. The friendships that eventually emerged were related to similarity of attitudes.

The evidence linking similarity of personality to attraction is not really as consistent. In long lasting relationships such as marriage, some studies emphasize the importance of similarity while others emphasize complementary needs. In fact, neither the 'birds of a feather flock together' nor the 'opposites attract' approach has received resounding support. In one investigation (Kerckhoff and Davis 1962), a number of university couples who were contemplating marriage were followed over a period of time. Initially, similarity of such attributes as socioeconomic status, religion and ethnic background were important. Later, similarity of family values became important, and only fairly late in the relationship did complementarity of needs emerge as an important determinant of the fate of the relationship.

Propinquity or physical proximity also generally leads to liking. Actually, it is not proximity *per se* but the opportunity to interact that appears to cause this effect. Festinger, Schachter, and Back (1950) discovered in their study of a new housing project that friendships were most likely to develop among the occupants of adjacent residences; the greater the distance between the residences, the less likely it was that the occupants would become friends. Moreover, friendship patterns reflected other aspects of architectural design, such as the location of mailboxes and whether residences faced the courtyard or the street, which gave some residents more opportunity for interaction than others. However, proximity does not always lead to attraction. If someone is boorish or irritating, our negative reaction to them can also be magnified by close contact. Therefore, although the general effect of proximity is attraction, proximity would appear to intensify both positive and negative reactions.

One final and intriguing consideration in our discussion of our likes and dislikes of others is the effects of our own behaviour on these evaluations. If we harm others, we may come to justify our actions by convincing ourselves that those we have harmed are dislikeable and deserved it. The opposite may also occur; if we reward someone more than they actually deserve, we may justify it by deciding that that person is more likeable and worthy than we originally thought.

SOME EXAMPLES OF SOCIAL BEHAVIOUR

COOPERATION AND COMPETITION

Competition is a familiar component of many of our activities; at school and university, we compete for grades, later for jobs, and in sport. Even when cooperation seems to be the most beneficial response for the parties involved, the result is sometimes competition, even conflict and hostility. How can we predict when people will cooperate and when they will compete? How can we promote the development of cooperative behaviour when it is clearly desirable?

In some laboratory studies of cooperation and competition, subjects play a **prisoner's dilemma game** which reflects many of the aspects of cooperation and competition in real life. This game is based on a situation in which two people (the prisoners) are being held for questioning about a crime which the police believe they have jointly committed. Each person is questioned separately and must decide, without knowledge of the other's response, whether to confess or not to confess, given the following set of outcomes. If neither confesses, neither can be convicted of this crime because of lack of evidence, but both will be charged with a minor offence and will receive a short jail sentence; if one confesses and the other does not, the one who confessed will go free for turning state's evidence, while the other will be convicted of the crime and receive the maximum sentence; and, if both confess, they will both be convicted of the crime but will get some leniency in sentencing. Clearly the best outcome for both occurs if neither one confesses. However, when each prisoner considers his or her own best outcome, confessing is an attractive alternative. But if both prisoners think this way, both will be convicted. Furthermore, if you believe that your fellow prisoner will confess, you yourself have to confess to avoid the maximum sentence. The basic question is – can you trust the other person not to confess.

In the laboratory, subjects are presented with a payoff matrix such as that which follows, which is an abstraction of the situation just described.

Subject 2

		A	B
		1. + 5	1. —10
A			
		2. + 5	2. + 10
Subject 1			
		1. + 10	1. —5
B			
		2. —10	2. —5

The numbers represent imaginary points or small amounts of money. Each subject must choose either A or B without the knowledge of the other's choice. Points are then awarded to each player on the basis of both of their choices. Typically, subjects are asked to play the game several times and therefore choices on one play can influence choices on subsequent plays. A choice of A is considered a cooperative response and a choice of B, a competitive one. The subjects are faced with basically the same situation and the same options as the prisoners.

A number of variables have been found to affect the rate of cooperation. For example, if the competitive aspects of the game are emphasized to the subjects, they will compete more often than when cooperation is emphasized. Subjects who play the game just once tend to compete more than those who play it a number of successive times. In addition, those who play against someone who gives a high rate of cooperative responses do not necessarily cooperate more in response. In this situation the belief that the other will cooperate leads some subjects to exploit the situation rather than respond similarly.

At this point you may be thinking that playing such a game in the laboratory is different in some respects from real life. Norms that regulate competition in the real world may not apply in the laboratory. Furthermore, the subjects may not be acquainted or even be able to see each other, and consequently may not be concerned about maintaining amicable relations. Therefore, they may be more prone to compete in the laboratory than they would in the real world, where consideration of personal gain is mitigated by social norms and interpersonal relationships. In fact, Wichman (1970) has shown that cooperation in a prisoner's dilemma game is much higher (87.0 per cent compared with 40.7 per cent) when subjects can see and hear each other while playing than when they are isolated. While the players are often isolated in experiments using prisoner's dilemma games, being able to see and hear the other person is typical of interaction in the real world.

Sherif studied cooperation and competition in the real life setting of a boys' summer camp (Sherif and Sherif 1969). First, a high level of competition and intergroup conflict was induced between two groups of boys. This stage of the experiment was accomplished with very little effort. Then, once these strong 'we-they' feelings (which often resulted in hostility) had been created, attempts were made to induce mutual cooperation and good will. This proved to be much more of a problem. The researchers tried several approaches, including bringing the two groups together under pleasant circumstances, but without success. The hostility between the groups persisted. In the end, good feeling was restored by introducing a series of **superordinate goals**; i.e. situations in which cooperation between the groups was required in order to solve a problem or reach a goal that was important to both groups. At first, the introduction of superordinate goals had little effect on other behaviour, but gradually the cooperation began to generalize to other activities and conflict decreased.

The role of mutual cooperation over time in reducing negative feelings was also studied in another experiment (Cook 1969), in which highly prejudiced white subjects played a management game with a black person and another white person over a period of time. The game required a high level of cooperation for success. Some time after this experience, 36 per cent of the subjects were less prejudiced compared with 9 per cent of a control group who had not played the game.

HELPING BEHAVIOUR

There are times when we are confronted with another person,

sometimes a stranger, who needs our help. What determines our reaction? When do we provide the needed help, sometimes at great inconvenience or risk to ourselves, and when do we ignore the need? An analysis of helping behaviour is very relevant to medical practice, since medicine is by its very nature a helping profession. Furthermore, financial rewards may not always be commensurate with the demands made on the doctor and his or her skills.

Social psychologists began to investigate systematically the conditions under which people help others after the brutal murder of a woman (Kitty Genovese) in Queens, New York in 1964. The murder, which took over thirty minutes, was witnessed by thirty-eight people from their windows in an apartment building. No-one helped the woman or even telephoned the police. The question, of course, was why one of these people didn't help.

In the numerous studies which followed, subjects were exposed to such events as smoke entering the laboratory, hearing a supposed subject in another room call for help because he was having a seizure, and people in the real world have witnessed a man collapsing on a subway, a woman on the side of a freeway with a flat tyre, and so forth, all in an effort to determine the conditions under which people will help.

Suppose that you were faced with a stranger who needed your help. What considerations would determine your response? You might quickly weigh the pros and cons of stopping to help. You may believe that there is a social norm of helping others; if you do help, others will think that you are a 'good' person and, generally, you will feel like a 'good' person. On the other hand, helping may be inconvenient; you may be in a hurry and not really have time to stop. Helping may involve risk. Furthermore if you help, you may get involved – with the person needing help, the problem, and perhaps even the police. Any aspect of the situation which affects your perception of the potential rewards and costs of helping may influence your decision.

Our willingness to help is also influenced by the attributes of the person in need. In one study (Piliavin, Rodin and Piliavin 1969), people responded more often and more quickly to a person who appeared to collapse because he was ill than to one who appeared to collapse because he was drunk. Apparently the perceived cause of the misfortune affects our response. This finding is of special interest when we consider that doctors are often called upon to treat patients whose problems are believed to be self-inflicted or not socially acceptable, such as alcoholism, drug addiction and venereal disease.

Also, the likelihood of a helping response increased with the salience or proximity of the collapsed person as well as his similarity to the potential helper: those passengers who were closer were more likely to help, and white passengers were more likely to help a white person while black passengers were more likely to help a black person.

Another determinant of whether or not we will help is the presence of other people. Those who witness an emergency alone are more likely to help than those who witness it with others (see for example, Darley and Latané 1968). In groups there is diffusion of responsibility; each individual feels no more responsible than anyone else, so why be the one to get involved. It has also been found that our decision to help can be affected by the reactions of others; if they calmly ignore what is happening we may be less inclined to help. When we are with others, the possibility that we might look silly if we 'overreact' may inhibit helping responses. On the other hand, the evidence indicates that exposure to a model of helping behaviour increases the likelihood of a helping response.

Our discussion of helping behaviour thus far has emphasized the conditions which elicit or inhibit acts of helping, without consideration of the motives of those who help. In both real life and in helping behaviour experiments some people do help, even when helping may involve inconvenience or risk. Why do these people help? Are they primarily concerned with the welfare of another or are they motivated by self interest? This brings us to the question of how **altruism** should be defined. To what extent must the act be devoid of self-interest to be considered altruistic? Few people would agree that help given to another person in anticipation of material reward is an example of altruism. Acts of helping performed primarily to gain the approval or praise of others may not be considered altruistic either. Even anonymous help could be motivated mainly by internal rewards, such as the feeling that one is a 'good' person. In fact, we can ask if any behaviour is really the result of the intention to help another, rather than to benefit the self. However, because of the difficulties involved in assessing the reasons for behaviour, research on helping has generally concentrated on conditions that elicit or inhibit helping behaviour itself rather than the intent of the act.

SUMMARY

Although both constant contact and isolation have detrimental effects on human behaviour, in general people do need to affiliate with others. Experimental research has not yet provided us with definite conclusions regarding the effects of density on human behaviour, but it is reasonable to assume that these effects will vary with the individual and with the situation. The presence of others enhances performance of tasks that are already learned, but interferes with the performance of new and unfamiliar tasks. Our attraction to those around us depends on a number of factors, including their provision of or association with rewards, their proximity, and their similarity to us in attitude but not necessarily personality.

Cooperation and competition have been investigated in the laboratory by having subjects play prisoner's dilemma games. Other research indicates that competition and conflict can be reduced through the introduction of a series of superordinate goals. Our response to another person who needs our help is determined by a number of variables, such as our view of the rewards and costs of helping, the attributes of the person in need, and the presence of others.

TERMS AND CONCEPTS

affiliation
density
crowding
social facilitation
prisoner's dilemma game
superordinate goals
altruism

FOR DISCUSSION

1.   Keep track of the amount of time you spend alone and with others for about a week (waking hours only). Note your *desire* to be with others or to be alone as well. What factors seem to affect your need for affiliation and your desire to be alone?

2.   To what degree do you think your attraction toward others is determined by the variables discussed in this chapter? Can you think of other variables that affect the level of attraction you feel toward others?

3. It seems easier to induce competition than cooperation. Why do you think this is so?

4. Have you ever been in a situation where a stranger needed your help? Analyse your reactions and the factors that influenced your decision to help or not to help. Do you think that there are instances of helping behaviour that are not at all motivated by self-interest?

5. To what extent do you think that the helping behaviour of doctors is affected by the variables discussed in this chapter?

SUGGESTED READING

Berscheid and Walster: a lucid and entertaining account of what we know about interpersonal attraction.

Langer and Saegert: an interesting field experiment on the effects of crowding.

Zajonc: on social facilitation.

REFERENCES

Altman, I. and Haythorn, W. 1967. The ecology of isolated groups. *Behav. Sci.* **12,** 169–82.

Altman, I., Taylor, D. and Wheeler, L. 1971. Ecological aspects of group behavior in social isolation. *J. appl. soc. Psychol.* **1,** 76–100.

Berscheid, E. and Walster, E. 1978. *Interpersonal Attraction* (2nd edn). Reading, Mass.: Addison-Wesley.

Cook, S. 1969. Motives in a conceptual analysis of attitude–related behavior. In W. Arnold and D. Levine (eds) *Nebraska Symposium on motivation* **17,** 179–235.

Darley, J. and Latané, B. 1968. Bystander intervention in emergencies: Diffusion of responsibility. *J. Person. Soc. Psychol.* **8,** 377–83.

Festinger, L., Schachter, S. and Back, K. 1950. *Social Pressures in Informal Groups: A Study of Human Factors in Housing.* New York: Harper & Row.

Freedman, J. L. 1975. *Crowding and Behavior.* New York: Viking Press.

Haythorn, W. and Altman, I. 1967. Together in isolation. *Trans-Action* **4,** 18–23.

Kerckhoff, A. C. and Davis, K. E. 1962. Value consensus and need complementarity in mate selection. *Amer. Soc. Rev.* **27,** 295–303.

Langer, E. J. and Saegert, S. 1977. Crowding and cognitive control. *J. Person. Soc. Psychol.* **35,** 175–82.

Newcomb, T. 1961. *The Acquaintance Process.* New York: Holt, Rinehart and Winston.

Piliavin, J., Rodin, J. and Piliavin, J. 1969. Good samaritanism: An underground phenomenon? *J. Person. Soc. Psychol.* **13**, 289–99.

Saegert, S. 1973. Crowding: Cognitive overload and behavioral constraint. In W. Preiser (ed.) *Environmental design research* **2.** Stroudsburg, Pa.: Dowden, Hutchinson and Ross.

Sarnoff, I. and Zimbardo, P. 1961. Anxiety, fear and social affiliation. *J. Abnorm. Soc. Psychol.* **62**, 356–63.

Schachter, S. 1959. *the Psychology of Affiliation.* Stanford: Stanford University Press.

Schettino, A. P. and Borden, R. J. 1976. Sex differences in response to naturalistic crowding: Affective reactions to group size and group density *Person. Soc. Psychol. Bull.* **2**, 67–71.

Sherif, M. and Sherif, C. 1969. *Social Psychology.* New York: Harper and Row.

Stokels, D. 1972. On the distinction between density and crowding. *Psychol. Rev.* **79**, 275–7.

Wichman, H. 1970. Effects of isolation and communication on cooperation in a two-person game. *J. Pers. Soc. Psychol.* **16**, 114–20.

Zajonc, R. 1965. Social facilitation. *Science* **149**, 269–74.

Chapter 14

Social Influence

Social influence is a common process in our everyday lives and therefore central to our study of social behaviour. Friends may try to change our views on an issue or talk us into attending a particular event; parents may try to influence their offspring on any number of topics from dress to field of study; doctors may try to induce patients to stop smoking; political candidates may try to convince people to vote for them either by personal appeal or appeal through the media; and of course the advertising industry is constantly trying to get us to buy a whole host of products. There is no denying that we are influenced by our social environment, but to what extent, and what are the bounds of this common process?

In an effort to answer this complex question, we first consider some conceptual formulations of social influence, then some examples of social influence research including both laboratory and field studies, and finally the effects of the mass media. At the end of Chapter 15, which also deals with the processes of influence and change, we will discuss the problem of inducing change in patients.

SOCIAL INFLUENCE: CONCEPTUAL PERSPECTIVES

Very generally speaking, we can say that **social influence** has occurred when one person or group induces a change in the behaviour (overt behaviour or internal thoughts and feelings) of another.

RESPONSES TO SOCIAL INFLUENCE

How can we tell when a social influence attempt has been successful? On the simplest level, we may merely observe the resultant overt behaviour and conclude on this basis that influence has or has not occurred. However, a behavioural response indicative of influence can be accompanied by a variety of 'internal states'. Sometimes we overtly conform while privately maintaining our own views, and other times our overt conformity is really a by-product of a true change in our opinions. On the other hand, no overt indication of influence may not necessarily mean that none has occurred: we may actually have changed our opinions in response to an influence attempt but publicly maintain our old opinion to save face.

Kelman (1961) defines three processes of social influence: compliance, identification and internalization. **Compliance** occurs when we conform to an influence attempt on a behavioural level while privately retaining our own attitudes and beliefs. What we say or do is not integrated with what we really think. Such behaviour is an expedient response which is adopted because those exerting the influence possess control, i.e. the ability to punish and reward us, and which will be maintained only as long as it is monitored by those who induced it.

Identification occurs when we adopt the attitudes and beliefs of others to establish or maintain a 'satisfying self-defining relationship' with them. In other words, we identify with them. Influence is dependent upon the salience of the relationship with these others, either persons or groups, regardless of their physical presence (i.e. ability to monitor behaviour), and will be maintained only as long as we desire to maintain the relationship. According to Kelman, it should be noted here that we may think the attitudes and beliefs adopted are our own but they are not really integrated with our enduring value system: if our identifications change, so will the particular associated attitudes and beliefs.

Internalization occurs when the induced attitudes and beliefs actually become our own; they are adopted on the basis of their content and become integrated with our enduring value system. Influence in this case is dependent upon the credibility of those exerting the influence, but the maintenance of the new response is independent of those who induced it. As such, internalization is probably the most stable and enduring form of influence.

THE ABILITY TO EXERT INFLUENCE: SOCIAL POWER

While Kelman has emphasized the response to social influence, French and Raven have considered the other side of the coin, the induction of social influence. What are the means through which influence can be exerted?

French and Raven (1959) discuss five common types of social

power that can be used to induce influence. (You can probably think of others as well.) **Reward power** and **coercive power** are fairly self-evident. To the extent that we believe that others can determine the rewards or punishments we receive, they have the ability to influence our behaviour (see Chapter 6 for a more detailed discussion of the effects of rewards and punishments). Rewards and punishments may be tangible, such as the sweet or the spanking administered to the child, or relatively intangible such as the compliment received from an acquaintance.

Legitimate power is more complex. Someone only possesses legitimate power to influence us if, because of our own value system, we *acknowledge* that that person has the legitimate right to influence us. Individuals can have legitimate power because of a particular position or role (see Chapter 17) which they occupy. Thus, government authorities, our superiors at work, and elected officials may influence us to a greater or lesser extent.

Referent power is based on our identification with others: to the extent that we are attracted by another person or a group and desire to be 'closely associated' with them, they are able to influence us. **Expert power** is based on the knowledge or expertise that we attribute to others: they are able to influence us to the extent that we perceive them to be knowledgable or expert.

Although these five types are described separately, it is possible, even likely, that more than one will be operating in any given situation. It is important to note that with each type of power, the ability of others to influence us is not so much based on their objective attributes but on our *perception* of these attributes in relation to ourselves, our needs and our values.

SOCIAL INFLUENCE: SOME REPRESENTATIVE RESEARCH

When the question 'are people influenced by those around them?' is asked there are two extreme answers that can be given. One is 'no – people are independent individuals and remain "themselves" regardless of the social situation.' The other is 'yes – of course, people are basically sheep, you can make almost anyone do anything'. Neither is correct: the answer, as usual, is very complicated. But, in general we can say that under certain conditions, some changes can be induced in some people.

To illustrate the complexity of this topic and to gain some

appreciation of the conditions that make social influence more likely, we will consider in detail some examples of research in this area.

THE INFLUENCE OF OTHERS ON BEHAVIOUR: CONFORMITY

In a now famous series of laboratory experiments, Asch (1952) presented his subjects with an interesting dilemma. At the start of the experiment, a subject may think that the task appears simple, if not trivial: he and seven other subjects are merely required to state which of three lines matches a comparison line in length. Each subject calls out an answer in turn. Everyone gives the right answer, there is no ambiguity. A second set of lines is presented and the process is repeated.

On the third set of lines, however, everyone in turn calls out what seems to him to be obviously the wrong answer. This is the dilemma: his own eyes are telling him one answer is correct, but other people are saying another is correct. What does he do? Does he conform and give the obviously wrong answer, or does he remain independent and give what he perceives to be the right answer?

The whole experiment has eighteen sets of lines or judgements for the subjects to make. On twelve of these, seven subjects unanimously give the wrong answer. Needless to say, these seven had met with the experimenter and were told when to give wrong answers and when to give right ones. The eighth subject is the 'real' subject and it is his behaviour that is being studied.

Asch found that over all subjects conformity was observed about one third of the time. However, there was a good deal of individual variation in the number of times a subject conformed: some subjects never conformed, others conformed once, twice, three times, etc. About one third of the subjects conformed more than half the time.

After the experiment, subjects were asked a series of questions in an attempt to determine the reasons behind their behaviour. The responses to these questions demonstrated further differences in individual reactions to this situation: not only did subjects behave differently in their rate of conformity, but there were different reasons for the same behaviour. Those who remained independent throughout fell into three main categories: confident independence, withdrawn independence based on a belief in the necessity of being an individual, and independence based on a belief that subjects should complete the experimental task adequately. Subjects who conformed more than half the time also fell into three main categories: those who claimed their conforming responses were actually correct (very few), those who believed that their own perceptions were for some reason inaccurate, and those who did not want to appear different from the group. Asch has shown that the conformity rate depends upon the situation. When he varied the number of other people opposing the subject, i.e. giving the wrong answer, he found that with one opposing person there was practically no conformity, with two the rate rose to 12.8 per cent, and with three the original rate was observed. Interestingly, he found that increasing the number of opposing subjects to ten to fifteen did not increase the rate of conformity.

In another variation of his original experiment, Asch found that if one of the confederates agreed with the subject, i.e. gave the correct answer when the other six confederates give the wrong answer, the percentage of conforming responses dropped to 5.5 per cent. If however, the one supporter left on some pretext in the middle of the experiment, the number of conforming responses increased to more or less the original rate.

Thus, from Asch's results alone, we can begin to see how complex the process of social influence is. Not only is there a good deal of variation in the responses of different individuals to the same situation, but also, variations in the situation itself will affect the amount of conformity obtained.

Whether or not you think you would have conformed in the Asch situation, it is reasonable to assume that in our everyday lives we are influenced to some extent by those around us. We then can ask *why* are others able to influence us? Our earlier discussion of the three processes of social influence, and particularly our discussion of social power, offer some insights into the 'why' of influence. Our understanding is also aided by considering two types of influence defined by Deutsch and Gerard (1955). The first is **informational influence**, defined as '... an influence to accept information obtained from another as *evidence* about reality.' (p. 629). We have two sources of information about the nature of reality: our own sensory experience and the reports and behaviour of those around us. A number of studies have shown that factors which increase our dependence on others, such as the ambiguity of the situation and our perceived competence relative to that of the others, increase the informational influence, i.e. the conformity rate.

The second type of influence, **normative influence**, is defined as '... an influence to conform with the positive expectations of another.' (p. 629). We are influenced to conform to the positive expectations of others because we desire their approval and acceptance, and wish to avoid the subtle and not so subtle punishments that others can inflict on a deviate (such as ridicule, scorn and social isolation).

Although conceptually distinct, normative and informational influence are not mutually exclusive and often operate in the same situation, such as in Asch's experiment as evidenced by the subjects' reasons for their responses.

THE INFLUENCE OF OTHERS ON BEHAVIOUR: OBEDIENCE

Milgram (1965a, 1965b) was interested in the conditions under which people would obey orders given by others; more specifically, in the question '... if X tells Y to hurt Z, under what conditions will Y carry out the command of X and under what conditions will he refuse?' (Milgram 1965a, p. 57) – an abstraction of the situation that exists in prison camps and during wars.

His experimental situation differs in important respects from that of Asch. You may have thought that the task used by Asch, the judgement of lengths of lines, was trivial; that perhaps subjects in his experiments thought their judgements were unimportant and would have little effect on their lives once the experiment concluded. In the Milgram experiments, however, the subject must decide whether or not to obey a command to hurt another person; an act of behaviour rather than a verbal judgement is required, and the situation in which the subject finds himself – the conflict he experiences – more dramatic.

In this experiment, subjects participated in pairs. They were told that the experiment was designed to test the effects of punishment on learning, and that one would assume the role of 'learner' and the other of 'teacher', as determined by drawing lots. In fact, one subject was a **confederate** (someone who cooperates with the experimenter). The drawing was rigged so that he always was the 'learner' and the **naive subject** (the real subject) always the 'teacher'. The task of the 'learner' was to memorize a list of paired associate nonsense syllables. The task of the 'teacher' was to punish wrong responses with electric shocks of increasing voltage for each successive mistake. For this purpose, the teacher was presented with what he was told was an electric shock generator with thirty levels of shock, ranging from 15 to 450 volts at 15 volt intervals, and verbal labels such as 'danger: severe shock'. Each shock was administered by the act of depressing a lever. As you have probably already guessed, the 'learner', or 'victim' as he was called, provided enough wrong answers so that an obedient subject would eventually have to administer a 450 volt shock. The learner, of course, was never actually shocked, but the teacher did not know this and believed the learner was receiving shocks as they were administered.

The experiment, as you have probably also guessed, had nothing at all to do with the effects of punishment on learning: its real purpose was to study obedience. Will the subject obey the experimenter and actually shock the victim, or will he refuse? Milgram systematically tested the effects of the proximity of the victim on the level of obedience using the four conditions below. It should be noted that an obedient subject is defined as one who completes the experiment as opposed to one who refuses to continue at some point.

1) *Remote feedback* – the victim, in a separate room from the subject pounds on the wall after the 300 volt shock. In this condition 66 per cent of the subjects obey the experimenter and complete the experiment.

2) *Voice feedback* – the victim is still in a separate room but makes verbal protests which can be heard by the teacher. In this condition 62.5 per cent obey.

3) *Proximity* – the victim is in the same room as the subject, 50 cm away from him, and makes the same verbal protests as in the 'voice feedback' condition. In this condition 40 per cent obey.

4) *Touch proximity* – following the 150 volt shock, the victim refuses to rest his hand on a plate through which he receives the shock, and demands to be set free. The experimenter then instructs the subject to force the victim's hand down on to the plate while he administers the shock. 30 per cent of subjects obey in this condition.

From these results it can be seen that the closer the victim is to the subject the lower the obedience, or, the greater the number of subjects who refuse to continue with the experiment. Milgram also found that the proximity of the authority, i.e. the experimenter, affected the level of obedience: twenty-six out of forty subjects obeyed when the experimenter sat about a metre from the subject, while only nine out of forty obeyed when the experimenter left the room after the initial instructions and continued to direct the experiment by telephone.

Let us pause for a moment and consider the response of Milgram's subjects to this experimental situation. Milgram, and probably many people who have read about his experiments, find the level of obedience obtained unexpectedly high, and it is reasonable to ask to what extent the levels of obedience obtained could have been predicted prior to knowing the actual response of the subjects. What would you have predicted? Well, to answer this question, Milgram presented psychiatrists and fourth-year university students with a description of the voice feedback condition and asked them to predict how many subjects would refuse to continue at each point during the experiment. The predicted level of obedience was a lot lower than the obtained level: it was predicted that practically no one would complete the experiment whereas in fact 62.5 per cent did.

Another point concerns the behaviour of the subjects. The average subject did not just sit there, silently and calmly administering the shocks until the end of the experiment. On the contrary, he experienced conflict, tension and stress. You might have assumed that there would be a one to one relationship between a person's internal state and behaviour, but this did not seem to be the case. Although many subjects actually wanted to leave the situation they did not seem able to do so, and continued to administer the shocks.

In another series of experiments (Milgram 1965b), two confederates in addition to the real subject assumed the role of teacher. The duties were divided amongst the three, so that the two confederates administered the learning task to the victim but the responsibility for administering the shock still rested with the real subject. How would the behaviour of these two additional teachers affect the behaviour of the subject?

In one condition, one confederate teacher refused to continue after 150 volts, and the other after 210 volts. Milgram reports that in this condition, thirty-six out of forty real subjects refused to continue with the experiment at some point, compared with the fourteen out of forty who refused when faced with this situation alone. Interestingly, the majority of those who refused to continue denied that the actions of the two confederates had any effect on their own behaviour. Milgram comments that this sharp drop in obedience is similar to the drop in conformity found by Asch when one confederate supports the subject by giving the right answer.

In a second condition, again using three teachers (two confederates and one real subject), Milgram instructed the two confederates to obey the experimenter throughout the experiment. If more subjects refused to continue when others refused, perhaps more subjects would obey when others obeyed. However, in this condition twenty-nine out of forty obeyed (eleven refused) which was not significantly different from the twenty-six out of forty when subjects participated alone.

At this point you may be thinking that perhaps the level of

obedience observed by Milgram is peculiar to his particular situation and not able to be generalized to situations that are likely to occur in everyday life. First of all, the power of the experimenter (see Chapter 2) in this situation would be likely to increase obedience. Furthermore, the situation is unusual in that subjects are experiencing strong conflict, but perhaps unlike everyday life, they do not have time to think about it, to weigh the alternatives, and to consider consequences of their actions. They must either continue or withdraw, and either action commits them to a particular resolution of the conflict.

Now we will consider another study, done in the field with subjects who thought they were in real life situations, not an experiment (Hofling *et al.* 1966). The situation is less dramatic, but the results are similar to those found by Milgram.

This experiment was conducted on hospital wards by nurses and psychiatrists who were studying doctor-nurse conflict. They found that twenty-one out of twenty-two nurses obeyed a doctor's order to administer twice the maximum dosage of a drug (as stated on the package). The doctor gave his order by telephone, claiming he would sign the order later when he arrived in the ward. This was clearly against hospital policy, which stated that all orders for drugs be signed first. The drug prescribed was actually a placebo and the nurse was stopped after she had prepared the medication but before she approached the patient. This level of actual obedience sharply contrasted with the responses of other nurses and student nurses who were asked to state what they *would* do in this situation: ten of the twelve nurses and all twenty-one of the student nurses said that they would not comply.

Once again in this study, the level of obedience in the actual situation seems higher than what we would have expected, and there is a discrepancy between the actual behaviour of the subjects and predicted behaviour based on description of the situation.

THE INFLUENCES OF OTHERS ON ATTITUDES AND BELIEFS: NORMS AND REFERENCE GROUPS

In a longitudinal field study, Newcomb (1958, 1963) examined the long term influence of a particular social environment on individual attitudes. Although the topic of attitudes will be closely examined in the next chapter, this study is included here because of its importance in illustrating the long term effects of the social environment on the individual in a real world setting. The social environment he chose was Bennington College, a small, private and expensive all-female tertiary institution, located in a somewhat isolated rural area of the northeastern United States. During the four years of his first study, from 1935 to 1939, he obtained data from the students who attended the college during that time. He focussed on their political attitudes – an interesting topic because the students typically came from wealthy conservative families but, while at Bennington, tended to adopt liberal attitudes.

From his investigation, Newcomb found that there existed a community norm of liberalism. A **norm** can be defined as a generally agreed upon pattern of appropriate behaviours, beliefs, attitudes, etc. Like all norms, there was consensus on what the norm was – most students agreed that it was 'good' to be liberal; and also enforcement of the norm – those who were not liberal were the targets of gossip, even ridicule, and found themselves isolated. Not surprisingly, prestige was associated with liberalism; those who were the most liberal were accorded the most prestige. Furthermore, the general trend over four years at Bennington was to become more liberal. This general trend was evident when first-year students were compared with fourth-year students and also when the attitudes of the same individuals were followed over four years.

However, despite the general trend, some students, a minority, retained their conservative attitudes. Although the shifts in attitudes shown by the majority could be predicted from the knowledge that a student was a member of Bennington College, membership group alone could not predict all of the responses. Thus Newcomb distinguished between **membership group** and reference group. The individual's actual membership groups (e.g. a particular family, a college student body, a group of friends) may or may not be reference groups for that individual. A group is a **reference group** (or point of reference) when the individual identifies with the group norms and uses them as standards for personal behaviour. Groups can serve as a positive point of reference or as a negative point of reference. Furthermore membership groups and reference groups need not necessarily overlap: a membership group may not be used as a reference group, and the individual may have reference groups that are not membership groups.

Newcomb concluded that attitude change or the lack of it over four years was not only a function of the individual's relationship to the total membership group, but also of the positive and negative reference groups, and that attitudes tended to be consistent with these positive and negative identifications.

During 1960–1961 Newcomb (1963) interviewed most of the women he had studied for three or four years in his earlier investigation. The purpose of the follow-up was to determine the extent to which those women who had become more liberal during their four years at Bennington remained so in later life. Newcomb hypothesized that present attitudes may determine the choice of future social environments, and that a recently changed attitude would be more likely to persist if an environment which supported it was chosen.

When the women interviewed were considered as a group, their political attitudes twenty years later were considerably more liberal than would be expected, considering their relatively high socioeconomic status level (i.e. family income, etc.). Newcomb then looked at one aspect of their social environment chosen by the women themselves, specifically their husbands. On the whole, the husbands, like the wives, were much less conservative than expected given their socioeconomic status.

Furthermore when those women who became more liberal at Bennington were considered, those who retained their liberal attitudes tended to have liberal husbands, while those who were middle of the road or conservative at the time of the follow-up tended to have husbands with similar views. The same pattern emerged when the minority who were conservative upon leaving Bennington were considered. Therefore, the evidence indicated that retention or change of the attitudes originally studied was related to the supportiveness of the social environment (i.e. the husband) chosen.

In summary, we can say that the original study indicated that reference groups are a determinant of attitudes, while the follow-up study indicated that perhaps present attitudes can determine the choice of future reference groups. Then, of course, the attitudes are maintained by the social support of the new reference groups. Insofar as this occurs, an attitude can become a self-maintaining system.

'BRAINWASHING' OR THOUGHT REFORM

The thought reform methods used by the Chinese constitute an extreme example of attempted social influence. We will consider two reports of the Chinese indoctrination programme: Schein's (1956) account of the attempted indoctrination of United Nations prisoners of war (during the Korean war); and Lifton's (1961) account of individual Westerners living in China who were subjected to intensive indoctrination.

In Schein's (1956) report of the experiences of POWs, we find the simultaneous application of several techniques, all designed to induce the prisoner to accept the communist point of view. The Chinese attempted to remove all supports for the prisoners' previous beliefs and to provide support only for the new, desired ones. Personal mail was censored, news sources and outside contacts restricted, and religious expression forbidden. Also, meaningful conversation among the prisoners, a potential source of support for previous beliefs, was made extremely difficult by the constant presence of Chinese spies and informers among the prisoners themselves. Groups that did form despite the prevailing feeling of mistrust were broken up by the Chinese. Schein (1956) reports that '... the most important effect of the social isolation which existed was the consequent emotional isolation, which prevented a man from validating any of his beliefs, attitudes, and values through meaningful interaction with other men at a time when these were under heavy attack from many sources, and when no accurate information was available.' (p. 155).

Within this atmosphere, direct indoctrination procedures were used, such as lectures, pamphlets and movies. But these consisted of propaganda and references to the United States which were generally naive and uninformed. The Chinese also used indirect techniques which demanded greater personal involvement on the part of the prisoners, including discussion groups, interrogations (even about the prisoners' previous life histories), and forced public confessions of trivial transgressions of camp rules. Rewards and punishments were systematically applied to elicit collaboration. But collaboration and its subsequent benefit of a more comfortable existence often aroused hostility in non-collaborators, which served to push the collaborator further in the direction of the Chinese.

In discussing the reactions of the POWs, Schein (1956) distinguishes between collaboration (defined as '... any kind of behavior which helped the enemy ...' (p. 164)), which is equivalent to compliance, and ideological change, which is more or less equivalent to internalization and which could range from mild doubts about previous beliefs to complete conversion. He contends that considerable collaboration did occur, but that the Chinese failed to induce much ideological change, considering their efforts. He admits however that the extent of ideological change was very difficult to assess.

The reactions of the POWs, like the reactions of the subjects in Asch's experiments, were varied. Furthermore, similar overt reactions were not always the result of similar motivations. Most men fell into a category which Schein labels the 'get-alongers'. These men '... establish a complex compromise between the demands of the Chinese and the demands of their own ideology.' (p. 165). They emotionally withdrew from the situation as much as possible and maintained their previous group identifications. Those classified as resisters differed: some were 'well-integrated resistance leaders,' others were 'obstructionists' (those who always resisted authority), and so forth. Similarly diverse were the motivations of the cooperators, a group which included (to use Schein's labels again) 'the opportunist', 'the weakling' and 'the bored or curious intellectual' among others.

Schein, in considering the lack of actual ideological change, points out that problems in administering the programme may have been at fault rather than the programme itself. The Chinese were not able to control the environment totally. They were not able to eliminate completely supports for previous beliefs. Their inadequate knowledge of English allowed the prisoners to ridicule them in subtle ways. Furthermore, the men faced this indoctrination programme in groups; there were not enough Chinese to carry out indoctrination on a one-to-one basis although this proved more effective when it was used.

In Lifton's (1961) account of the indoctrination procedures used on individual westerners living in China, these technical problems were absent. There was no language difficulty since these prisoners spoke Chinese. Also, indoctrination was carried out on the individual level; appeals and attacks were tailored to the particular individual. In short, the control of the social environment and the support it could provide for previous beliefs or for the new desired beliefs was much more complete. Attacks were aimed at the individual's whole sense of self-identity; the 'old self' had to be destroyed and a 'new self' built up in its place.

Individual reactions to this intensive indoctrination varied. Of the people he interviewed shortly after their release, Lifton classified a few as 'apparent converts', others as 'apparent resisters', and the majority as 'obviously confused'. Most of these people eventually reverted to their 'western selves'. However, as we saw in the Bennington studies, the social environments must be considered when we talk about the maintenance, or change of attitudes. These people returned to the western world, an environment that was supportive of their previous selves and not of their new selves. We can only speculate about what would have happened had these people remained in China.

EFFECTS OF THE MASS MEDIA

The research examples we have discussed all involve face-to-face influence; here we will consider influence via the mass media. Think for a moment what proportion of each day you spend watching television or movies, listening to the radio, or reading newspapers, magazines, etc. To what extent are we influenced by this exposure to the mass media?

The effects of mass media have been the topic of numerous investigations, but McGuire (1969) concludes that 'The outcome has been quite embarrassing for proponents of the mass media, since there is little evidence of attitude change, much less change in gross behavior such as buying or voting.' (p. 227). Nonetheless, this does not mean that we can conclude that the mass media have no effects. It would be a rare outcome indeed to find that we are not affected at all by something which takes up so much of our time.

Quite apart from direct influence attempts such as advertising and political campaigns, the media are an important source of information about the world around us. Through the media, we learn about places and events which we do not directly experience. If this added information changes our view of the world, our attitudes, etc., then, in a general sense, we have been influenced. Furthermore, the media (e.g. newspapers, news broadcasts, etc.) select the information to which we will be exposed and can emphasize or de-emphasize the importance of an event, and therefore, to a greater or lesser extent, structure our view of this indirectly experienced world.

We will now consider a few general findings that are particularly relevant to our discussion of social influence.

Often when public officials or other organizations decide that the public should change its behaviour (stop smoking, wear seatbelts, have blood pressure checked, and so forth), an information campaign is launched through the media. But do these campaigns actually bring about the intended changes? Hyman and Sheatsley (1947) cast doubt on the effectiveness of such campaigns. They contended that an increase in the amount of information presented will not necessarily result in a corresponding increase in public awareness. First of all, not all people are equally exposed to the information presented; some are more difficult to reach than others. Hyman and Sheatsley argued that there is 'a hard core of chronic "know-nothings" ' who are generally uninformed regardless of the issue. Furthermore, exposure to information is related to interest; those that are interested acquire the most information while the apathetic remain uninformed. The authors also claimed that people seek out information consistent with their point of view and avoid information which is not. However, McGuire (1969) contends that only the 'seeking out' part of this selective exposure hypothesis is supported, and that there is little evidence for the 'avoidance' part. Even given exposure, Hyman and Sheatsley maintained that people will interpret the same information differently depending upon their previous point of view. Last but not least, even if the information is assimilated as intended, knowledge does not necessarily result in the intended change. The authors emphasized the role of survey research as a source of valuable information in both planning and assessing the effectiveness of such campaigns.

One recent study, however, (Farquhar *et al.* 1977) has found that mass media education campaigns can be effective in reducing the risk of cardiovascular disease. In this study, two communities (in Northern California) were exposed to an extensive mass media campaign, aimed at reducing risk by providing information about the probable causes of risk and about specific behaviours which may reduce risk. Prior to designing the campaign, the 'knowledge deficits' and the 'media-consumption patterns' of those who would be exposed to it were assessed. In one community, a small sample of high risk subjects also received face-to-face counselling. The risk of cardiovascular disease in these communities was then compared with that in a third control community over a two-year period. Those exposed to the mass media campaign showed a decrease in risk compared with those in the control community. Those who received face-to-face counselling initially showed a greater reduction in risk than those who were only exposed to the mass media campaign, but this difference decreased by the end of the second year.

Another area of research on the effects of mass media has centred around the **two-step flow of communication hypothesis**. According to this hypothesis, we are not directly influenced by the media, but indirectly influenced through opinion leaders who communicate to us what they have assimilated from the media. This hypothesis developed from a study of voting behaviour (Lazarsfeld, Berelson and Gaudet 1948) which found that personal contact appeared to have more impact on voting decisions than the mass media. Furthermore, opinion leaders could be identified throughout society who showed more interest in the election and were more exposed to the media than others. This hypothesis, which emphasizes that we are more influenced by those around us than we are by the media, generated considerable interest and research.

Katz (1957), in reviewing the original voting study as well as some subsequent research concerned with other areas of influence, contends that opinion leaders are generally members of the same group as those influenced. Within a group, different individuals may be opinion leaders for different areas of interest, and particular opinion leaders are more exposed to media information in their area than other group members.

With regard to the effects of the mass media on voting behaviour, Weiss (1969) concludes that the role of the media appears to be limited to the reinforcement of existing preferences rather than bringing about conversions. But he makes the point that little attention has been given to the effects of the media *between* campaigns, and it is possible that the media have a cumulative effect over time.

The possibility that the mass media have effects more subtle than was originally proposed need not be confined to the area of voting behaviour. It is quite possible that the media, particularly in their role as an important source of information, do affect our behaviour, our attitudes, our values, etc. in ways that have yet to be properly assessed.

SUMMARY

Social influence occurs when one person or group induces a change in the behaviour (overt behaviour and/or internal thoughts and feelings) of another. Three types of influence are compliance, identification and internalization, depending upon the nature of the change. We can be influenced by reward power, coercive power, legitimate power referent power or expert power.

We are influenced in a complicated way by those around us. From the examples of research discussed, we can see that individuals do vary in their response to social influence attempts. Some situations also induce more influence than others.

Although it has been difficult to demonstrate the effects of the mass media on attitudes and behaviour, their effects may be more subtle than originally supposed. Information campaigns in the media are not necessarily an effective way of inducing change in the public. The effects of the media appear to be mediated by opinion leaders, and in general we are influenced more by those around us than by the media.

TERMS AND CONCEPTS

social influence
compliance
identification
internalization
reward power
coercive power
legitimate power
referent power
expert power
informational influence
normative influence
confederate
naive subject
norm
membership group
reference group
two-step flow of communication

FOR DISCUSSION

1. Think of examples of compliance, of identification, and of internalization in real life situations. What types of social power do you think were exercised in these situations?

2. List some of the norms that the (medical) students at your university adhere to. Do upper-level students conform to these norms more or less than first-year students? Is adherence to these norms related to status? What happens to those that do not conform?

3. Why do you think there is a discrepancy between the actual level of obedience (Milgram 1965; Hofling *et al.* 1966) and the predicted level of obedience (either of others or one's self)?

4.   Why do you think the levels of conformity (Asch) and obedience (Milgram) dropped when one or two (in the case of Milgram) others did not conform or obey?

5.   Do you agree that we are more influenced by those around us than we are by the mass media?

SUGGESTED READING

Kelman: analysis of three processes of social influence.

Lifton: fascinating account of thought reform or 'brainwashing'.

Weiss: comprehensive review of research on the effects of mass media.

REFERENCES

Asch, S. 1952. Effects of group pressure upon the modification and distortion of judgments. In G. E. Swanson, T. M. Newcomb and E. L. Hartley (eds) *Readings in Social Psychology*, rev. edn., 2–11. New York: Henry Holt and Company.

Deutsch, M. and Gerard, H. B. 1955. A study of normative and informational social influences upon individual judgment. *J. Abnorm. Soc. Psychol.* **51,** 629–36.

Farquhar, J. W., Maccoby, N., Wood, P. D., Alexander, J. K., Breitrose, H., Brown, B. W. Jr., Haskell, W. L., McAlister, A. L., Meyer, A. J., Nash, J. D. and Stern, M. P. 1977. Community education for cardiovascular health. *The Lancet*, **1,** p. 1192–5.

French, J. R. P. Jr. and Raven, B. H. 1959. The bases of social power. In D. Cartwright (ed.) *Studies in Social Power* 150–67. Ann Arbor: University of Michigan, Institute for Social research.

Hofling, C. K., Brotzman, E., Dalrymple, S., Graves, N. and Pierce, C. M. 1966. An experimental study in nurse-physician relationships. *J. Nerv. Ment. Dis.* **143,** 171–80.

Hyman, H. H., and Sheatsley, P. B. 1947. Some reasons why information campaigns fail. *Public Opinion Quart.* **11,** 413–23.

Katz, E. 1957. The two-step flow of communication: An up-to-date report on an hypothesis. *Public Opinion Quart.* **21,** 61–78.

Kelman, H. C. 1961. Processes of opinion change. *Public Opinion Quart.* **25,** 57–78.

Lazarsfeld, P. F., Berelson, B. and Gaudet, H. 1948. *The People's Choice* (2nd ed). New York: Columbia University Press.

Lifton, R. 1961. *Thought reform and the psychology of totalism: A study of "brainwashing" in China.* New York: W. W. Norton & Company, Inc.

McGuire, W. 1969. The nature of attitude and attitude change. In G. Lindzey and E. Aronson (eds) *The Handbook of Social Psychology* (2nd edn) *III. The Individual in a Social Context,* 136–314. Reading, Mass.: Addison-Wesley.

Milgram, S. 1965a. Some conditions of obedience and disobedience to authority. *Human Relations,* **18,** 57–76.

Milgram, S. 1965b. Liberating effects of group pressure. *J. Person. Soc. Psychol.* **1,** 127–34.

Newcomb, T. 1958. Attitude development as a function of reference groups: The Bennington study. In E. E. Maccoby, T. M. Newcomb and E. L. Hartly (eds) *Readings in Social Psychology.* 265–75. New York: Holt, Rinehart and Winston.

Newcomb, T. 1963. Persistence and regression of changed attitudes: long-range studies. *J. Soc. Issues* **19,** 3–14, No. 4.

Schein, E. H. 1956. The Chinese indoctrination program for prisoners of war: A study of attempted brainwashing. *Psychiatry* **19,** 149–72.

Weiss, W. 1969. The effects of the mass media of communication. In Lindzey, G. and Aronson, E. (eds) *The Handbook of Social Psychology.* (2nd edn) **V.** *Applied Social Psychology* 77–195. Reading, Mass.: Addison-Wesley.

Chapter 15

Attitudes: Their Organization and Change

'I really like that sports car', 'I can't stand that lecturer', 'I disagree with raising membership fees'. These are expressions of attitudes. We all have a variety of attitudes: towards objects, individuals, groups, issues, and so on. We seldom view the world around us with complete neutrality; we have likes and dislikes.

Furthermore, under certain conditions, we find that attitudes change. In this chapter, like the preceding one, we focus on the processes of influence and change. But here we will take a more detailed look at the internal mechanisms involved, the individual's positive and negative evaluations and beliefs.

First we consider how attitudes are organized, then the conditions under which they change, and finally the application of some of the principles of this chapter and of the preceding one to the problem of inducing change in patients.

ATTITUDE ORGANIZATION

ATTITUDES, BELIEFS AND BEHAVIOUR

Although there are many definitions of the concept of attitude, we can consider an **attitude** to be a general predisposition to respond positively or negatively toward an object or a person. In other words, attitudes entail evaluation. There are different degrees of positive and negative evaluation, as well as a neutral point where there is no affective reaction at all. Attraction to particular people, intense dislike of certain commercials, opposition to some government policies, mild preference for a given brand of deodorant, these are all examples of attitudes.

Attitudes are usually associated to a greater or lesser extent with **beliefs**. As Bem (1970) states, 'If a man perceives some relationship between two things or between some thing and a characteristic of it, he is said to hold a belief' (p. 4). If you were asked why you were attracted to a particular person or opposed a particular government policy, you could probably list a number of reasons, perhaps having to do with the attributes of the person and the consequences of the government policy. These reasons are the beliefs associated with the positive or negative attitude. In some cases the attitude may be the result of a set of beliefs. In others, the beliefs may serve to justify the affective reaction which is really based on different factors. It is a mistake to assume that all likes and dislikes result from informed consideration of the available information.

Sometimes, a strong affective reaction is associated with few beliefs. Such an attitude is exemplified by the statement, 'I hate that commercial – I don't know why but I just can't stand it'. These attitudes are often referred to as irrational and can be difficult to change. Sometimes the reverse occurs, i.e. a mild affective reaction associated with a complex set of beliefs. For example, you may have some preference for one newspaper over another, based on your detailed knowledge of the editorial policies, news reporting, features, etc. of both, but which lacks any strong emotional investment.

Attitudes and beliefs vary in the extent to which they are expressed in actual behaviour. You can probably think of some instances when your own behaviour followed directly from your attitudes and beliefs, and others when it did not. Sometimes the behaviour that we would expect, given particular attitudes and beliefs, is inconsistent with what actually happens. These inconsistencies occur because actual behaviour is also determined by other factors, such as other attitudes and beliefs that are relevant to the same behaviour, and by situational constraints. A highly favourable attitude toward the good works of a particular charity implies a monetary contribution, but a negative attitude towards the excessive pressure used to elicit contributions, or one's financial situation, may preclude it.

ATTITUDE FORMATION

Why do we hold certain attitudes? How do we come to evaluate both positively and negatively different aspects of our environment? Certainly our attitudes are dependent upon a wide variety of inputs from our environment. As was said in Chapter 14, we have two basic sources of information about the 'world': our own experience of it and what others tell us about it.

In some cases, our own experience will largely determine our attitudes. Certainly you can think of instances where the sum total of your experience with some aspect of your environment has been the direct determinant of your attitude towards it. Perhaps every time you bought a product made by a certain company you found it to be well designed, well made, durable, easily repaired etc. From these experiences you have developed a liking for the company and its products, formed a set of beliefs about the company and its products (the reasons why you like it), and will buy other products made by this company in the future. In cases like this, our attitude forms a convenient summary of all our particular experiences and allows us to predict (to some degree) future experiences.

Researchers have found that experience does affect our attitudes, sometimes in ways that are less obvious than this example. For instance, a number of experiments have found that under some conditions our familiarity with something is related to how favourably we view it. In these experiments, subjects are typically exposed to different stimuli (such as nonsense words) different numbers of times and are then asked to indicate their attitudes toward each of these stimuli. The general finding is that those stimuli which have been presented more often are rated more favourably.

Furthermore, the principles of both operant and classical conditioning (see Chapter 6) have been found to apply to attitude formation. That attitudes can be affected by operant conditioning comes as no surprise. If an opinion we express receives positive reactions from others, this reinforcement increases the likelihood that we will express the same opinions again in similar circumstances. In general, people do try to elicit positive reactions from others and to avoid negative ones.

You will recall from Chapter 6 that in classical conditioning, a conditioned stimulus (CS) which is paired with an unconditioned stimulus (UCS) then comes to elicit the same response as the UCS. When this principle is applied to attitude formation, the UCS is some environmental stimulus which already elicits an affective response; the CS is some new stimulus which when paired with the UCS, elicits the same affective response. In one experiment, words that were paired with aversive stimuli came to be negatively evaluated (Staats, Staats and Crawford 1962). In another context it was found that subjects who were supplied with soft drinks and peanuts showed more acceptance of an advocated position than those that were not (Janis, Kaye and Kirschner 1965). Furthermore, Staats (1967) claims that the principle of higher-order conditioning applies as well – that the CS then acts as an UCS when paired with other new stimuli.

Since many of our attitudes concern aspects of our environment with which we have no direct experience, the 'information' provided by others about the world is perhaps the most important determinant of our attitudes. Attitudes toward people we have never met, countries we have never visited and movies we have never seen are all the result of what others have told us about these things. The term 'others' can refer to immediate others, such as parents and peers, or more remote others such as the mass media. The earliest influence on our attitudes (as with other cognitive and behavioural variables) is our parents, and certainly the mechanisms of socialization (described in Chapters 6 and 9) such as modelling and identification are relevant to the formation of attitudes. The Bennington studies described in Chapter 14 were an excellent example of the influence of peers on both the change and the maintenance of attitudes, in this case political attitudes. And, even though it is difficult to demonstrate consistently direct effects of the mass media, the possibility that we are influenced by exposure to the attitudes and values conveyed by the media over a long period of time cannot be discounted. For example, to what extent are the conceptions of the roles of male and female, or even of doctor, influenced by the media's portrayal of these roles? This effect would be extremely difficult to test, particularly when the attitudes and values conveyed by the media are consistent with those expressed by parents and peers. In fact, when all of the 'others' around the individual consistently uphold a particular view of the world, the result is what Bem (1970) terms a **non-conscious ideology**, '... a set of beliefs and attitudes which he accepts implicitly but which remains outside of his awareness because alternative conceptions of the world remain unimagined.' (p. 89).

FUNCTIONS OF ATTITUDES

The functional approach to attitudes attempts to explain why we hold certain attitudes by investigating their motivational bases, the needs that they fulfil for us. Katz (1960) describes four major functions that attitudes can serve.

1) The **adjustive function**. An attitude can be held because of its instrumental, utilitarian value; because it enables individuals to

minimize punishments and maximize rewards when dealing with those around them. This function is related to the learning theory approach to attitudes discussed in the previous section.

2) The **ego-defensive function**. This function is related to Freudian psychology (see Chapter 11 for a discussion of Freudian concepts, including defence mechanisms). Here, the attitude 'defends' the individual from unpleasant or threatening information that might otherwise have to be coped with. Unlike attitudes which serve the adjustive function, ego-defensive attitudes follow from the internal conflicts of the individual rather than actual experience with the object of the attitude.

3) The **value expressive function**. Some attitudes are held because they express the individual's central values and his or her self-concept. We all like to think of ourselves as being this or that kind of person (whether or not we actually are), and holding certain attitudes enables us to do so. The rewards derived from such attitudes do not come from the environment, i.e. reactions of others, but from within the individual.

4) The **knowledge function**. Individuals need to understand and structure the world around them. An attitude which serves this function enables them to organize and structure some aspect of their experience.

The same attitude can serve different functions for different people. Racial prejudice has been said to serve the ego-defensive function for some people; for others it may serve the adjustive function, i.e. prejudiced attitudes are held because they are rewarded by others. Furthermore, the same attitude can serve more than one function for an individual.

The functional approach has important implications for attitude change. Katz (1960) states 'The most general statement that can be made about the conditions conducive to attitude change is that the expression of the old attitude or its anticipated expression no longer gives satisfaction to its related need state. In other words, it no longer serves its function and the individual feels blocked or frustrated' (p. 177). Consequently, prior to any attitude change attempt, the function that attitude serves for the individual should be determined. The particular approach used to induce change should depend upon the attitude's function; approaches that may be effective when one function is being served may not be when others are. For example, providing relevant information may help change knowledge function attitudes but have little effect on ego-defensive ones.

ATTITUDE CHANGE

CONSISTENCY AND ATTITUDE CHANGE

Attitudes are not unrelated to each other. You probably know from your own experience that knowledge of a person's attitude on one issue often enables you to predict his or her attitudes on other issues – they are somehow consistent with one another. A number of theories about this consistency among attitudes have been proposed and they have certain general characteristics in common. They all define a state of consistency which is assumed to be comfortable and desirable, and a state of inconsistency which is assumed to be uncomfortable and undesirable. Further, it is assumed that the individual is motivated to eliminate (or at least reduce) this uncomfortable state of inconsistency when it exists. One way that inconsistency can be eliminated is by changing the attitude or attitudes that are inconsistent. However, as we shall see, this is not the only possible way of eliminating or reducing the discomfort of inconsistency.

Here we will concentrate on one of these theories, Cognitive Dissonance Theory (Festinger 1957), which has been particularly influential and has generated a great deal of research. The basic idea of this theory is relatively simple. We all carry around a vast number of cognitions, defined as '... any knowledge, opinion, or belief about the environment, about oneself, or about one's behavior.' (Festinger 1957, p. 3). **Cognitive dissonance** exists when two of these cognitions are 'psychologically' inconsistent, i.e. one implies the opposite of the other. The uncomfortable state of dissonance can be reduced, either by changing one cognition so that it is consonant with the other or by adding new cognitions that help to reduce or to justify the inconsistency.

Festinger's (1957) common everyday example of cigarette smoking can be used to illustrate these basic principles. Consider these two cognitions: a) I smoke cigarettes, and b) cigarette smoking is harmful to my health. These two cognitions are dissonant because one implies the opposite of the other: if cigarette smoking is harmful to my health, then I should *not* smoke. One way to reduce dissonance is to change one of the elements. Changing the first cognition means giving up smoking. If this alternative is not appealing, you may work on the second cognition and perhaps convince yourself that the evidence linking smoking with lung cancer is really very weak. The dissonance can be reduced by adding cognitions. In this case, you may minimize the risk you take in smoking, by comparing it with other everyday risks; you may find other intelligent people who smoke, preferably doctors, and be convinced that it cannot be all that bad if such people smoke; or the inconsistency may be justified in the same way as one optimistic medical student did, believing that by the time he got lung cancer there would be a cure for it.

Some applications of dissonance theory

This relatively simple theory is applicable to a variety of situations and often makes non-obvious predictions about the outcomes. We will now consider some of its major applications.

Dissonance theory predicts that decision-making often arouses dissonance. When you must choose among alternatives that each have positive and negative aspects, the positive aspects of the alternatives not chosen, as well as the negative aspects of the chosen alternative, are dissonant with your choice. A number of studies have indicated that dissonance is then reduced by concentrating on the positive aspects of the chosen alternatives and on the negative aspects of the ones not chosen. As a result, the chosen alternative becomes more desirable and the ones not chosen less desirable, even though they might have been almost equal in desirability prior to the choice. (Have you ever seen anyone who just spent his savings on stereo equipment who did not think that his set-up was superior to the comparable alternatives?)

Furthermore, this post-decisional distortion seems to be greater when the decision is irrevocable. In one ingenious field experiment (Knox and Inkster 1968), two groups of people at a race track were interviewed: those about to bet on a particular horse and those who just had bet on a horse. All of the people had made a decision, but the former group could still change their minds, while the latter group could not. Those who had already made the bet gave their horse a better chance of winning than those who were about to bet.

Dissonance is also related to effort: the more effort you expend to attain some desired goal, for example group membership, the more likely you will feel positively about its attainment. In other words, we convince ourselves that those things that we have worked hard for are really worth it, even if they really are not. Deciding in the end that something was not really worth all the effort would be dissonant with the knowledge that the effort had been expended; it would be like deciding after you had made the bet that the horse was not going to win.

Experimental support for this relationship was obtained by Aronson and Mills (1959), who varied the severity of the initiation that female university students had to undergo before being admitted to a group which, they were told, would be discussing the psychology of sex. Those in the severe initiation condition were required to read a list of obscene words and two vivid sexual passages out loud to a male experimenter (an embarrassing experience for most female university students in the late fifties), while those in the mild initiation condition read a list of sexual but not obscene words. Those in the control condition received no initiation. Then all subjects listened to a boring discussion, which they were told was the group they would be joining subsequently. Although subjects in both initiation conditions, as well as those who had received no initiation, listened to the same discussion, those who had gone through more effort to join rated the discussion more positively than those who had invested little or no effort.

Perhaps the most intriguing application of dissonance theory concerns the consequences of forced compliance. It has been popularly assumed that behaviour follows from attitudes: if a behaviour change is required, the relevant attitudes must first be changed. However, a number of experiments have demonstrated that the opposite can occur: i.e. if behaviour is changed under certain conditions, attitude change will follow. Furthermore, the less force used to elicit behavioural compliance, the more likely it is that attitude change will occur.

In a now classic experiment (Festinger and Carlsmith 1959), the researchers offered some subjects $1 and others $20 to tell another subject, waiting to participate in the experiment, that the experimental task was interesting, whereas in fact it was boring. When subsequently asked to rate the experimental task, those in the $1 condition rated it more positively than those in the $20 condition. Why? The subjects' knowledge that the task was dull is dissonant with the knowledge that they told someone else that it was interesting. In the $20 condition, this dissonance can be reduced by adding another cognition, a justification, the fact that they were paid $20 to lie. Consequently there is no need for attitude change. One dollar, however, provides little justification for the lie, but dissonance can be reduced by deciding that the task *was* interesting.

Likewise when subjects were induced to eat fried grasshoppers (a disliked food) by an unpleasant experimenter, their attitude towards the fried grasshoppers changed more in the positive direction than in subjects induced to do so by a pleasant experimenter (Zimbardo, Weisenberg, Firestone and Levy 1969). In another experiment (Aronson and Carlsmith 1963), children who were told not to play with a highly desirable toy, and subsequently did not play with it, changed their evaluation of the toy in the negative direction more when the command was accompanied by a mild threat than by a severe threat.

The basic principle is the same in each of these experiments. People who are somehow induced to behave in ways that are inconsistent with their attitudes will experience dissonance, particularly if there was little reason or justification for their behaviour. The discomfort of dissonance is then alleviated by changing their attitudes, so that they are consistent with the induced behaviour. But, it would seem, only when alternative ways of reducing dissonance, i.e. adding cognitions that justify or rationalize the behaviour, are not available.

COMMUNICATION AND PERSUASION

Persuasive communications – messages intended to change our attitudes – are a part of our everyday life. When are they successful? Under what conditions are we likely to change an attitude as a result of such a communication? Any number of studies have been conducted in an effort to identify these conditions. Although there is no simple answer, and no formula for changing an individual's attitude on a given issue, we can now cite some general principles of attitude change that seem to work most of the time (but not with every individual and not even in every experiment).

In our analysis of persuasive communication we must consider: a) its source, i.e. the communicator, b) the communication itself, and c) its target, i.e. the audience.

The communicator

It is a fact of life that some people are more influential than others. But how can this difference be explained? What factors are involved? One factor is **credibility**. Generally, the more credible the communicator, the more likely it is that others will be influenced. But what is credibility? It is generally accepted that credibility depends upon two other factors: the expertise and the trustworthiness of the communicator. A particular communication is more likely to be convincing if it is presented by an expert in the field than if it is presented by someone with no relevant qualifications. Communicators tend to be perceived as trustworthy (and therefore able to influence) to the extent that they have no vested interest in their point of view, and when they do not appear to be trying to exert influence.

Another characteristic of the communicator that affects persuasiveness is attractiveness, or likeability. We tend to be influenced by those we like, find attractive, and with whom we can identify. Advertisers are certainly not blind to this principle, judging by their use of movie stars and sports personalities to sell a whole range of products (many of which are unrelated to movies or sport).

The communication

The same message may be presented in a variety of ways. A number of different aspects of the presentation have been found to affect the persuasiveness of the message. One is the degree of discrepancy between the view of the target audience and the view advocated by the message. Generally, it has been found that moderately discrepant communications induce more change than either slightly or greatly discrepant ones. It seems as though change increases as discrepancy increases, up to a point, and then further increases in discrepancy actually result in decreased change. One explanation for this relationship can be found in dissonance theory. Exposure to an opinion which differs from your own may arouse dissonance. When the discrepancy is not great, dissonance may be reduced by changing your own attitudes. However, when the opinion is very discrepant from your own, the dissonance may be reduced by derogating the communicator – telling yourself that the communicator is uninformed, ignorant, etc. – thus eliminating the need for any attitude change.

The degree of fear aroused in the target audience by the communication has also been found to effect the amount of induced change. We will discuss **fear arousal** in greater detail than the other aspects of persuasive communication in this section, because of its particular relevance for medical practice. You, as a doctor, will be trying to induce patients to do things that you believe are good for their health – to stop smoking, to have a chest X-ray, to exercise more, and so on. But as we have emphasized before, merely presenting people with the information may not bring about the intended change in either attitudes or behaviour; people can block out unpleasant information, misinterpret it, minimize its importance, and even if the information registers in fairly unadulterated form, it may not necessarily lead to action.

Now bodily malfunctions, their treatment and their consequences are capable of arousing great fear in many people. So the question arises: to what extent should a doctor use fear to motivate patients to adhere to his or her recommendations? As you will see, there is no simple answer to this question.

In one well-known experiment (Janis and Feshbach 1953), which tested the effects of fear arousal on the subsequent dental hygiene behaviour of high school students, an inverse relationship between fear arousal and reported improvement in dental hygiene behaviour was found. Those who received the most fear-arousing presentation changed least, and those who received the least fear-arousing one changed most.

However, many studies have been done since this one on a variety of fear-arousing topics (such as driving safety, and the relationship between smoking and lung cancer). As Aronson (1976) states: 'The overwhelming weight of the experimental data suggests that, all other things being equal, the more frightened a person is by a communication, the more likely he is to take positive preventive action.' (p. 65).

But the answer is really more complicated when other variables are considered. For instance, the relationship between fear arousal and change is affected by the chronic anxiety of the individual: those with low chronic anxiety seem to respond better to high fear appeals, while those with high chronic anxiety do not. For these latter people, strong fear arousal increases the anxiety level to the point where it motivates defensive avoidance rather than action.

Furthermore, the probability of actual behavioural change is affected by the provision of clear, specific instructions. In one experiment (Leventhal, Singer and Jones 1965), it was found that although high fear arousal produced more attitude change (toward tetanus shots, in this case), it did not affect actual behaviour: more subjects who received instructions about how to obtain tetanus shots actually got them than those who received no instruction, regardless of the level of fear arousal. Also, a group of subjects who only received the instructions without any fear appeal took no action.

Thus we can tentatively conclude that a communication will be most effective when an optimal level of fear is aroused, i.e. one which induces action but not defensive avoidance, and when clear, specific instructions for avoiding the feared condition are provided.

The target audience

Some audiences or individuals are more easily influenced than others. What variables determine the ease with which people will be persuaded? One factor is the individual's ability to counterargue. A forewarned audience, particularly if they disagree with the speaker's position, has time to counterargue and therefore changes less than one that listens to the message 'cold'. Likewise, it has been found that people who are distracted while listening to a persuasive communication show more change than those that are not, presumably because the distraction interferes with their ability to counterargue.

The persuasibility of individuals can also be decreased by **inoculation** (McGuire 1969). The procedure used is analogous to medical inoculation. Subjects undergo a mild attack on their beliefs which they refute. Then, when they are subsequently confronted with a severe attack, they are less affected by it than those who have not experienced the mild attack.

A FINAL NOTE ON ATTITUDE CHANGE

Despite all we have said in this chapter and in the preceding one, generally speaking, attitudes are difficult to change, particularly when the issue is an important or involving one. Most likely your attitude toward your toothpaste would be easier to change than your attitude towards increases in student fees. Furthermore, even if we just consider one specific attitude, the emotional investment in it, like its function, can vary from one individual to the next, and therefore the effect of any persuasive communication aimed at groups of individuals will vary as well.

Despite the vast numbers of experiments investigating attitude change, relatively little work has been done on the long term effects of persuasive communication. However, role playing, which can be a very involving activity, does seem to produce a surprisingly long term effect. In one experiment (Mann and Janis 1968) subjects who played the role of a smoker with lung cancer were still smoking less eighteen months after the experiment. In some other studies, a so-called 'sleeper-effect' has been obtained: under certain conditions, some subjects show little change directly following a persuasive communication but do show change some time later.

All things considered, it is not surprising that attitudes are difficult to change, particularly as a result of a persuasive communication. Changed attitudes must exist in the social environment beyond the communication, where other communications from other sources may refute, or at least not support, the newly changed attitude. Perhaps this future support or the lack of it from the individual's social environment is the most important consideration in attitude maintenance and change.

ATTITUDE AND BEHAVIOUR CHANGE IN PATIENTS

COMPREHENSION AND RETENTION OF INFORMATION

Needless to say, no change can be expected if the information or instructions intended to induce change are not understood and remembered. The problems of comprehension and retention have been discussed in Chapter 5, and with regard to the effects of mass media in Chapter 14, but one basic point bears repetition in this context: the mere provision of information or instructions does not necessarily lead to change. First, the message can be ignored or distorted. As we saw in Chapter 14, there is no one-to-one relationship between the message presented and the message received. Although the problems discussed in Chapter 14 pertain to messages presented in the media, in general we would expect them to occur with face-to-face communication as well. Moreover, messages correctly received can be subsequently distorted or minimized in importance. A patient who understands the doctor's instructions and then does not follow them may experience dissonance. We can anticipate some typical dissonance reduction tactics: 'I feel fine now so there is no reason to bother taking the rest of these pills'; 'John Smith is twenty years older than I am, has smoked all of his life, and seems perfectly healthy, so why should I stop smoking?'; 'Breaking my special diet just this once can't hurt all that much'; and so on. A clear explanation of instructions, their likely side effects and the consequences of not following instructions should make it more difficult for the patient to engage in such cognitive manoeuvres.

FACTORS AFFECTING CHANGE

We can view doctor-patient interaction as a persuasive communication situation, with the doctor as the communicator, the instructions as the communication, and the patient as the target audience. Although the principles of persuasive communication must be applied with caution, as noted at the end of the discussion above, a couple of fairly obvious applications deserve mention. Under most circumstances, the doctor will be viewed as a highly credible source, and may be someone the patient likes and can identify with if the doctor-patient relationship is good. This puts the doctor in a powerful position as a communicator. Fear arousal has already been discussed; it is worth mentioning again that in general change is directly related to fear arousal, but that the level of fear arousal should be matched to the individual (considering his or her level of anxiety, coping ability, etc.) and coupled with clear specific instructions.

When we consider the patient, we must ask what function or functions a particular attitude or behaviour serves for the patient. Sometimes attitudes and behaviour serve important but non-obvious functions, which must be taken into account if change is to occur. A man may drink at the pub, not because of the taste of the beer, but because his friends are there. Going to the pub, which entails drinking, serves a social function for him. Telling this man to stop drinking may be equivalent to asking him to give up his main social acitivity (unless of course he drinks lemonade at the pub, but this may cause other difficulties for him).

Lastly, we must consider the social environment of the patient and its compatibility with the doctor's instructions. The patient is acted upon by a variety of forces: personal needs, motivations, attitudes, etc. as well as forces from the social environment. All too often doctors seem to assume that their instructions are the only force acting on the patient, and are then surprised by the relatively low rate of compliance. At least for non-hospitalized patients, such instructions are only one force; there may be others that counteract them. One simple example is that of the patient who does not take a prescribed drug because it produces unwanted side effects. The situation becomes more complicated when long-established behaviour patterns must be altered, such as eating, drinking, smoking and physical activity. In these cases, the chances of actual change could be improved perhaps if both doctor and patient were aware of the sources of resistance to the change. Only through such awareness can the doctor's instructions be realistically integrated with the patient's social environment.

SUMMARY

An attitude can be considered to be a general predisposition to respond positively or negatively towards an object, a person, etc. Attitudes can be the result of direct experience with the environment or of what others tell us about the environment. They can serve various functions for the individual, such as the adjustive function, the ego-defensive function, the value-expressive function and the knowledge function. Attitudes tend to be consistent or consonant with each other and, when they are not, people are often motivated to eliminate or reduce the inconsistency or dissonance through attitude change. The process of attitude change can also be analyzed in terms of the persuasive communication situation: specifically, the communicator, the communication and the audience. Numerous aspects of this situation, including level of fear arousal, have been found to affect attitude change. Many of the principles of change discussed in this chapter and in the preceding one are relevant to the problem of inducing compliance and change in patients.

TERMS AND CONCEPTS

attitude
belief
non-conscious ideology
adjustive ⎫
ego-defensive ⎪ functions
value-expressive ⎬ of
knowledge ⎭ attitude
cognitive dissonance
credibility
fear arousal
innoculation

FOR DISCUSSION

1. Think of one of your attitudes. How did that attitude develop?

What function or functions do you think that it serves? Do you think it could be changed? If so, how?

2. What do you think are some of the factors that determine whether or not an attitude will be directly expressed by behaviour?

3. Think of some other situations besides those discussed in this chapter where dissonance reduction attempts could lead to attitude change.

4. Why do you think that the provision of the appropriate information alone does not necessarily result in the intended attitude or behaviour change?

5. Discuss some of the ways that doctors could make use of the principles of persuasive communication in their efforts to change patient attitudes and behaviour.

SUGGESTED READING

Bem: lucid paperback on attitudes and beliefs – highly recommended.

Festinger (1962): good introduction to cognitive dissonance theory.

Katz: classic article on the functions of attitudes.

McGuire: a complete, if at times tedious, review of the attitude change literature.

REFERENCES

Aronson, E. 1976. *The Social Animal.* (2nd ed) San Francisco: W. H. Freeman and Company.

Aronson, E. and Carlsmith, J. 1963. Effects of the severity of threat on the devaluation of forbidden behavior. *J. Abnorm. Soc. Psychol.* **66**, 584–8.

Aronson, E. and Mills, J. 1959. The effect of severity of initiation on liking for a group. *J. Abnorm. Soc. Psychol.* **59**, 177–81.

Bem, D. 1970. *Beliefs, Attitudes, and Human Affairs.* Belmont, Calif.: Brooks/Cole.

Festinger, L. 1957. *A Theory of Cognitive Dissonance.* Stanford: Stanford University Press.

Festinger, L. 1962. Cognitive dissonance. *Sci. Amer.* **207**, 93–107.

Festinger, L. and Carlsmith, J. 1959. Cognitive consequences of forced compliance. *J. Abnorm. Soc. Psychol.* **58**, 203–10.

Janis, I. and Feshbach, S. 1953. Effects of fear-arousing communications. *J. Abnorm. Soc. Psychol.* **48,** 78–92.

Janis, I., Kaye, D. and Kirschner, P. 1965. Facilitating effects of 'eating-while-reading' on responsiveness to persuasive communication. *J. Person. Soc. Psychol.* **1,** 181–6.

Katz, D. 1960. The functional approach to the study of attitude. *The Public Opinion Quart.* **24,** 163–204.

Knox, R. and Inkster, J. 1968. Postdecision dissonance at post time. *J. Person. Soc. Psychol.* **8,** 319–23.

Leventhal, H., Singer, R. and Jones, S. 1965. The effects of fear and specificity of recommendation upon attitudes and behavior. *J. Person. Soc. Psychol.* **2,** 20–29.

Mann, L. and Janis, I. 1968. A follow-up study on the long-term effects of emotional role playing. *J. Person. Soc. Psychol.* **8,** 339–42.

McGuire, W. 1969. The nature of attitudes and attitude change. In G. Lindzey and E. Aronson (eds) *The Handbook of Social Psychology.* (2nd edn) *III. The Individual in a Social Context* 136–314. Reading, Mass.: Addison-Wesley.

Staats, A. W. 1967. An outline of an integrated learning theory of attitude formation and function. In M. Fishbein (ed.) *Readings in Attitude Theory and Measurement,* 373–6. New York: John Wiley and Sons.

Staats, A. W., Staats, C. K. and Crawford, H. L. 1962. First-order conditioning of meaning and the parallel conditioning of a GSR. *J. Gen. Psychol.* **67,** 159–67.

Zimbardo, P., Weisenberg, M., Firestone, I. and Levy, B. 1969. Changing appetites for eating fried grasshoppers. In P. Zimbardo (ed.) *The Cognitive Control of Motivation* 44–54. Chicago: Scott, Foresman.

Chapter 16

Perception of Self and Others

In Chapter 4 we discussed the general topic of perception. Here we concentrate on how we perceive other people and how we perceive ourselves; two processes, as we shall see, which are highly interdependent. We are constantly observing those around us – what they say, what they do – and on this basis form impressions of who they really are and how they are likely to behave. We also form impressions of ourselves – what we are really like.

We first consider the perception of others, then the perception of ourselves, and finally the relevance of these processes to behaviour in medical settings.

PERCEPTION OF OTHERS

THE FORMATION OF IMPRESSIONS

As we constantly observe those around us, we make assumptions about them, about their personality, their motivations, their attitudes, their future behaviour and so on. Often these assumptions, which can be very elaborate, are based on little objective information. Consider the following description of one individual's behaviour:

> Jim left the house to get some stationery. He walked out into the sun-filled street with two of his friends, basking in the sun as he walked. Jim entered the stationery store which was full of people. Jim talked with an acquaintance while he waited for the clerk to catch his eye. On his way out, he stopped to chat with a school friend who was just coming into the store. Leaving the store, he walked toward school. On his way out he met the girl to whom he had been introduced the night before. They talked for a short while, and then Jim left for school. (Luchins 1957, p. 34).

Suppose you were given this description but no other information about Jim, and were then asked to answer questions about him, such as how friendly or unfriendly he is, how social or unsocial, how he is likely to behave in particular situations, etc. Could you answer these questions? Most of the subjects in a series of experiments by Luchins (1957) did. Furthermore, their answers were remarkably consistent.

Let us take another example. Suppose that, rather than a description of a person's behaviour, you were told that an individual possessed the following characteristics: intelligent, skilful, industrious, warm, determined, practical, cautious. Then you were presented with a series of pairs of traits and asked to select from each pair the one most likely to be possessed by the person, and finally, to write a character sketch of this person. This procedure was followed by Asch (1946). Once again, subjects tended to form similar impressions of this person: 91 per cent thought he was generous, 90 per cent happy, 91 per cent sociable, 100 per cent persistent, etc. The character sketches showed that complex detailed impressions were formed on the basis of just these seven characteristics. One subject described the person as '... a scientist performing experiments and persevering after many setbacks,' another as 'a person who believes certain things to be right, wants others to see his point, would be sincere in an argument and would like to see his point won.' (Asch 1946, p. 263).

Two main points emerge from our discussion so far. First of all, most people can form detailed and complicated impressions of others on the basis of very little information. And secondly, at least for these tasks, there does seem to be some agreement among the subjects; in other words, different people tend to form the same impression from the same cues.

If you think about the impressions you form of people, you will probably agree that these findings are not confined to laboratory experiments. In our everyday experience we constantly make assumptions about people from very few cues and, if we compare our assumptions with those made by our friends, they are often similar. For example, consider the impressions we form on the basis of physical appearance. A number of studies have demonstrated that we are quite willing to attribute a whole host of traits, likely behaviours, etc. merely on the basis of physical appearance cues, and often in the absence of any social contact with the person being judged. Some of these studies have investigated the effect of physical attractiveness (or the lack of it) on our impressions. In one study (Dion, Berscheid and Walster 1972), subjects were shown photographs of three people, one physically attractive, one of average physical attractiveness and one physically unattractive. They were then asked to rate these people on a number of personality characteristics, future happiness and occupational success. Attractive people were judged to have more socially desirable personality traits, happier marriages, more prestigious occupations, etc. than those of lesser attractiveness. Furthermore, in another study (Walster, Aronson, Abrahams and Rottmann 1966) which involved computerized dating, it was found that physical attractiveness was the most important determinant of how well people liked their date (as opposed to a number of personality characteristics measured prior to the date).

How do we form these impressions? How do we combine the different bits of information to form a consistent impression that allows us to make these elaborate extrapolations? Asch (1946), contends that '... the characteristics forming the basis of an impression do not contribute each a fixed, independent meaning, but that their content is itself partly a function of the environment of the other characteristics, of their mutual relations.' (p. 268). Thus the total impression is assumed to be more than merely the sum of its parts. Let us now consider some of the specific ways in which we combine the information to form an overall impression.

First impressions: Primary versus recency effects
How important are first impressions? To what extent are our opinions of people determined by our first contact with them? Consider the person described by another set of adjectives used by Asch: A) intelligent industrious impulsive critical stubborn envious. Now consider the person described by this set: B) envious stubborn critical impulsive industrious intelligent. The two lists are identical except for the order of the traits: the first list progresses from positive to negative traits, and the second from negative to positive. Asch (1946) found that the order of presentation does make a difference. Subjects presented with the first order formed a very different impression from those presented with the second, even though the total information available was the same. 'The impression produced by A is predominantly that of an able person who possesses certain shortcomings which do not, however, overshadow his merits. On the other hand, B impresses the majority as a "problem", whose abilities are hampered by his serious difficulties.' (Asch 1946, p. 270). As you can see, in both cases the adjectives presented first had the most effect on the impression formed. The latter adjectives are interpreted within the frame of reference established by the former adjectives.

Luchins (1957) found much the same effect using descriptions of behaviour. In addition to the earlier paragraph about Jim, Luchins also wrote the following one:

> After school Jim left the classroom alone. Leaving the school he started on his long walk home. The street was brilliantly filled with sunshine. Jim walked down the street on the shady side. Coming down the street toward him, he saw the pretty girl whom he had met on the previous evening. Jim crossed the street and entered a candy store. The store was crowded with students, and he noticed a few familiar faces. Jim waited quietly until the counterman caught his eye and then gave his order. Taking his drink, he sat down at a side table. When he had finished his drink he went home. (Luchins 1957, p. 35.)

When subjects read both paragraphs, some with the friendly Jim first and some with the withdrawn Jim first, the first paragraph exerted the most influence on their impressions as indicated by their answers to the questions about Jim. Luchins asked some subjects if they had noticed inconsistencies and if so, how they had resolved them. Although many subjects did not notice inconsistencies, or thought them too minor to worry about, Luchins (1957) reports that, 'When attempts to reconcile the two blocks were reported, they usually revealed that the first block was taken as portraying the 'real' Jim while the subsequent information was regarded as describing behaviour that had to be explained away.' (p. 54).

Although there is considerable support for the occurrence of **primacy effects**, it should be noted that under some conditions **recency effects** (relying more on the last bits of information presented) or no effects at all have been obtained. Some studies have shown that when the experimental procedure induces the subjects to attend to all of the information provided, the primacy effect disappears. These results suggest an alternative explanation for primacy effects to that proposed by Asch; specifically, rather than interpreting the latter information within the context of the former, subjects simply do not pay as much attention to latter information as they do to former information.

Central traits

Asch believed that not all the characteristics of the person would equally contribute to the total impression – some would be more important or more **central** than others, and affect the interpretation of less central ones. He presented subjects with one of the two following lists of traits: intelligent skilful industrious warm determined practical cautious; and intelligent skilful industrious cold determined practical cautious. The only difference between the lists is that cold is substituted for warm in the second. But this one difference produced substantial differences in the impressions formed by subjects, as indicated by the character sketches they wrote and the adjectives they checked. Impressions of the 'warm' person were more positive than those of the 'cold' person. The attribution of some characteristics, such as wisdom, humour, popularity and imaginativeness, were consistently related to the warm-cold variation, but others, such as reliability, honesty and physical attractiveness were not. Asch (1952) concluded that '... a change in one quality produces a fundamental change in the entire impression.' (p. 210). But this effect had its limitations. The warm person was not always viewed more positively than the cold person, as evidenced by the adjectives that did not differentiate the two. Also, the differences observed when 'polite' and 'blunt' were substituted for 'warm' and 'cold' were not nearly as impressive, indicating that traits vary in their ability to influence the overall impression. Finally, when warm and cold were combined with another set of adjectives: obedient, weak, shallow, unambitious and vain, they did not influence impressions to the same degree.

Other views of impression formation

Some attempts (Wishner 1960 for example) have been made to explain the effects of central traits in terms of the patterns of intercorrelations among traits, rather than the greater influence of some traits in determining the total impression. Some pairs of traits are more highly correlated than others: you may think that someone who is kind is also very likely to be gentle, but may or may not be intelligent. Moreover, some traits may be related to a greater number of traits than others. Wishner contends that the results obtained by Asch can be explained by looking at the intercorrelations between the traits presented to subjects and those on Asch's check list; warm-cold was correlated with many, but not all, of the adjectives on this list, and so appeared to have a large effect on subjects' impressions. It should be noted that this correlational approach does not necessarily contradict Asch's conception of central traits, but rather enables us to predict when a trait will be central.

Another more general approach to impression formation which has received considerable experimental support is known as **information integration**. Contrary to the holistic approach of Asch, the information integration approach considers each trait to make an independent contribution to our overall evaluation of the person. The traits possessed by an individual have various positive and negative values: intelligence may have a high positive value, absentmindedness a slight negative value, and so forth. These values are then combined to form our general evaluation of the person. All traits need not necessarily make an equal contribution to the overall evaluation; some may be weighted more heavily than others. This weighting makes sense in terms of our own experience with impression formation: whether or not a person has a sense of humour may have a greater effect on your evaluation than his or her punctuality.

ATTRIBUTION THEORY

Attribution theory views the individual as an amateur psychologist trying to understand the behaviour that he or she observes. As we have already explained, we are not content merely to observe behaviour; we want to know the 'why' behind the behaviour, the reason for it. Attributing causes to behaviour enables us to introduce structure and predictability to our environment. However, not all behaviour is indicative of underlying dispositions. So how do we decide which behaviour to count and which to discount in constructing our general impressions of others? And how do we decide which disposition to attribute on the basis of a particular act?

Heider (1958) describes how people in everyday life infer these underlying, relatively stable dispositions from their observations of behaviour and its effects. According to Heider the outcomes or effects that we observe are the result of a combination of environmental and personal forces. The relative contribution of each to the outcome can vary, and the environmental forces may aid or oppose personal forces. In perceiving others, we try to decide to what extent the outcome was caused by each of these types of forces.

Heider also distinguishes between personal and impersonal causality. **Personal causality** refers to acts intended by the person and **impersonal causality** to those that are unintended or caused by external forces. When we believe that effects are the result of personal causality, we think (under certain conditions) that it can tell us something about what the person is like, his or her motives, etc. But to the extent that we perceive the effects to result from impersonal causes, we tend to discount them as being representative of any underlying disposition of the person.

Jones and Davis (1965), in their analysis of the attribution process, assume that when inferring a general disposition we first look at the person's behaviour and its effects, and then decide to what extent the various effects were intentional. In attributing intention, we must believe that the person had both the knowledge of the effects and the ability to produce them. Then, from intentions, we infer underlying and relatively constant dispositions.

Even assuming that the behaviour and its effects were intentional, they are probably open to a wide range of interpretations. We still must decide what, if anything, a particular act tells us about the person. Jones and Davis (1965) use the term **correspondence** to refer to '... the extent that the act and the underlying characteristics or attitude are similarly described by the inference.' (p. 223); in other words, the extent to which a particular act is perceived to be indicative of a more general disposition. Some acts are very informative while others are not.

The degree of correspondence is dependent upon a number of factors. To begin with, the person must be perceived as having a choice: if the action was not done independently, or was severely constrained by the situation, the behaviour will be discounted. Also, to the extent that the act was the socially desirable thing to do, little information about the person is obtained; extreme behaviour, or behaviour which is not socially desirable, is more likely to result in a correspondent inference about the person. Another consideration is the extent to which a given act produces effects not produced by other acts. The fewer effects the observed act has in common with the person's other acts, the more likely we are to make a correspondent inference. If you observe that a person does favours for others, you may be unsure if he or she is kind and helpful, or trying to 'buy' friendship. If, however, you observe that this person does an unsolicited and anonymous favour for someone, your possible interpretations may be narrowed to kind and helpful.

Our discussion so far has assumed that the perceiver is a neutral, unbiased observer. But when the behaviour we are perceiving involves us, as it often does, we can hardly be considered objective observers or impartial 'inferers'. Jones and Davis (1965) contend that as our personal involvement increases, so does the likelihood that we will make a correspondent inference. If an observed act has positive or negative consequences for us, or if we perceive that the act was at least partly the result of our presence, we are more likely to assume that the act was the result of an intention and represents an underlying disposition.

In our efforts to identify the causes of behaviour, we tend to attribute our own actions to situational influences, while we tend to attribute the actions of others to underlying dispositions (see Jones and Nisbett 1971). Consequently, in forming our impressions of others, we may be too inclined to conclude that their behaviour is the result of personal dispositions while underestimating the effects of situational pressures and constraints.

ACCURACY OF IMPRESSIONS

Now that we have considered some of the mechanisms involved in the formation of impressions, we can ask how accurate these impressions are. When we make these sweeping assumptions about someone, how do they compare with the 'real' person?

Personality characteristics

A good person perceiver should be able to make accurate judgements about a range of characteristics of many different people: in other words, skill in person perception should be a general ability which is manifested in a wide variety of situations. It would seem reasonable to assume that some people are better at person perception than others. Early research attempted to identify the good person perceivers and the characteristics that differentiated them from those less skilled. In these studies, subjects were typically asked to make judgements about the attributes of another person or persons, which were then compared with some standard of accuracy (such as the other person's self ratings, evaluations of trained clinicians, personality tests, etc.).

However, there were a number of ways to make accurate judgements without really being a good person perceiver, i.e. to be right for the wrong reasons. For example, Bender and Hastorf (1953) contend that projection and similarity might partially account for accuracy scores. The assumption that another is similar to oneself provides a basis on which self-perceptions may be used to judge others. If the assumption is correct, the judgement will be correct; if the assumption is incorrect, the judgement, too, will be wrong. Here, accuracy depends upon the similarity of the judge and the person being judged rather than any skill at person perception. Another way to achieve accuracy without really being a good person perceiver is to base your judgements on your knowledge of the group being judged, rather than on your perceptions of its individual members (Brown 1965). To the extent that your knowledge of the group's average position or norm is accurate, your judgements of its individual members will tend to be accurate as well. The point of interest here, however, is that these ways of being right for the wrong reasons may actually reflect some of the ways that people make judgements in the real world. For instance, if you know that a man is a business executive and your knowledge of the average business executive is accurate, your judgements about the particular man may be accurate as well. However, your judgements based on similarity and projection, or on knowledge of the group, will only be accurate if you are similar to those being judged, or if your knowledge of the group is correct.

The question of who the accurate person perceivers are still remains, although interest in it seems to have declined. Brown (1965) sums up the research in this area by stating '... we do not know in what respects accurate person perception is a general characteristic and also do not know the qualities of an accurate judge.' (p. 647).

Approaching the problem from a somewhat different perspective, we can ask to what extent accurate person perception matters. Initially, it might be assumed that accurate person perception would be a useful skill, enabling one to deal more effectively with the people one encounters. However, the evidence has not always supported this assumption. Steiner (1955) cites some contradictory results: happily married couples were better than unhappily married ones at predicting each other's responses to the MMPI (Dymond 1953); ratings of group efficiency were related to the average ability of its members to predict each other's self ratings (Cottrell and Dymond 1949); but the ability of naval officers to judge the attitudes of their men was not related to their popularity (Campbell 1949); and the ability of office supervisors to perceive their subordinates accurately was not related to their popularity either (Sprunger 1949). Steiner suggests that this seemingly contradictory evidence can be explained by considering whether or not the group operates with a system of roles (see Chapter 17 for a discussion of the concept of role). When behaviour can be predicted from knowledge of the roles involved, accurate person perception may not improve the interaction. However, when there are no relevant roles from which to predict behaviour, accurate person perception may be important for smooth interaction.

Emotions

In addition to attributing personality characteristics, we also make assumptions about the more transitory states of emotion experienced by those around us. Once again, such assumptions, if correct, should promote smooth, predictable interactions. But how do we make these assumptions and how accurate are they?

In many early experiments, subjects were presented with a series of faces (for example, photographs from magazines, drawings, photographs of actors) each presumably portraying a particular emotion, and had to guess which emotion was being portrayed. But these studies did not consistently demonstrate that subjects could accurately perform this task. Woodworth (1938) examined the results of these studies and grouped together those emotions most often confused, and then ordered the groups so that mistakes were made most often between adjacent categories. The result was a one-dimensional scale of emotions with six categories: love-happiness-mirth; surprise; fear-suffering; anger-determination; disgust; and contempt. When these broader categories of emotion were used, subjects were found to be more accurate in their judgements than some of the early studies had indicated.

Schlosberg (1952) noting that the two end categories (love-happiness-mirth and contempt) tended to be confused, suggested a two-dimensional circular representation of these six categories and labelled the two dimensions pleasantness-unpleasantness and attention-rejection.

The research discussed so far has been confined to the recognition of emotion from faces, but in real life we use a variety of cues in addition to faces, such as voice and bodily movements. Such cues as tone of voice and sweating hands can be indicative of emotions, sometimes when facial expressions are not. Furthermore emotion does not usually occur in a vacuum but in the context of a particular situation, which also adds to our information about the emotion being experienced. Munn (1940), using pictures from *Life* magazine, showed that the accuracy of subjects' judgements of emotion increased when they were shown the context, i.e. the whole picture rather than just the face.

PERCEPTION OF SELF

In addition to perceiving others, we also perceive ourselves – what we say and what we do, and we make inferences about what we are really like – our personality traits, motivations, attitudes and so on. How do we make these inferences about ourselves, what information do we use? As discussed in Chapter 7, Schachter and Singer (1962) found that in defining our own emotional states, we use external cues, specifically the situational context, as well as internal ones.

Bem (1972) in his **self-perception theory** emphasizes the role played by our observations of our own behaviour, and the circumstances under which it occurs in the inferences we make about ourselves. This theory was originally developed as an alternative explanation for some of the results of cognitive dissonance experiments (see Chapter 15). Like cognitive dissonance theory, it claims that attitudes can follow from, rather than cause, behaviour. More generally, Bem contends that if we want to know what we think or how we feel, we use many of the same cues that others use when they decide what we think or how we feel, specifically our behaviour and the circumstances that surround it. However, it should be noted that when we do have clear and strong internal cues, our inferences can reflect this information which may not be available to an external observer.

We have stated before that other people are an important source of information about the world around us (see Chapters 14 and 15). **Social comparison theory** (Festinger 1954) contends that they are also an important source of information about ourselves, our opinions and abilities. Festinger (1954) claims that we have a need to evaluate our opinions and abilities. When we cannot do so in an objective, non-social way, we compare our opinions and abilities to those of others (usually others similar to ourselves), and thereby gain knowledge about ourselves.

One important point in these approaches, and in the discussion of self-perception which follows, is that much of our conception of who we are comes from our observations of the world external to us (including our own behaviour) rather than from within us.

INTERACTIVE APPROACH TO SELF PERCEPTION

Perception of ourselves is interrelated with our perception of others. When we perceive others, part of what we perceive is their perception of us, or more specifically, their reactions to us. Our perception of these reactions helps to determine our perception of ourselves and our self-concept – who we are, what we are really like.

Others not only react, but they also develop expectations for our behaviour. These reactions and expectations influence our view of ourselves and our subsequent behaviour. We saw one example of this effect in Chapter 2, when we discussed how the expectations of the experimenter could influence the behaviour of the subjects. However, this effect is not confined to the laboratory; it occurs in everyday life as well. Exactly how these reactions and expectations are communicated to us still remains unclear, but their influence on our conception of ourselves and on our behaviour is not disputed.

The relationship between our behaviour on the one hand, and our perceptions of these reactions and expectations on the other, is not simple: each can affect the other. Not only can our behaviour affect the reactions and expectations of others, particularly when their information about us is limited, but these expectations and reactions can also influence our behaviour. Over time, behaviour and expectations become fairly consistent, as exemplified by our occasional description of someone as 'acting out of character'. Moreover, when we interact with much the same people over long periods of time, such as our family, our friends, our teachers, etc., we tend to get locked in to certain behaviours and certain ways of responding.

Sometimes we can get locked in to a behaviour pattern or role that we would subsequently like to change. But those around us tend to keep us in the old familiar role. Consider the high-school student who has always attracted attention by being the class clown, but eventually decides that other, more serious aspects of his personality are more important, and would like some recognition for them. Changing his image may prove to be remarkably difficult. Others expect him to make jokes and simply may not attend to other aspects of his actions and conversation or, in other subtle ways, promote the continuance of his expected role.

These expectations can become self-fulfilling prophecies, regardless of whether or not they are accurate. If you believe that someone is friendly, you will be friendly toward them, thereby eliciting the behaviour you expected. Similarly, if you expect that someone is hostile toward you, your behaviour toward them may in fact elicit the expected hostile reaction. Furthermore, we attend to behaviour that supports our impressions and confirms our expectations. Behaviour that does not may be distorted and interpreted to fit our original impressions and expectations, particularly when the behaviour itself is open to many interpretations.

As discussed in Chapter 8, Rosenthal and Jacobson (1968) found direct experimental support for the effects of expectations on behaviour in a classroom setting. Teachers were led to believe that certain pupils would bloom intellectually. Despite the fact that these students were selected randomly, they actually did show more subsequent intellectual gains than other students.

Another somewhat frightening experiment demonstrated the effects of expectations on subsequent interpretations of behaviour (Rosenham 1973). Eight sane people were admitted to a psychiatric hospital and labelled schizophrenic, on the basis of an interview during which they feigned symptoms of mental illness. Regardless of their subsequent 'normal' behaviour in the hospital, the staff interpreted their actions in terms of their label, that is as symptomatic of their 'illness'.

IMPRESSION MANAGEMENT

This interactive process of person perception and self-perception is more complicated still. According to Goffman (1959), not only are we aware that others are forming impressions of us, but we try, to a greater or lesser extent, to structure these impressions. We try to present others with a view of ourselves that will lead them to conclude what we want them to conclude, (**impression management**). To this end, we manipulate what we say and what we do. However, those who perceive us are not completely taken in. They realize that some aspects of our behaviour are relatively easy to control, such as what we say, while others, such as non-verbal behaviour, may not be. According to Goffman, others use the latter, presumably more difficult to control, behaviours as a check on the image presented by more easily controlled behaviours. However, as you might have anticipated, clever people are aware of these checks and attempt to control their 'spontaneous' behaviour as well, thus presenting a totally consistent image. But others may suspect this added control and look for some flaw in the performance which is indicative of the 'true' self. *The Selling of the President 1968* (McGinniss 1970), a detailed description of Nixon's 1968 presidential campaign, is a good real-life example of this image manipulation process.

A NOTE ON SELF-ESTEEM

We not only perceive the self, we also evaluate the self. These evaluations, like other aspects of self-perception, are to a large extent dependent on information from external sources. As we have already discussed, our own evaluation of our opinions and abilities often comes from a comparison with those of others. Level of **self-esteem** has been found to be related to many aspects of social behaviour;

people who believe in their own worth do tend to behave differently from those who do not (also, see discussion in Chapter 9). To mention just a few findings, people with low self-esteem are more persuasible, conform more, have lower goals, and report higher levels of anxiety than people with high self-esteem. These differences are captured well by Ziller's contention that 'persons with high self-esteem as opposed to those with low self-esteem tend to control the environment, whereas persons with low self-esteem tend to be controlled by the environment.' (1973, p. xv).

PERCEPTION IN DOCTOR-PATIENT INTERACTIONS

Knowledge of the processes of person perception and self perception can contribute to our understanding of doctor-patient interactions. Before the doctor can decide on treatment, the condition of the patient must be assessed. To a greater or lesser extent assessment may be based on information provided by the patient during an interview. While the patient is describing the complaint, the doctor is observing the patient, interpreting the description, and forming an impression of the patient and his or her condition. In other words, the factors which influence our perceptions and misperceptions of others can, to some extent, affect the diagnosis and consequently the treatment.

When confronted with a new patient, the doctor rapidly forms an impression. Cues such as physical appearance, tone of voice and other non-verbal aspects of behaviour, as well as what the patient actually says, may contribute to this impression; and this first impression, as we have seen, can have a significant effect on the subsequent overall impression. What would be a doctor's first impression of a new patient who requests a medical certificate despite being perfectly healthy and merely feigning symptoms? Most likely a negative one, perhaps accompanied by assumptions that the person is generally lazy, deceitful, irresponsible, and so forth. Although this behaviour may be atypical, the doctor's impression, once formed, may affect future interactions with this patient. Furthermore, if such behaviour were displayed by another patient whom the doctor had known and respected for twenty years, his interpretation of it would probably be quite different.

Another factor which may affect impression formation, and which we have not considered, is the resemblance of the perceived person to others we have encountered. Most of us have had the experience of meeting a new person who, for some reason, reminds us of someone else. We then tend to attribute to the new person those characteristics attributed to the other person, regardless of whether or not they are applicable. For example, if a male patient reminds a doctor of a middle-aged uncle who is domineering and overbearing, the doctor may assume that this patient has these traits and act toward him as if towards the uncle. Assumption and attributions made on this basis have the potential to interfere with smooth doctor-patient interaction and communication.

Impressions formed on this erroneous basis, or any other basis for that matter, tend to be self-perpetuating and resistant to change (as we discussed before), whether or not they are accurate. Consider a patient who has presented the doctor with many minor trivial complaints over a period of time and consequently has been labelled a 'hypochondriac'. If this patient actually becomes ill, how will the doctor's expectations affect the seriousness with which the complaint is viewed? An extreme example of the effects of expectations on reactions is found in the Rosenham (1973) study cited above.

Doctors must remember that patients also are perceiving, and forming impressions and expectations. Many of the same cues used by doctors, such as physical appearance, can contribute to the impressions of doctors formed by patients. In addition, patients will be deciding from their observations whether or not to attribute to the doctor such qualities as competence, genuine concern with their condition, concern with fees etc; needless to say, such attributions can potentially affect the treatment outcome.

Many more examples could be given to illustrate the importance of the processes discussed in this chapter. The main point here is that only through an awareness and an understanding of these processes can we attempt to control them and their potential detrimental effects on health care situations.

SUMMARY

When we perceive others, we often form detailed complicated impressions of what they are like on the basis of very little information. Generally, first impressions exert greater influence on our total impression than later information. Some traits may influence our impression more than others, although there is evidence for some alternative views of the impression formation process. When we attribute underlying dispositions on the basis of our observations, we must first decide to what extent the outcome was intended by the person, and if intended, what the behaviour tells us about the person's dispositions. Research on our ability to perceive personality characteristics accurately has been inconclusive, but we do tend to be able to distinguish among broad categories of emotions.

Our main source of information about ourselves is our perceptions of those around us. Their reactions and expectations to some extent determine our impressions of ourselves and our behaviour. Once formed, such expectations for the behaviour of others are very difficult to change and can become self-fulfilling prophecies.

Awareness of the processes of person perception and self-perception can contribute to our understanding of doctor-patient interactions.

TERMS AND CONCEPTS

primary and recency effects
central traits
information integration
attribution theory
personal causality
impersonal causality
correspondence
self-perception theory
social comparison theory
impression management
self-esteem

FOR DISCUSSION

1. Assume that you have just met someone for the first time and conversed with them for five minutes. On what sorts of information would your impression of that person be based? To what extent would you feel confident in attributing personality characteristics and predicting future behaviour on the basis of this information? Do you think that your first impression would be modified by future information that is inconsistent with it?

2. Why do you think that people are willing to attribute so many positive characteristics solely on the basis of physical attractiveness?

3. What information do you think doctors would use in forming a first impression of a patient? What information do you think patients would use in forming a first impression of a doctor?

4. To what extent do you think that the expectations of those around you (parents, friends, etc.) influence your own behaviour? What do you think their reactions would be if you radically modified some aspect of yourself, for example your style of dress?

SUGGESTED READING

Asch (1946): classic series of studies on impression formation.

Dion, Berscheid and Walster: interesting study of the effects of physical attractiveness on impressions and attributions.

Goffman: interesting analysis of interpersonal behaviour and perceptions.

Rosenham: essential reading for medical students.

REFERENCES

Asch, S. 1946. Forming impressions of personality. *J. Abnorm. Soc. Psychol.* **41,** 258–90.

Asch, S. 1952. *Social Psychology.* New York: Prentice-Hall.

Bem, D. 1972. Self-perception theory. In L. Berkowitz (ed.) *Advances in Experimental Social Psychology* **6.** New York: Academic Press, Inc.

Bender, I. E. and Hastorf, A. H. 1953. On measuring generalized empathic ability (social sensitivity). *J. Abnorm. Soc. Psychol.* **48,** 503–6.

Brown, R. 1965. *Social Psychology.* New York: Free Press.

Campbell, D. T. 1949. Ohio State University, Personal Research Board. *Studies in Naval Leadership.* Columbus: Ohio State Univ. Research Foundation.

Cottrell, L. and Dymond, R. 1949. The empathic responses: A neglected field for research. *Psychiatry* **12,** 355–9.

Dion, K., Berscheid, E. and Walster, E. 1972. What is beautiful is good. *J. Person. Soc. Psychol.* **24,** 285–90.

Dymond, R. 1953. The relation of accuracy of perception of the spouse and marital happiness. *Amer. Psychol.* **8,** 344 (Abstract).

Festinger, L. 1954. A theory of social comparison processes. *Human Relations* **7,** 117–40.

Goffman, E. 1959. *The Presentation of Self in Everyday Life.* New York: Doubleday-Anchor.

Heider, F. 1958. *The Psychology of Interpersonal Relations.* New York: Wiley.

Jones, E. E. and Davis, K. E. 1965. From acts to dispositions: The attribution process in person perception. In L. Berkowitz (ed.) *Advances in Experimental Social Psychology* **2** 219–66. New York: Academic Press.

Jones, E. E. and Nisbett, R. E. 1971. The actor and the observer: Divergent perceptions of the causes of behavior. In E. E. Jones *et al.* (eds), *Attribution: Perceiving the Causes of Behavior.* Morristown, New Jersey: General Learning Press.

Luchins, A. 1957. Primacy-recency in impression formation. In C. Hovland, W. Mandell, E. Campbell, T. Brock, A. Luchins, A. Cohen, W. McGuire, I. Janis, R. Feierabend and N. Anderson, *The Order of Presentation in Persuasion* 33–61. New Haven: Yale University Press.

McGinniss, J. 1970. *The Selling of the President 1968.* New York: Pocket Books.

Munn, N. 1940. The effect of knowledge of the situation upon judgment of emotion from facial expressions. *J. Abnorm. Soc. Psychol.* **35**, 324–38.

Rosenham, D. L. 1973. On being sane in insane places. *Science* **179**, 250–8.

Rosenthal, R. and Jacobson, L. 1968. *Pygmalion in the Classroom: Teacher Expectation and Pupils' Intellectual Development.* New York: Holt, Rinehart and Winston.

Schachter, S. and Singer, J. 1962. Cognitive, social and physiological determinants of emotional state. *Psychol. Rev.* **69**, 379–99.

Schlosberg, H. 1952. The description of facial expression in terms of two dimensions. *J. Exp. Psychol.* **44**, 229–37.

Sprunger, J. A. 1949. Relationship of a test of ability to estimate group opinion to other variables. Unpublished Master's Thesis. Ohio State University.

Steiner, I. 1955. Interpersonal behavior as influenced by accuracy of social perception. *Psychol. Rev.* **62**, 268–74.

Walster, E., Aronson, V., Abrahams, D. and Rottman, L. 1966. Importance of physical attractiveness in dating behavior. *J. Person. Soc. Psychol.* **4**, 508–16.

Wishner, J. 1960. Reanalysis of 'impressions of personality'. *Psychol. Rev.* **67**, 96–112.

Woodworth, R. S. 1938. *Experimental Psychology.* New York: Holt.

Ziller, R. C. 1973. *The Social Self.* New York: Pergamon Press, Inc.

Chapter 17

Roles

The concept of 'role' enables us to understand and predict behaviour in a variety of social situations. At times, knowledge of a person's role can be more important in predicting behaviour than knowledge of personality. This is usually the case in medical settings, where the roles of doctor and patient are well defined and the personalities of the individuals playing these roles may have relatively little effect on the course of the doctor-patient interaction.

In this chapter we first consider the concepts of role and role conflict in general terms, and then apply these concepts to behaviour in medical settings.

This chapter considers formal roles – those positions prescribed by society that can be occupied by a number of persons. Informal or emergent roles, those that result from the social interaction of particular people and generally apply only to the individuals involved, will be discussed in Chapter 18.

THE CONCEPT OF ROLES

DEFINING ROLES

A **role** can be defined as a set of norms for the behaviour of a person in a particular position, such as mother, teacher, judge, doctor, clergyman, student, prime minister, child, shop assistant, etc. The term role applies to *achieved* positions – those we work to attain, such as occupation – as well as *ascribed* positions – those we have no control over, such as age and sex. These norms for behaviour are usually not written down in any formal sense, but rather are generally agreed upon by the members of society. Sometimes, the fact that such norms exist may not be given a great deal of attention until some violation of them occurs, such as a mother abandoning her child or a judge accepting a bribe.

Roles, like other social behaviour, must be learned (see Chapters 6 and 9), and the amount of learned behaviour for acceptable role performance varies. Some roles, such as that of customer at a grocery store, do not require a great deal of complicated behaviour and are easily mastered. Others, such as that of doctor, require very complex patterns of behaviour, which may necessitate a formal training period and some sort of official admission to the role.

Individuals typically occupy more than one, and often many, roles at the same time. One person may simultaneously occupy the roles of father, husband, son, brother, teacher, chairman of a citizen's committee on the environment, boy scout leader and soccer coach, among others. Furthermore, individuals occupy different roles at different stages of life: a person is first a child, then a student, then perhaps a doctor or a teacher, and finally a pensioner, in addition to the other roles he or she may occupy at any given time. But regardless of the individuals who pass in and out of a role, the role itself remains. In other words, roles transcend the individuals who occupy them. The role of company vice-president is a well established position requiring a particular pattern of behaviour, independent of the individuals who are appointed to that position and subsequently resign, retire or are fired. In this sense, role is a structural concept and society can be viewed as a complex system of roles.

Although roles are prescribed by society they are enacted by individuals, and each person will have his or her own conception of what a particular role involves – of what it means to be a good mother, a good doctor or a good student. This conception may be very close to what most people think the role involves, or it may deviate from the majority opinion to a greater or lesser extent. Furthermore, actual role behaviour may or may not be consistent with a person's conception of the role, mainly because the actual behaviour will depend upon other factors as well, such as the person's personality and other roles.

As we saw in Chapter 16, the expectations of other people do influence our behaviour, and role behaviour is no exception. Other people have expectations for the behaviour of an individual in a given role – they have their own ideas about how a good mother, a good doctor or a good student should act. These expectations may or may not be in accordance with the individual's actual role behaviour: role performances that agree with the expectations of the relevant others are generally reinforced and those that do not, are not.

ROLES AND INTERACTION

Roles typically exist in complementary or reciprocal pairs such as mother-child, teacher-student, doctor-patient, employee-employer, husband-wife. Two roles are termed complementary or **reciprocal** if the nature of one cannot be fully described without reference to the other. It is very difficult to describe the role of mother without mentioning the role of child, or the role of doctor without mentioning the role of patient.

Role behaviour generally involves interaction between persons occupying reciprocal roles, and the course of this interaction is prescribed by the norms associated with each of these roles: each person not only knows how to behave, but also what behaviour to expect from the occupant of a reciprocal role. In this sense, roles can be viewed as rules for the interaction of positions; they set bounds on the possible events that can occur in interaction sequences which involve those roles. Ordinarily, a doctor is not expected to ask the patient to make the diagnosis and prescribe the treatment, nor is a teacher expected to make sexual advances to his or her students.

Therefore, when we interact with people who occupy given roles, we can predict their behaviour on the basis of their role, or at least rule out the possibility of certain types of inappropriate behaviour occurring. Being able to predict the course of interaction makes us feel more comfortable. When you interact with your family and friends you know what to expect. You have known these people for a long time – you can predict their behaviour and your interaction with them because of your past experience with them and your knowledge of their personalities. But most of us have to interact every day with a variety of people we have never met before. Imagine how chaotic and confusing life would be, if predicting the behaviour of these people depended upon detailed knowledge of their individual personalities rather than knowledge of their roles.

ROLE AND PERSONALITY

Roles differ in the amount of individual variation that will be accepted as a good role performance; for the role of priest carrying out High Mass, very little individual variation will be allowed, whereas for the role of student, a range of idosyncratic behaviour will be accepted. In addition, roles also vary in the amount of the individual's total behaviour that is prescribed: the role of prisoner prescribes much of the daily behaviour of the occupant, whereas the role of chairman of a committee that meets once a week does not.

Certainly an individual's personality affects his interpretation of his role, and therefore some individual variation in performance will be present in even the most explicitly prescribed roles. However, roles also have an effect on the individual. Some roles, particularly those which prescribe a great deal of daily behaviour, or those which the individual has occupied for a period of time, can become an integral part of an individual's self identity. As a result, they can affect not only behaviour but attitudes and values as well. Loss or removal of such a role can cause feelings of loss of identity, as experienced by some people upon retirement when suddenly they are no longer a teacher, or a doctor, or a policeman.

The relationship between role and individual attitudes was the subject of an interesting field study conducted in a factory (Lieberman 1956). Initially, a number of workers in this factory completed a questionnaire designed to assess their attitudes towards both management and unions. By about fifteen months later, some of these workers had become foremen while others had been elected stewards. When the same questionnaire was administered again, the expected results were obtained: generally speaking, new foremen became more pro-management and new stewards more pro-union when compared to control groups of workers who had not changed their positions. In two years time, some of the new foremen and some of the new stewards had returned to the role of rank-and-file worker. Compared with those who remained in these positions, those who had been foremen appeared to return to the attitudes they had expressed on the first questionnaire, although the results for those who had been stewards were not as consistent.

The influence of occupational roles on individuals is obvious to many people uninitiated in social psychology, as evidenced by the familiar comment 'he's really changed since he's been promoted'. However, roles which the individual has not occupied for a long period of time, nor is particularly committed to, can also have a substantial effect on that individual – a fact that is not so obvious.

In a study involving a simulated prison situation, Zimbardo *et al.* (1973) demonstrated that such roles could have a profound effect on people. Student volunteers, who were screened for emotional stability and paid $15 a day for their participation in this 'live-in' experiment, were randomly assigned to the role of either prisoner or guard. Although they knew they were in an experiment, the situation was constructed to simulate most of the psychological conditions found in real prisons. After only six days, the students had internalized their roles to such an extent that the experimenters ended what was to have been a two week experiment. The following passage illustrates the effects of the reciprocal roles of guard and prisoner on the subjects:

> You cannot be a prisoner if no one will be your guard, and you cannot be a prison guard if no one takes you or your prison seriously. Therefore, over time a perverted symbiotic relationship developed. As the guards became more aggressive, prisoners became more passive; assertion by the guards led to dependency in the prisoners; self-aggrandizement was met with self-deprecation, authority with helplessness, and the counterpart of the guards' sense of mastery and control was the depression and hopelessness witnessed in the prisoners. As these differences in behavior, mood and perception became more evident to all, the need for the now 'righteously' powerful guards to rule the obviously inferior and powerless inmates became a sufficient reason to support almost any further indignity of man against man ... (p. 40–2).

ROLE CONFLICTS

Role conflicts arise when an individual finds it difficult or impossible to meet the expectations that others have for his or her behaviour as an occupant of a particular role. When this happens, smooth predictable interaction is disrupted to a greater or lesser extent, and the people involved may experience considerable discomfort. In addition, the general goals of the interaction, such as production in a factory, medical treatment in a hospital, or child care in a family may be impeded as a result.

Brown (1965) has described three general types of role conflict, although these are by no means the only ones that can occur.

Inter-role conflict. Individuals usually occupy more than one role, but in most cases these different roles are enacted at different times or places. Occasionally, however, two roles may prescribe behaviour for the same situation and these prescriptions may be mutually exclusive. The individual cannot meet the demands of both roles at once. An example of this type of conflict is the situation where a university lecturer finds that his daughter has enrolled in his class; the roles of lecturer and parent make inconsistent demands regarding behaviour toward the student-daughter.

Intra-role conflict. There are two types of intra-role conflict, and in both cases the conflict results from inconsistent expectations for the behaviour associated with one role. Usually a role will have more than one reciprocal role, for example the role of teacher has the reciprocal roles of both student and principal, and a woman may have reciprocal roles with both her child and her husband. Role conflict can occur when these different reciprocal roles make incompatible demands on the person in the middle, i.e. the teacher or the woman. The second type of intra-role conflict occurs when different occupants of the *same* reciprocal role have different expectations, which may or may not agree with the role occupant's conception of the role. In a restaurant, a waiter may be attending to several customers at once and some may expect him to make jokes and conversation, while others expect him to serve quietly and unobtrusively.

Role-personality conflict. Individuals can find themselves in roles that prescribe behaviour that is incompatible with their personalities. Some soldiers, for example, may find the regimentation of army life difficult to adjust to; an insurance salesman who is not aggressive or gregarious may not be particularly happy or successful in his work. Those who value the ideal of equality may find it difficult to enact roles which emphasize status differences, for example roles typically found in military organizations.

ROLES AND ROLE CONFLICTS IN MEDICAL SETTINGS

THE ROLES OF PATIENT AND DOCTOR

The reciprocal roles of doctor and patient are well-defined and the course of doctor-patient interaction is governed by the norms associated with these roles. The ability to predict this interaction, at least within certain limits, enables doctors and patients who have never met before to interact with relative ease, even when a patient must undergo a physical examination or reveal very personal information.

The sick role: *prescriptions for behaviour during illness.* Parsons (1951) lists four prescriptions of the sick role:

First is the exemption from normal social role responsibilities, which of course is relative to the nature and severity of the illness. This exemption requires legitimation by and to the various alters [others] involved and the physician often serves as a court of appeal as well as a direct legitimatizing agent ...

The second closely related aspect is the institutionalized definition that the sick person cannot be expected by 'pulling himself together' to get well by an act of decision or will ... This element in the definition of the state of illness is obviously crucial as a bridge to the acceptance of 'help'.

The third element is the definition of the state of being ill as itself undesirable with its obligation to want to 'get well' ...

Finally, the fourth closely related element is the obligation – in proportion to the severity of the condition, of course – to seek *technically competent* help, namely, in the most usual case, that of a physician and to *cooperate* with him in the process of trying to get well. (p. 436–7).

Implicit in this description is the child-like dependency of the patient on the all-knowing 'parent' doctor. The patient is expected to accept without question the prescribed treatment, and to relinquish the decision making function he or she ordinarily exercises.

Individuals vary in their willingness to adopt the sick role. Sometimes their desire, or lack of it, to adopt this role, i.e. define themselves as ill, does not agree with the medical evaluation of the situation (see Chapter 11). Some people attempt to gain admission to the sick role when in fact their state of health does not warrant it. For these people the sick role is probably very attractive: they are relieved of everyday responsibilities and receive more attention and concern from those around them than they would ordinarily. Other people, who are quite ill from the medical point of view, find it very difficult to think of themselves as ill, perhaps because of the conflicting demands of family or work, or because to them, admission of illness is equivalent to the admission of weakness, or for other reasons.

What determines how an individual will respond to symptoms and at what stage will personal illness be recognised and medical help sought? Mechanic (1966) lists seven factors that can affect **illness behaviour**.

1) the number and persistence of symptoms; 2) the individual's ability to recognize symptoms; 3) the perceived seriousness of symptoms; 4) the extent of social and physical disability resulting from the symptoms; 5) the cultural background of the defining person, group or agency in terms of the emphasis on tolerance, stoicism, etc.; 6) available information and medical knowledge; and 7) the availability of sources of help and their social and physical accessibility. Here we include not only physical

distance and costs of time, money and effort, but also such costs as 'fear', stigma, social distance, feelings of humiliation and the like. (p. 17).

The degree to which these sick role prescriptions apply depends upon how sick the patient actually is. The more serious the complaint the more the patient will be expected to adhere to the sick role. Needless to say, hospitalized patients will experience greater dependency and less control over their daily activities than outpatients, and in their case the sick role takes precedence over any other roles. Brown (1963), in describing the experience of hospitalization from the patients' point of view, claims that the patients, already experiencing anxiety over a variety of problems, are faced with an impersonal, unfamiliar environment which robs them of their identities. Brown writes: 'The patient is frequently not known as a college professor, an expert steel riveter, an exceptionally fine homemaker, or a champion fisherman; he is the occupant of the second bed in Room 34, or the patient with gallstones, a broken hip, "Ca" or "CVA". The individual has been reduced to the anonymity of a horizontal figure between white sheets.' (p. 119).

It is interesting to speculate about the desirability of these expectations for sick role behaviour, particularly with the decline in acute illness coupled with the increase of conditions requiring long term active participation of the patient in his or her treatment. Although Parsons' conception of the patient role may apply to seriously ill patients who may or may not be hospitalized, much of the actual behaviour of non-hospitalized patients does not conform to this conception. For example, patients do not always follow doctors' instructions. Stimson (1974) reviews nineteen studies of the use of prescribed drugs in non-hospitalized patients, and reports that the percentage of patients 'defaulting' from doctors' instructions varies from nineteen to seventy-two per cent, and is usually thirty per cent or more. In attempting to account for this patient behaviour, he argues that patients are decision makers who evaluate both the prescribed drug and the doctor in terms of their own experience and the experiences of those around them. The advice of the doctor is only one of many sources of influence on the patient's decision to take the drug as prescribed or not. From this point of view, the three models of doctor-patient interaction proposed by Szasz and Hollender (1956) may have wider applicability than Parsons' (1951) description of the sick role.

They propose three types of doctor-patient relationships depending upon the severity of the patient's condition. The first they describe as **activity-passivity**. This type of relationship applies when the patient is acutely ill, or injured and helpless, and the treatment proceeds without any real effort on the patient's part. The second type of relationship, **guidance-cooperation**, applies to less acute situations where the patient is ill but aware of the situation and capable of participating in the treatment, to the extent of acknowledging that the doctor 'knows best' and following doctor's orders. **Mutual participation**, the third type of relationship, is applicable to the treatment of chronic diseases such as diabetes and high blood pressure where the patient actively participates in the treatment, and doctor and patient approach each other more as equals than in the other two types of relationship.

Role of doctor

The traditional doctor-patient relationship is asymmetrical: in sharp contrast to the dependency and helplessness of the patient role described by Parsons (1951) is the power associated with the role of doctor.

Parsons (1951), in discussing the role of doctor, states 'The primary definition of the physician's responsibility is to "do everything possible" to forward the complete, early and painless recovery of his patients.' (p. 450). In addition to this very general statement he describes various aspects of the doctor's professional attitude towards patients, perhaps the most important of which is **affective neutrality**. By this he means that a doctor must 'stand back' emotionally from his patients; he must not display the same degree of involvement in the patient's plight as would family and friends. He must be detached, and keep any emotional reactions he does have in check so that they do not affect his judgement as a medical practitioner. This essential aspect of the professional role is not always easily learned. According to Leif and Fox (1963), medical students typically have difficulty at first in considering patients in non-emotional, medical terms; they pass through a stage of detachment characterized by '... a pseudoscientific attitude in which students imitate their instructors, talk professional jargon, and try to act as impersonally as possible toward their patients. They are all business: "I admitted two coronaries last night." "Did you hear that great aortic insufficiency on Dr B's ward?"' (p. 34); and, finally they achieve an appropriate balance in attitude.

Parsons (1951) also discusses two other aspects of professional attitude – universalism and functional specificity – which are both closely related to affective neutrality. The term **universalism** refers to the norm that doctors should treat all patients alike and not let the particular non-medical details, such as race and social class, influence the treatment. The closely related norm of **functional specificity** prescribes that the doctor should only be concerned with those aspects of the patient that are directly relevant to his or her medical problem – the disease must be treated, and not necessarily the person.

Bloom and Wilson (1972) suggest that these two aspects of professional attitude may not be as applicable to the role of doctor as they once were, because of the current trend to 'treat the whole person', while also pointing out the applicability of functional specificity to the trend toward specialization. Menke (1971) also suggests that the role of doctor is changing, but in a way different from, although not incompatible with that suggested by Bloom and Wilson. He contends that the ideal of the family doctor in his individual private practice is being superseded (due to technological necessity) by other medical roles. In addition to specialization and group practice, Menke writes: 'By virtue of changing work environments, a physician may be a healer, a scientist, a bureaucrat, an organization man and a businessman as well as a professional. In some circumstances, he may even be a clerk, an auditor, a book-keeper and a bill collector. One of the difficulties of being a bureaucrat, if a doctor practises in a hospital environment, is that he is also a professional and a healer; he may be an administrator and a supervisor as well.' (1971, p. 63).

ROLE CONFLICTS IN MEDICAL SETTINGS

Role conflicts in medical settings are not at all uncommon. It is important that the source of both existing and potential conflicts be understood, so that their disruptive effects on social interaction can be eliminated or at least minimized. All of the types of role conflict discussed earlier can be found in medical situations. We will now consider some examples, but these are not meant to constitute an exhaustive list of the conflicts that can occur.

Perhaps the classic inter-role conflict occurs when a doctor's own child arrives as an accident victim in Casualty. The role of doctor demands affective neutrality but the role of parent implies emotional concern (perhaps to the point of panic) over the child's condition. It is precisely to avoid this type of conflict that doctors seldom treat members of their own family, at least for serious ailments.

An example of intra-role conflict resulting from the inconsistent expectations of two reciprocal roles is that experienced by the nurse, when directions from a doctor (one reciprocal role) contradict those of the nurse's superior (another reciprocal role) representing the hospital administration. This conflict was the subject of the field study of the behaviour of nurses discussed in Chapter 14 (Hofling *et al.* 1966). As mentioned in Chapter 14, the resolution of this conflict for the vast majority was to follow the doctor's directions.

Intra-role conflict, produced by inconsistent expectations of those individuals occupying the same reciprocal role, can be experienced by the general practitioner who treats a variety of patients whose expectations for a doctor's behaviour do not agree. Some may expect a friendly, casual approach while others expect a certain degree of cool aloofness; some may expect a detailed explanation of the cause of the complaint while others may not. Expectations may vary depending upon the age and social class of the patient as well. Consequently it is not unusual to find general practitioners adjusting their role behaviour from one patient to another.

Role-personality conflict may be experienced by a hospitalized patient. Adaptation to the sick role, particularly the child-like dependence and acceptance as well as the lack of control over the environment, may be very difficult for a person who is normally dominant, and is used to exercising a high degree of environmental control. However, Lorber (1975) reports that of 103 surgical patients, only 28 expressed attitudes about hospital patient behaviour that deviated from 'good patient' behaviour. Nonetheless, it has often been said that doctors make the worst patients!

SUMMARY

A role can be defined as a set of norms for the behaviour of a person in a particular position. Knowledge of the roles that are relevant to a given situation enables us to predict the behaviour of the people involved, without detailed knowledge of their personalities. Not only the individual's behaviour but personal attitudes and values can be influenced by the roles occupied.

Role conflicts occur when an individual finds it difficult or impossible to meet the expectations that others have for his role behaviour. Three common types of conflict are inter-role, intra-role and role-personality conflict.

A great deal of the behaviour in medical settings can be understood in terms of roles and role conflicts. The reciprocal roles of doctor and patient are well defined and govern the interaction of individuals who occupy these roles. Potentially disruptive role conflicts of each of the types discussed can occur in medical settings.

TERMS AND CONCEPTS

role
reciprocal role
inter-role ⎫
intra-role ⎬ types of role conflict
role-personality ⎭
the sick role
illness behaviour
activity-passivity ⎫
guidance-cooperation ⎬ models of the doctor-patient relationship
mutual participation ⎭
affective neutrality
universalism
functional specificity

FOR DISCUSSION

1. Think of the role of medical student. What are the generally agreed upon norms for behaviour associated with this role? What areas of behaviour are open to individual interpretation? To what extent do you think your own concept of the role of medical student agrees with that of your fellow students, and with that of the faculty?

2. Can you think of a time you experienced role conflict? If so, what type of conflict was it? How do you think such conflicts can be minimized or eliminated?

3. Have you ever been in the 'sick role'? How well did you adjust to this role? What part did those around you play in putting you in the role and reinforcing appropriate role behaviour? What do you think can be done to help bridge the gap between normal participation in society and the sick role, particularly with hospital patients?

4. Consider the examples of role conflict in medical settings given in this chapter. What other specific examples of such conflicts can you think of? How would you go about minimizing these?

SUGGESTED READING

Bloom and Wilson: comparison of different models of the doctor-patient relationship.

Brown: hospitalization from the patient's point of view.

Lief and Fox: development of the attitude of detached concern.

Parsons, chapter 10: a bit long, but a classic sociological analysis of medical practice.

Mechanic: factors affecting illness behaviour and the adoption of the role of patient.

REFERENCES

Bloom, S. W. and Wilson, R. N. 1972. Patient-practitioner relationships. In H. E. Freeman, S. Levine and L. G. Reeder (eds) *Handbook of Medical Sociology* (2nd end) Englewood Cliffs, New Jersey: Prentice-Hall.

Brown, E. L. 1963. Meeting patients' psychosocial needs in the general hospital. *Annals of the American Academy of Political and Social Science* **346**, 117–25.

Brown, R. 1965. *Social Psychology.* New York: The Free Press.

Hofling, C. K., Brotzman, E., Dalrymple, S., Graves, N. and Pierce, C. M. 1966. An experimental study in nurse-physician relationships. *J. Nerv. Ment. Dis.* **143**, 171–80.

Lieberman, S. 1956. The effects of changes in roles on the attitudes of the role occupants. *Human Relations* **9**, 385–402.

Lief, H. I. and Fox, R. C. 1963. Training for 'detached concern' in medical students. In H. I. Lief, V. F. Lief and N. R. Lief (eds) *The Psychological Basis of Medical Practice*, 12–35. New York: Harper and Row.

Lorber, J. 1975. Good patients and problem patients: Conformity and deviance in a general hospital. *J. Health Soc. Behav.* **16**, 213–25.

Mechanic, D. 1966. Response factors in illness: The study of illness behavior. *Soc. Psychiat.* **1**, 11–20.

Menke, W. G. 1971. Medical identity: Change and conflict in professional roles. *J. Med. Educ.* **46**, 58–63.

Parsons, T. 1951. *The Social System.* New York: The Free Press.

Stimson, G. V. 1974. Obeying doctor's orders: A view from the other side: *Soc. Sci and Med.* **8**, 97–104.

Szasz, T. S. and Hollender, M. H. 1956. A contribution to the philosophy of medicine: The basic models of the doctor-patient relationship. *Arch. Int. Med.* **97**, 585–92.

Zimbardo, P. G., Banks, W. C., Haney, C. and Jaffe, J. D. L. 1973. A Pirandellian prison. *New York Times Magazine*, April 8, Sec. 6, pp. 38–60.

Chapter 18

Group Processes

Groups play an extremely important part in our lives. First, we are born into a group, our family. Then, during childhood, both education and play usually occur in groups. Throughout adulthood, many leisure activities and most work situations involve some degree of group participation, be it in a sports team, a bridge club, a union, a medical practice, or in the committee meetings that are an integral part of many occupations in our society.

Not surprisingly, many of the decisions that affect our lives are made by groups, in government, in business, as well as in medical and health care areas. Therefore, it is extremely important that we have some understanding of how groups function. As we shall see, many of the social processes we have explored thus far are relevant to our understanding of groups, such as social influence, attitude change, interpersonal perception, as well as social roles.

In this chapter we first consider the formation and development of group structure and then go on to discuss factors that affect group functioning and group decision making.

GROUP STRUCTURE

THE DEVELOPMENT OF NORMS AND ROLES

Let us consider this common situation. A number of individuals who are previously unacquainted with each other come together and interact as a group over a period of time. Initially each member has no knowledge of any of the others – no knowledge of their personality, their occupation, their family, their status, etc. In other words, the members begin on an equal footing; no one has any firm expectations for anyone else's behaviour. Actually, some expectations may exist because people do tend to make inferences about others purely on the basis of their physical appearance, as we saw in Chapter 16.

As these individuals interact over time, group norms governing group activities and the behaviour of individual members will develop. For example, Newcomb's (1958) study of Bennington College (see Chapter 14) revealed the existence of identifiable specific group norms governing the behaviour of Bennington students, and the fact that these norms were enforced by gossip and isolation of violators.

Some group norms prescribe behaviour that is applicable to all members, such as the norm of being politically involved at Bennington in the 1930s, while other norms prescribe the behaviour of individual members, i.e. the social roles that they are expected to play. As our group of previously unacquainted people interacts, they will begin to assume different roles such as leader, secretary, joke-maker, big-talker and so on. We call these *informal* roles (as opposed to the formal roles discussed in chapter 17) because they develop through the interaction of particular individuals rather than being predetermined by society's prescriptions. Nonetheless, they allow us to predict the behaviour of those around us (and therefore feel comfortable in our interactions with them) in much the same way as formal roles do.

In fact, we very rapidly develop expectations for the behaviour of the other people in groups to which we belong (see Chapter 16). This process can be observed in tutorial groups or seminars that meet regularly over a term. When the person who talks a great deal but has very little to contribute begins another monologue, other group members may lean back in their chairs, stretch, yawn and look at the clock; they have developed expectations for this person's behaviour. Conversely, when a member who makes infrequent but valuable contributions wants the floor, he or she may have little difficulty in getting it, because the other members have developed expectations for this person's behaviour as well. The fact that different roles develop in a group may not be noticed or acknowledged by the group members until some change in roles occurs, such as a normally shy member attempting to dominate the discussion or the absence of a person whose role is valued, such as the leader.

The development of these roles is a very complex process. As we saw in Chapter 16, they develop not only because a given member *chooses* to act in a particular way but because the other members come to *expect* him to act in that way. The pressures that these expectations can exert become only too apparent when an individual tries to change his or her role in the group: for example, the group clown may have difficulty in being taken seriously; a quiet member of the group who suddenly decides to be a big contributor may have difficulty in getting the floor.

Tuckman (1965) has proposed a model of four developmental stages common to small groups that interact over time. His model is based on evidence from studies of therapy groups and T-groups, as well as natural groups (those in real world settings such as a committee) and laboratory groups. He refers to the stages as **forming, storming, norming** and **performing**. The forming stage is characterized by the orientation of the group members to each other and to the group's task, as they test the boundaries of acceptable group behaviour. During the storming stage, intra-group hostility develops as members resist the formation of group structure and the demands of the task. In the norming stage, resistance gives way to group cohesiveness as the members accept each other's roles and the group, and openly exchange information about the task. Finally, the group reaches the performing stage where interpersonal relationships have been established and the group's energies can be directed towards the task. Although it would be an oversimplification to claim that all groups in all settings pass through these four stages, Tuckman's model does contribute to our understanding of the process of group development.

THE LEADERSHIP ROLE

In most groups, the role of leader is particularly important to the functioning of the group. Not surprisingly, the phenomenon of group leadership has generated a great deal of interest and research among social scientists. We will be concerned with **emergent leadership** – leadership which develops out of group interactions, as opposed to the situation where the group meets with a leader already appointed. Situations can occur, however, where the formally appointed leader performs inadequately and another group member emerges as informal leader.

How can we predict which group member will emerge as the group's leader? The first attempt to answer this question, referred to as the **trait approach**, focussed on individual characteristics: that is, what characteristics distinguished leaders from non-leaders? This approach remained popular for a while, probably because it was consistent with the conception of a leader as a 'great man', and also with the late 19th and early 20th century notion of people as individuals who succeed or fail on their own merits.

Despite the great number of studies which attempted to demonstrate relationships between leadership and other individual characteristics, the evidence for such relationships remained weak at best. A person who emerged as leader in one situation did not always emerge as leader in another when the group members or the group task were different. In short, the trait approach did not enable researchers to predict who would emerge as leader in a given group with any great accuracy.

A more complicated approach, the **situational approach**, contends that in addition to the attributes of individuals, the group situations must be taken into account in predicting emergent leadership. For example, the needs of the group and the requirements of its task will vary from one group to the next, and sometimes over time in the same group. The person who will emerge as leader will be the person with abilities best suited to the needs of the group at the time.

Another important question about emergent leadership concerns the extent of the influence of the leader. Specifically, does the leader impose his or her views on the group or does the leader reflect the views that are held by the group? Does the group follow the leader or does the leader follow the group?

In one study (Merei 1949) which investigated this issue, children who were 'leaders' were introduced to groups of children who were not leaders. Prior to the introduction of the leader, the groups of non-leaders had met and established their own traditions or norms regarding play patterns, use of available objects, etc. Merei sought to determine whether the leader's own new traditions would be imposed on the group, or whether the group would force its traditions on the leader. He found (with the exception of a few extreme cases where the leaders either were totally absorbed by the group or were able to change group traditions substantially) that the group managed to force its traditions on the leader. But, most leaders did assume the leadership role within the group's traditions. Some ordered the other children to do what they would have done anyway, some took possession of the available objects and then allocated them for their usual use to the appropriate children, and still others accepted group traditions and then proceeded to introduce new variations. The issue of who follows whom is further complicated by the fact that leadership is emerging at the same time that group traditions are being formed.

MORE ON EMERGENT ROLES AND LEADERSHIP: THE BALES
APPROACH

Bales (1958) has put forth an interesting approach to the whole issue
of emergent roles, particularly leadership. He has distinguished three
attributes of the behaviour of individuals in groups: a) *activity* – the
amount of participation a given person initiates, i.e. how often he or
she talks; b) *task ability* – the degree of knowledge and competence
possessed by each group member with regard to the specific group
task (as rated by the other group members); and c) *likeability* – the
degree to which each member is liked by the others in the group
(again, as rated by the other group members). Over large numbers of
groups, these three factors tend to be relatively independent; a high
rating on one is not consistently related to high ratings on the other
two.

By varying these three attributes, a number of role types that can
emerge in groups can be generated.

1) A member who is high on all three of the factors corresponds to the
traditional conception of the good leader, or the 'great man'. Such men are
found, but, if the factors are uncorrelated, are rare.

2) A member who is high on activity and task-ability ratings but less high
on likeability is a familiar type who may be called the 'task specialist'.
This type is not so rare as the first type and may operate effectively in
cooperation with the third.

3) A member who is high on likeability but less high on activity and task
ability may be called the 'social specialist'. This type is much less rare
than the first type, and groups which operate under the dual leadership of
a man of this type and of the second type are common.

4) A member who is high on activity but relatively low on task ability and
likeability ratings may be called an 'overactive deviant'. This type is not
rare. This is the person who, in the leadership literature, is said to show
'domination' rather than 'leadership'.

5) A member who is low on all three may be called an 'underactive
deviant' and may indeed be a kind of scapegoat. On the assumption that
the factors are uncorrelated, this type should be as rare as the first type,
but since the lack of correlation traces mainly to discrepancies at the upper
end of the scales, this type is not actually so rare as the first type and is, in
fact, probably very common. (Bales 1958, p. 447).

FACTORS THAT AFFECT GROUP FUNCTIONING

Although the personalities and abilities of individual group members, and in particular the roles that they assume in the group, are important determinants of what actually happens in that group, other factors are important as well. These factors to some extent transcend individual members and specific group tasks (but may, in fact, affect the emergence of different roles). We consider some of these factors here.

GROUP COHESIVENESS

If you think about your own experiences in groups, it is likely that you will remember some groups that really worked well – everyone enthusiastic, interested in the purpose of the group (its task), and making good contributions, and some that did not work so well – members bored and disinterested in the group's task, making minimal contributions, wasting time and generally accomplishing little. Most university instructors who have conducted many tutorials and seminars would agree that there is this variation over groups, even if factors like the group size and task remain the same.

This group spirit (or 'we-ness') variable is called **group cohesiveness** – some groups are highly cohesive and some are not. We can think of group cohesiveness as the desire of the group members to remain a part of the group, their attraction to the group.

And what determines the attraction of the group member toward the group? Cartwright (1968) states:

> ... a person's attraction to a group is determined by four interacting sets of variables: a) his *motive base for attraction* consisting of his needs for affiliation, recognition, security, money or other values that can be mediated by groups; b) the *incentive properties of the group*, consisting of its goals, programs, characteristics of its members, style of operation, prestige or other properties of significance for his motive base; c) his *expectancy*, the subjective probability, that membership will actually have beneficial or detrimental consequences for him; and d) *his comparison level* – his conception of the level of outcomes that group membership should provide.' (p. 96).

The attraction of each member toward the group depends not only on that member's own needs but also on his perception of the ability of the group to satisfy those needs.

Cohesiveness is a very important variable in terms of our understanding of group behaviour, because of the effects it appears to have on other aspects of group functioning. Shaw (1971), in summarizing the research on group cohesiveness, states: 'Relative to low-cohesive groups, high-cohesive groups engage in more social interaction, engage in more positive interactions (friendly, cooperative, democratic, etc.), exert greater influence over their members, are more effective in achieving goals they set for themselves, and have higher member satisfaction'. (p. 205).

GROUP SIZE

As group size increases, not only must each member contend with a greater number of interpersonal relationships but also, assuming a time limit for discussion, there is less time available for each member to be heard (Bales and Borgatta 1955). As you probably know from your own experience in groups, participation is rarely equal among group members, even in small groups. But, as group size increases, fewer and fewer members either can or are willing to participate actively. The discussion becomes dominated by a few and the others may become dissatisfied with the group.

Slater (1958), in a study designed to find the optimum group size, presented groups ranging from two to seven members with a summary of a problem facing an organization administrator and asked the groups to discuss how it should be solved. He found that five was the optimum size for this task in the eyes of the group members. He also concluded that groups rated as too large tended to have different problems from groups rated as too small. In larger groups, members were viewed as, '... too aggressive, impulsive, competitive and inconsiderate, and the group as too hierarchical, centralized and disorganized.' (p. 138), while in smaller groups, members tended to be '... too tense, passive, tactful and constrained ... Their fear of alienating one another seems to prevent them from expressing their ideas freely.' (p. 138).

STATUS OF MEMBERS

Individual status or power is generally derived from sources external to the group (one notable exception being the role of leader); members bring it in with them. Even if such status is irrelevant to the particular group task, its influence on group processes such as the emergence of leadership and the communication pattern within the group can be observed.

Strodtbeck, James and Hawkins (1958) used mock jury deliberations to study the effect of status on group processes. They found that: 'Men, in contrast with women, and persons of higher status, in contrast with lower status or occupations, have higher participation, influence, satisfaction, and perceived competence for the jury task.' (p. 387). Furthermore, the foremen selected were more often of high occupational status than low, and were males more often than females.

The relative status of group members can influence the group's communication pattern as well. In a field experiment (Hurwitz, Zander and Hymovitch 1953), subjects who were ... 'mainly social workers (including executives), teachers, counseling and guidance workers, psychiatrists, psychologists, and nurses' (p. 484), attended a one-day conference on mental hygiene problems. These professions represented a range of prestige: half of the subjects chosen were classified as high prestige and the other half as low. During the day each subject participated in discussions groups which were observed by the experimenters.

They found that, generally speaking, high prestige members both initiated and received more communication than low prestige members. They also found that when the subjects were asked to rate the amount of participation by others in their group, both high and low prestige members overrated the participation of the lows significantly more than they did the highs.

When these two results – the actual and the perceived rates of participation – are considered together, interesting implications for group discussion and decision making can be drawn. Often a number of individuals, for example in the medical profession, are brought together in a group for the purpose of making a particular decision. The group may well include people of different status, such as a nurse, a visiting specialist, a psychiatric social worker, a physiotherapist, etc. They all are there because they have specific information to contribute to the decision-making process. Although the meeting is officially 'democratic', everyone perceives the status hierarchy and contributes accordingly, thus inhibiting the free flow of information. The end result may be a group decision based on less information than was potentially available. However, everyone leaves the meeting believing that participation was more equal than it was and therefore may not even be aware that this is happening.

SPATIAL CONFIGURATION

The spatial configuration of the group members can affect various aspects of group functioning, such as the communication pattern, influence and leadership. Let us consider a group assembled around a round table. When a given member stops talking, the members most likely to start are those directly opposite the speaker. The likelihood of responding decreases as we move around the table, and those sitting next to the given member are the least likely to speak (Steinzor 1950).

All positions are at least potentially equal at a round table, but this is not the case at oblong tables. Oblong tables typically have two end positions, four corner positions, and some middle positions (between the corners) depending upon the size of the group. Studies of jury groups of twelve have found that the foreman chosen (after the group is seated) is about three times as likely to occupy an end as a corner position, and about twice as likely to occupy a corner as a middle position. The occupants of end positions also participate significantly more in the discussion than those of other positions. (Strodtbeck and Hook 1961).

However, there are some indications that those who are more influential, and more likely to be elected foreman, do tend to select the end positions. One recent study (Nemeth and Wachtler 1974) has found that the influence of the end position is due to the act of *choosing* it rather than to the position itself. In this experiment, an individual exerted more influence in the end position than in other positions, but only when that position was chosen by the individual, and not when it was assigned by the experimenter. The researchers claim that those who choose end positions are seen as consistent and confident by other group members as a result, and are therefore better able to exert influence.

GROUP DECISION MAKING

GROUP CONSENSUS

Influence and the deviant
As we saw in Chapter 14, groups can exercise enormous pressures on their members to conform and are usually quite ready to exercise sanctions for non-conformity. In one study (Schachter 1951), which

examined the reactions of groups to a deviant member, groups were instructed to reach a decision on the action to be taken regarding a juvenile delinquent, after having read the case history. One group member, a stooge, disagreed with the general group consensus throughout the discussion period, as pre-arranged with the experimenter. When the pattern of communication (that is, who talks to whom during the discussion) was analysed, it was found that more communication was directed towards the deviate than towards conforming group members. Assuming that communication represents influence attempts, we can conclude that the group was putting greater social pressure on this member than on the other conforming members. Furthermore, in some instances, this relatively high level of communication directed toward the deviate, would, at some point, decline. It was as though some of the group, realizing that they could not change the deviate, ignored him, 'psychologically' excluding him from the group. After the group discussion, each member was asked to rank the others according to how much they wanted them to remain in the same group as themselves. In other words, how much each member liked each of the others, and predictably the deviate usually was rated below the conforming group members.

Another study (Homans 1965), this time in the field rather than the laboratory, also illustrates these group pressures towards conformity and group reactions towards non-conformity. This study looked at factory workers and found that even when they were paid on a piece-rate basis, group norms evolved, limiting the number of units each person was to produce. Yet most workers chose to adhere to the group norms rather than make more money. Those that did not adhere were called 'rate killers' and faced overt group disapproval.

Groupthink

Janis (1971) in his analysis of a number of important government decisions including the decision of the Kennedy administration to launch the Bay of Pigs invasion, identified a phenomenon he termed **groupthink**, '... the mode of thinking that persons engage in when *concurrence-seeking* becomes so dominant in a cohesive ingroup that it tends to override realistic appraisal of alternative courses of action.' (p. 43). In such groups, individual members suppress rather than express their doubts and misgivings about group decisions, and do not properly weight the pros and cons of various alternatives.

Since decisions made when groupthink is occurring are usually not optimal, it is important that ways be found for groups to guard against it. Janis has suggested a number of procedures that might be effective. Basically they are designed to encourage group members to express objections, doubts, disagreements and different points of view; in other words, to maximize opinion input and encourage the critical evaluation of a range of alternatives, using the information and opinions available.

GROUPS VERSUS INDIVIDUALS

On task performance

If you were given the choice of completing a behavioural science project on your own or with a group of your fellow students (where each member would receive the group grade), which alternative would you choose? You might feel that pooling your knowledge with that of others would be an advantage; some members may excel in areas where others are weak, and vice versa. Obviously several people could accomplish more than one individual (or, the same amount as one individual but with less work per person). You might consider your ability to complete the project relative to that of the potential group members. An above-average behavioural science student may have little to gain from working with others, but an average student might benefit from working in a group with one or more above-average students. You can probably think of other considerations as well.

Generally it has been found that groups are superior to one individual working alone. The group has the advantage of the skills and knowledge of several people rather than just one. Therefore it is more likely that the group will have the required skills and knowledge than that any one individual will. Moreover, incorrect judgements and errors are more readily corrected in groups. However, groups often take more time than individuals to complete the same task – this is particularly true when the total number of person-hours is considered.

Although groups generally perform better than the average individual, there are very able individuals who may perform better than the group. One experiment (Tuckman and Lorge 1962), in which subjects completed a complex task requiring a series of solutions, first alone and then in groups, found that the group solutions did not always make use of the best solutions of the individual members.

On matters of opinion

How does group consensus on an issue differ from individual opinions on that issue? Once again there has been a great deal of research on this question and a good deal of it has concerned individual versus group risk taking. Quite the contrary to the stereotype of group decisions (particularly in business) being more conservative than those reached by individuals, the results of a number of these studies showed that in general groups made riskier decisions than individuals.

Typically, subjects individually would indicate the degree of risk they were willing to take in a given situation, and then reach a group consensus on the acceptable level of risk. Usually, the group consensus was riskier than the average of the individual decisions. This phenomenon was referred to as **risky-shift** and a number of explanations for its occurrence were put forward. However, some researchers found occasional shifts towards caution during group discussions on certain issues, which seemed to contradict the general shift to risk findings.

More recently, these results have been subsumed under a more general hypothesis, the **group polarization** hypothesis. According to this view, 'The average postgroup response will tend to be more extreme in the same direction as the average of the pregroup responses.' (Myers and Lamm 1976, p. 603). This hypothesis, which has been in general supported over a variety of tasks (Myers and Lamm 1976), is quite consistent with the group shifts toward both risk and caution that have been found.

SUMMARY

When a group of previously unacquainted people meet to perform a task or make a decision, different roles will emerge, including the role of leader. Evidence linking leadership to other traits is weak. Who will emerge as leader in a particular group seems more dependent on the group situation at the time. Group functioning is influenced by a number of factors, including the level of cohesiveness, group size, the status relationships of the members and their spatial configuration. There are strong pressures toward uniformity in groups; deviates tend to be rejected. When these pressures are strong, the phenomenon of groupthink can occur and the quality of group decisions can suffer. When groups are compared to individuals, in general, group task performance is better than average individual performance; group decisions on matters of opinion tend to be more polarized.

TERMS AND CONCEPTS

forming ⎫
storming ⎪ stages
norming ⎬ of group
performing ⎭ development

emergent leadership
trait approach to leadership
situational approach to leadership
group cohesiveness
groupthink
risky-shift
group polarization

FOR DISCUSSION

1. Think of two separate groups in which you have participated – one which functioned well and one which did not. Try to explain the differences in terms of the points discussed in this chapter.

2. Do you think that some people are more likely to emerge as leaders than others? Why? Think of an instance where someone, perhaps yourself, has emerged as group leader. To what extent was the emergence of this person due to his or her special knowledge and abilities and to what extent to the particular situation?

3. Do you agree that five is the optimal size for discussion-decision making groups? Why?

4. Why do you think that the spatial configuration of group members affects the communication pattern and emergent leadership?

5. What advice would you give to a group composed of doctors (some specialists), nurses, and a psychiatric social worker, etc., which was to discuss possible treatment alternatives for patients?

SUGGESTED READING

Bales: discussion of emergence of roles, including the leadership role, in groups.
Janis: interesting article on the phenomenon of groupthink.
Shaw: complete and detailed text on group dynamics.

REFERENCES

Bales, R. F. 1958. Task roles and social roles in problem solving groups. In E. E. Maccoby, T. M. Newcomb and E. L. Hartley (eds) *Readings in Social Psychology* 437–47. New York: Henry Holt and Co.

Bales, R. F. and Borgatta, E. 1955. Size of group as a factor in the interaction profile. In A. Hare, E. Borgatta and R. Bales (eds), *Small Groups: Studies in Social Interaction* 396–413. New York: Knopf.

Cartwright, D. 1968. The nature of group cohesiveness. In D. Cartwright and A. Zander (eds) *Group dynamics: Research and theory* 91–109. (3rd edn) New York: Harper & Row, Publishers.

Homans, G. 1965. Group factors in worker productivity. In H. Proshansky and B. Seidenberg (eds) *Basic Studies in Social Psychology* 592–604. New York: Holt, Rinehart and Winston.

Hurwitz, J. I., Zander, A. F. and Hymovitch, B. 1953. Some effects of power on the relations among group members. In D. Cartwright and A. Zander (eds) *Group Dynamics: Research and Theory* 483–92. Evanston, Illinois: Row, Peterson and Co.

Janis, I. 1971. Groupthink. *Psychology Today* 5, 43–6, 74–6.

Merei, F. 1949. Group leadership and institutionalization. *Human Relations* 2, 23–39.

Myers, D. G. and Lamm, H. 1976. The group polarization phenomenon. *Psychol. Bull*, 83, 602–27.

Nemeth, C. and Wachtler, J. 1974. Creating the perceptions of consistency and confidence: A necessary condition for minority influence. *Sociometry* 37, 529–40.

Newcomb, T. 1958. Attitude development as a function of reference groups: The Bennington study. In E. E. Maccoby, T. M. Newcomb and E. L. Hartley (eds) *Readings in Social Psychology* 265–75. New York: Henry Holt and Co.

Schachter, S. 1951. Deviation, rejection and communication. *J. Abnorm. Soc. Psychol.* 46, 190–207.

Shaw, M. E. 1971. *Group Dynamics: The Psychology of Small Group Behavior*. New York: McGraw-Hill.

Slater, P. E. 1958. Contrasting correlates of group size. *Sociometry* 21, 129–39.

Steinzor, B. 1950. The spatial factor in face-to-face discussion groups. *J. Abnorm. Soc. Psychol.* 45, 552–5.

Strodtbeck, F. and Hook, L. 1961. The social dimensions of a twelve man jury table. *Sociometry* 24, 397–415.

Strodtbeck, F. L., James, R. M. and Hawkins, C. 1958. Social status in jury deliberations. In E. E. Maccoby, T. M. Newcomb and E. L. Hartley (eds) *Readings in Social Psychology* 379–88. New York: Henry Holt and Co.

Tuckman, B. W. 1965. Developmental sequence in small groups. *Psychol. Bull.* **63**, 384–99.

Tuckman, J. and Lorge, I. 1962. Individual ability as a determinant of group superiority. *Human Relations* **15**, 45–51.

Chapter 19

Groups in Society

In this chapter we broaden our focus to consider groups in society as a determinant of behaviour. Most of us will be members of many groups throughout our lives, such as families, peer groups, professional, religious, political and community service groups, and social classes. The study of such groups is important because knowledge of group membership often allows us to predict other behaviour as well.

Following a brief discussion of the classification of groups, we will look at primary groups, including the family, and associations, including the modern hospital. Next, we will consider social stratification and its relationship to illness and health care. Finally, our discussion will turn to collective behaviour, that is, non-normative behaviour which occurs outside of the accepted social structure.

The term 'group' is typically used to refer to a great variety of groupings or collections of people who have something in common. However, some groups, such as families, have a lot more in common than others, such as all owners of colour television sets. Consequently, before we begin our discussion of groups in society, it is necessary to introduce some specific terms that allow us to distinguish among different types of groups. The term **social group** is used when social relationships exist among individuals who share similar beliefs and values, and a common sense of identity that sets them apart from others who do not belong to the group. Families, friendship groups, labour unions and the employees of a hospital are examples of social groups. **Social category** is used to refer to a number of individuals who do not necessarily have social relationships with each other, but who nonetheless share a common identity and occupy the same role. Middle-class families, pensioners, bank managers, doctors and shop stewards constitute social categories. A **statistical aggregate** is a collection of individuals with some common attribute but without social relationships or a sense of common identity. Owners of colour television sets, readers of the London *Times*, victims of automobile accidents, people over six feet tall, and fans of the Rolling Stones are statistical aggregates. The distinctions among social groups, social categories and statistical aggregates are sometimes blurred; statistical aggregates and social categories sometimes become social groups. In any case, it is assumed that knowledge of memberships in such groups or groupings enables us to predict other behaviour to a greater or lesser extent.

Primary groups and **associations** are two types of social groups. Although both involve social relationships, the quality of these relationships differs. Primary groups, like families and friendship groups, are characterized by close personal relationships that are valued for themselves, while associations, such as a modern hospital or a large motor company, are characterized by impersonal relationships based on fairly narrow role prescriptions and oriented towards achieving defined goals. More will be said about this distinction between primary groups and associations in the sections that follow.

Societies differ in the extent to which the daily activities of their members take place in the context of primary groups or associations. At one end of the continuum are communal or folk societies, typically small, where primary relationships are predominant. At the other end of the continuum are urban industrial societies where associational relationships are common. It should be noted that primary groups do also exist within urban industrial societies and even within associations, such as the friendship groups that form among the workers in large corporations.

PRIMARY GROUPS

CHARACTERISTICS OF PRIMARY GROUPS

Cooley (1909), the first to introduce the concept of the primary group, gave this description:

> By primary groups I mean those characterized by intimate face-to-face association and cooperation. They are primary in several senses, but chiefly in that they are fundamental in forming the social nature and ideals of the individual. The result of intimate association, psychologically, is a certain fusion of individualities in a common whole, so that one's very self, for many purposes at least, is the common life and purpose of the group. Perhaps the simplest way of describing this wholeness is by saying that it is a 'we'; it involves the sort of sympathy and mutual identification

for which 'we' is the natural expression. One lives in the feeling of the whole and finds the chief aims of his will in that feeling. (p. 23).

Today, however, sociologists do not necessarily consider 'face-to-face' interaction to be a distinguishing feature of primary groups. We can think of face-to-face relationships such as that of a supervisor and a worker, which we would not consider to be primary, as well as non-face-to-face relationships, such as that among family members who are geographically separated, that we would consider to be primary.

The main emphasis in characterizing the primary group is on the quality of the relationships. People interact as complete individuals and are accepted as unique individuals in primary relationships, while in associational relationships, individuals are regarded as the occupants of roles, such as salesman or manager, with little attention given to their individual personalities. This does not mean that roles do not exist in primary relationships; certainly the roles of mother, wife, husband and so forth do enter into primary relationships. In addition, people in primary groups, such as friendship groups, may adopt informal roles as described in Chapter 18. However, the roles that exist in primary groups typically encompass many areas of daily living, and permit candid communication on a variety of topics, while those relevant to associational relationships only involve a narrow range of behaviour and communication, such as the relationship between a department store clerk and a customer. Primary relationships are valued for the intrinsic satisfaction derived by those involved rather than for their utility in attaining specific goals, as in associational relationships. In addition, primary relationships tend to persist over a period of time, while associational relationships tend to be transitory.

The primary relationship as described here is something of an ideal; actual relationships in real life will vary in how closely they approximate it.

THE FAMILY: AN EXAMPLE OF A PRIMARY GROUP

Sociologists have distinguished the **nuclear family** from the **extended family**. The nuclear family unit consists of one husband, one wife and their children. The extended family is composed of a number of related nuclear family units and often spans more than two generations. Although urban industrial society favours the nuclear family, in other societies it is common for mother, father, children, grandparents, aunts, uncles, etc. to live together as one household. The family unit can also be based on polygamy, one husband with more than one wife, or, in rare cases, on polyandry, one wife with more than one husband and their children.

The family unit serves a variety of societal needs. Reproduction takes place predominantly in the family. The family also plays a vital role in the socialization of the young members of society, as discussed in Chapter 9. Furthermore, the family unit cares for dependant family members, such as children and the aged, who are unable to look after themselves. In addition it is the family to a greater or lesser extent (somewhat lesser in western societies) that determines an individual's position within the society. Families, of course, also help the individual to fulfill personal needs for affiliation, love, social support and so forth. It must be emphasized that the family is a major source of social support for the individual throughout life. Individuals who receive adequate social support when facing life crises, including illness, are generally better able to cope with their situation than those who do not.

With industrialization, family patterns have changed; the nuclear family rather than the extended family has become the predominant unit. There is greater geographic and social mobility in industrial societies. Since work roles are typically performed outside the family (as opposed to communal societies where the family was usually an economic unit as well) people must reside where there are jobs. This often necessitates geographical separation between the nuclear family unit and the grandparents, aunts, uncles, etc. who, in earlier days, would all have been part of one household. Social mobility can also weaken extended family ties. Children who achieve higher status than their parents may adopt new life styles and values that are neither appreciated nor understood by the older generation.

While the extended family was replaced by the nuclear family, the number of primary relationships outside the family tended to decrease and be replaced by associational relationships. In urban societies today, for example, neighbours often are not even acquainted, and work relationships can be fairly impersonal. The result is that individuals tend to depend more on primary relationships within the family for satisfaction of their social needs, but at the same time there are fewer relationships in the nuclear than in the extended family than can provide this satisfaction. Therefore, we would expect the marital relationship to be the main source of satisfaction of these needs, but also a main source of frustration when it does not meet them.

Recent changes in the role of women are likely to have an impact on the marital relationship. Changes in one role, such as wife, are likely to be accompanied by changes in the reciprocal role of husband. At least in some marriages, there seems to be less emphasis on the specific rights and duties of each partner as defined by the traditional roles of husband and wife, and more emphasis on an egalitarian relationship where such activities as household chores, child rearing and income earning are shared. However, whenever norms are changing, there is always the potential for conflict. The values and expectations of different individuals are likely to change at different times and to different degrees, or perhaps not at all. Therefore, it would seem to be important that the expectations of both husband and wife for the performance of both their own role and that of the other coincide, no matter how traditional or how liberated. A traditionally oriented male and a liberated female are not likely to agree on their expectations for behaviour in the marital relationship.

ASSOCIATIONS

CHARACTERISTICS OF ASSOCIATIONS

Associations have become a common part of our everyday lives; in business, in government and in health care, just to mention a few major areas, we must deal with large organizations. As we have previously stated, relationships in associations tend to be impersonal and relatively narrowly defined as compared with those in primary groups. Also, these relationships are oriented toward achieving the specific goals of the association, such as profit making, treatment of patients and so on.

Associations have a **formal organization** or structure. Etzioni (1964) states that '*Formal organization* generally refers to the organizational pattern designed by management: the blueprint of division of labor and power of control, the rules and regulations about wages, fines, quality control, etc.' (p. 40). These elements of formal structure are specifically created and modified to enable the organization to achieve its goals most efficiently. Within the organization, there is division of labour, and therefore many specific roles. The formal structure which is created and modified is composed of these roles, not of individuals; for example the role of assistant manager is well defined and has specific relationships with other roles, regardless of the particular individual who is assistant manager at any given time. These roles can be diagrammed hierarchically: board of directors – president – three vice-presidents – two assistant vice-presidents under each vice-president – and so on down to lowly supervisors and workers. Thus chains of authority and responsibility are well defined, as are the accepted channels of communication. For example it would be unusual if not unacceptable for a vice-president to bypass the president and communicate directly with the board of directors.

However, within the framework of the formal organization, there exists the **informal organization** or structure. Friendship or primary groups do develop among the workers. Informal leaders emerge who may have more power than formal supervisors. Organizational rules are interpreted and informal unspecified relationships develop, so that individuals can deal effectively with situations not specifically covered by the formal organization. Sometimes these informal relationships are more effective than those formally specified by the organization ('you have to know the ropes to get anything done around here'). And, informal relationships may enable some members to get vital information ('the inside story') without going through formal communication channels. The informal structure protects the individual from the cold impersonality of the association; it mediates between the individual and the larger formal organization. Identification with informal groups can encourage greater loyalty and commitment to the association itself. However, the informal organization can also be detrimental to the association when it limits the production rate or encourages socializing rather than work.

Early work on organizational management, known as **scientific management**, emphasized the formal organization, while the more recent **human relations approach** emphasizes the informal organization. Scientific management assumed that worker productivity was limited only by the physical capabilities of the workers, and that they could be motivated to work to full capacity by monetary incentives. But a now famous and influential series of studies, known as the Hawthorne studies (Roethlisberger and Dickson 1939), demonstrated that these assumptions were false. From these studies it was evident that informal groups of workers set norms for the production rate. Those who deviated from group norms by producing too much or too little were sanctioned by the group (as were the deviates in the studies discussed in Chapter 18). The social rewards and punishments provided by informal friendship groups were more important to most workers than the economic incentives offered for increased productivity. These studies as well as other research (Coch and French 1948) have demonstrated that workers must be considered members of groups rather than independent individuals; individual behaviour (i.e. production rates, the acceptance of new methods of production, etc.) will not change unless the group norms are changed.

THE HOSPITAL: AN EXAMPLE OF AN ASSOCIATION

Hospitals, like other associations, have goals, formal organization and informal organization. Modern hospitals usually have more than one goal; in addition to the treatment of patients, many are also involved in teaching and research. Within this extremely complex organization, there are a great number of different roles based on narrowly defined specialities and areas of expertise: doctors, nurses, physiotherapists, laboratory technicians, administrators, dietitians, clerks and cleaners are among the diverse groups employed by the hospital. Not surprisingly, in hospitals as in other associations, relationships can be relatively impersonal. As we saw in Chapter 17, the patient experiences the impersonality of these associational relationships just at the time when emotional support from primary relationships is most essential.

One distinctive feature of the formal organization of the hospital is that authority does not emanate from a single source, as it does in many other associations. In hospitals, there are typically two power hierarchies or lines of authority, one medical and one administrative. The hospital administrator, in turn, supervises various other hierarchies including the nursing staff. There also exists the doctor's expectation (which is usually met) of obedience without question and of being given precedence in setting patient treatment goals. This atypical power structure is not surprising in view of the doctor's special expertise and unique relationship with patients, as well as Wilson's (1963) observation that both doctor and patient are really 'guests' of the organization.

This power structure increases the potential for certain types of conflicts. One typical conflict, that of the nurse who must choose to obey the doctor *or* to obey hospital rules, has already been discussed (see Hofling *et al.* 1966, Chapter 14). This conflict and others like it arise because the doctor is giving orders to those under other lines of authority. Even apart from the doctor and his or her informal power, we would expect potential conflict when individuals under different lines of authority must interact in the same situation in which the power distribution may be unclear. Each will have a personal point of view which reflects the rules and policies of his own power hierarchy.

However, Wilson (1963) contends that problems such as these are mitigated by the informal organization that develops among hospital employees. Relationships, not specified by the formal structure and transcending aspects of it such as specialization and status, do develop. These relationships not only serve the social needs of the employees but enable them to deal more effectively with work situations as well, thus promoting the goals of the larger organization.

SOCIAL STRATIFICATION

THE BASES OF SOCIAL STRATIFICATION

Even in small communal societies, people occupy different positions or roles, if only that of male as opposed to female, or old as opposed to young. In urban industrial societies, there are numerous positions, and individuals usually occupy more than one in the course of their lives or simultaneously. As mentioned earlier, these positions may be ascribed, such as sex, or achieved, such as occupation. Furthermore, members of society evaluate these positions; some are clearly superior to others in terms of the privileges and rewards accorded to the occupant. Positions also differ in their importance to society as a whole and in the number of individuals who are able (or qualified) to occupy them. The evaluation of these different positions results in the stratification of society. The members of a particular stratum or social class tend to have similar life experiences, values, attitudes, behaviour patterns and so forth. Therefore, on the basis of social class, we are able to predict a remarkable amount of other behaviour.

How do sociologists go about establishing the class structure of a community? And how do they decide who belongs to what class? One method is the subjective approach; individuals are simply asked to what class they think that they belong. Another approach is to ask the people in the community to classify each other. The class structure that results from these methods reflects how the people being studied actually perceive themselves.

Sociologists also use a third method, the objective approach, in which a community is divided into classes on the basis of one or a combination of objective criteria, such as income, occupational status, education level, power, type of housing, etc. Although the rankings based on these objective criteria do tend to correlate with each other, there are instances in which they do not. Some occupations with relatively high status ratings, such as minister, do not have comparably high incomes. On the other hand, some people, such as movie stars, may earn high incomes but not necessarily have high occupational status or level of education. The divisions found by the objective approach may not necessarily be those that are perceived by the people themselves (they may perceive a different structure or none at all), but even so may be related to aspects of behaviour that the researchers wish to predict.

Societies differ in the extent to which **social mobility**, or movement between strata, is possible. In India, movement between castes is relatively rare, while in the United States, where social class is more determined by achieved than by ascribed criteria, social mobility is much more common.

One's place in the social order is related to a host of other variables including voting behaviour, patterns of child rearing, family stability, as well as illness and health care.

SOCIAL CLASS AND HEALTH

Although social class is related to many aspects of illness and health care, it should be noted that the evidence is correlational and not necessarily causal. Because social class is associated with other variables that affect health, for instance diet and nutrition, hygiene, education and life style, the reasons *why* these relationships exist are often difficult to determine.

To begin with, lower classes have higher infant mortality rates and lower life expectancies than higher social classes. Although the higher incidence of some diseases in the lower classes was noticed first, the upper classes have their characteristic diseases as well. Susser and Watson (1971) report that '... coronary disease, poliomyelitis, the leukaemias and a miscellany of other disorders such as alcoholism and cirrhosis of the liver (in Britain), cancer of the breast, cancer of the prostate and duodenal ulcer have been more common in the upper social classes ...' (p. 138). Rates of other diseases, such as epidemic and infectious diseases, bronchitis and tuberculosis have been higher in the lower classes, as is psychosis but not neurosis.

In addition, particular occupations have their own special risks. 'For example, doctors have a low mortality from all causes but a fairly high one from suicide and cirrhosis of the liver. High on the list of mortality from all causes are occupations such as glass blowing, mining and sandblasting, while low on the list are such occupations as teaching and herding sheep. Publicans and innkeepers have a high rate of mortality from all causes and the highest from cirrhosis of the liver.' (Jones and Jones 1975, p. 168).

Although it would appear that working class people have greater need of health care facilities, their use of these facilities is generally less than that of the higher classes. Rainwater (1968) notes that the lower classes tend to deal with illness in terms of crisis rather than prevention. Furthermore, the health care that people actually receive is to some degree related to their social class. The existence of government health care schemes goes part way towards eliminating discrepancies based on class differences. However, to the extent that one must pay for services provided, the ability to pay will correspondingly determine the health care received.

A NOTE ON COLLECTIVE BEHAVIOUR

Thus far we have focussed on patterns of social behaviour that are institutionalized and accepted within the societies in which they occur. But non-normative behaviour, behaviour that is outside of the existing social structure and not completely controlled by it, can occur as well. Such behaviour is referred to as **collective behaviour**. Demonstrations, riots, panics, fads, revival meetings, flying saucer cults, revolutions, etc. are all examples of collective behaviour. Some types of collective behaviour, like flying saucer cults, are more organized, structural and long lasting than others, such as panics.

Collective behaviour usually arises spontaneously to meet the situations, problems and needs that are not met by the present accepted normative institutions of society. Therefore, instances of collective behaviour are often indicative of impending change; what is considered non-normative today can become an institutionalized part of society tomorrow. Some of the present established religious denominations had their origins in collective behaviour. And a number of revolutionary groups have now become accepted governments.

Instances of collective behaviour which focus on aspects of illness and health are not uncommon, for example faith healing groups which promise cures outside of the accepted medical establishment. Fads such as jogging, consuming 'health foods' and taking large doses of certain vitamins are less dramatic examples of collective behaviour.

SUMMARY

The groups of collections of people in society can be categorized as social groups, social categories or statistical aggregates. Social groups can be subdivided into primary groups and associations, mainly on the basis of the quality of the relationships among the members. Primary groups are characterized by personal and intrinsically valued relationships, while associations are characterized by impersonal relationships that are structured to achieve specific goals. The family is an example of a primary group, whereas the modern hospital is an example of an association. Social class is related to a variety of other variables including illness and health care. Collective behaviour is non-normative behaviour that arises spontaneously outside of the existing social structure.

TERMS AND CONCEPTS

social group
primary group
association
social category
statistical aggregate
nuclear family
extended family
formal organization
informal organization
scientific management
human relations approach
social mobility
collective behaviour

FOR DISCUSSION

1.   What future changes (if any) would you anticipate in the family in urban industrial society?

2.   On the basis of either your own work experience in a large organization or that of someone you know, evaluate the effects of the informal organization on individual workers, work situations and on the organization as a whole.

3.   How do you think that the potential conflicts resulting from the unique structure of the hospital can be minimized or avoided?

4.   Are there different social classes in your community? On what criteria are they based? How do they affect attitudes and behaviour?

SUGGESTED READING

Susser and Watson, Chapter 7, Medicine and bureaucracy: description of some organizational aspects of the hospital and of the medical profession.

Susser and Watson, Chapter 4, Social class and disorders of health: detailed discussion of the relationships between illness and social class as well as some possible explanations for such relationships.

Wilson: good article on the social organization of hospitals.

REFERENCES

Coch, L. and French, J. R. P. 1948. Overcoming resistance to change. *Human Rel.* **1,** 512–32.

Cooley, C. H. 1909. *Social Organization.* New York: Charles Scribner's Sons.

Etzioni, A. 1964. *Modern Organizations.* Englewood Cliffs, New Jersey: Prentice-Hall, Inc.

Hofling, C. K., Brotzman, E., Dalrymple, S., Graves, N. and Pierce, C. M. 1966. An experimental study in nurse-physician relationships. *J. Nerv. Ment. Dis.* **143,** 171–80.

Jones, R. K. and Jones, P. A. 1975. *Sociology in Medicine.* New York: John Wiley & Sons.

Rainwater, L. 1968. The lower class: Health, illness and medical institutions. In I. Deutscher and E. J. Thompson (eds)*Among the People: Encounters with the Poor.* New York: Basic Books.

Roethlisberger, F. J. and Dickson, W. J. 1939. *Management and the Worker.* Cambridge: Harvard University Press.

Susser, M. W. and Watson, W. 1971. *Sociology in Medicine.* London: Oxford University Press.

Wilson, R. N. 1963. The social structure of a general hospital. *Ann. Amer. Acad. Polit. Soc. Sci.* **346,** 67–76.

Chapter 20

Cross-Cultural Perspectives

In this last chapter we focus on the cultural determinants of behaviour. From our basic beliefs about the nature of the universe and in the existence (or non-existence) of the supernatural, to the particular foods we eat and the utensils we use for eating, we think and act in accordance with our own particular **culture**. We may not even be aware of the pervasive influence of our culture until we are confronted with ways of thinking and behaving that differ from our own. However, through a consideration of the concept of culture and some specific practices of other cultures, we can better understand our own culture and its far-reaching effects on our lives.

First we discuss the general concept of culture as it is used by anthropologists, and then we consider some specific views of illness and treatment in different cultures which, by comparison, should enable us to understand our own better.

THE CONCEPT OF CULTURE

WHAT IS CULTURE?

Kluckhohn (1949) states that 'By "culture" anthropology means the total life way of a people, the social legacy the individual acquires from his group.' (p. 17). There are numerous different cultures and 'Each specific culture constitutes a kind of blueprint for all of life's activities.' (p. 18). Knowledge of a particular culture therefore allows us to predict many of the beliefs and much of the behaviour of its individual members.

The members of a given society share a common culture which enables them to deal with each other and with the physical world which they inhabit. Culture must be learned. Children are socialized into the particular culture of their group; all will learn language but some will learn English, some Greek, others Chinese and so forth. Furthermore, culture is transmitted from generation to generation. Each new member does not have to devise his or her own solutions to the problems of existence, but rather benefits from the accumulated knowledge of past generations.

Because so much of our life is affected by our culture, there is a tendency to assume that our way of life is the usual or the best way, that our particular beliefs and behaviour are 'human nature'. When people lack knowledge of other cultures, they often assume that their ways are the only ways, and that they are common to people everywhere. When confronted with cultural patterns that differ from their own, they may respond by downgrading them and considering them to be inferior to their own, which are naturally best. This orientation, which assumes that one's own culture is the natural or the best one and degrades those that differ, is known as **ethnocentrism**.

So much of what we take for granted, what we believe to be human nature, is in fact culturally determined and varies from culture to culture. Although to us in western industrial society, monogamy is 'natural' and polygamy is frowned upon if not outlawed, there are other societies in which polygamy is an accepted way of life. The competition to 'get ahead' and to be successful that is so prevalent in our society is not found everywhere. Furthermore, the scientific concepts of illness and treatment which we regard as the correct ones are by no means viewed as such by people in all cultures, as we shall see below.

As we consider examples of beliefs and behaviour that differ from our own, we must bear in mind that these particular segments of culture cannot be evaluated on their own; they must be viewed within the context of the whole culture of which they are a part. Kluckhohn (1949) observed that having many wives is an economic advantage among people who herd but not among those who hunt. The different aspects of a particular culture form an integrated and unified whole. Therefore, an isolated element from one culture (such as western scientific medicine) is likely to induce resistance or unintended changes in the system when is is introduced into another culture.

THE PERVASIVENESS OF CULTURE

Although people in all cultures must attend to the same biological needs such as thirst, hunger, sex, etc., there is great variety in the cultural prescriptions for meeting these needs. Foods regarded as

322 *Behavioural Science in Medicine*

delicacies in one culture may be considered inedible by another. At one time Americans believed that tomatoes were poisonous. People everywhere experience hunger, but whether hunger induces images of thick rare steaks, fried grasshoppers or raw fish is determined by culture. Acceptable sexual expression differs as well: while some societies condone and even encourage premarital sex, others strongly forbid it; homosexuality is considered normal in some societies but not in others. Mead (1957) observes that even the incidence of morning sickness is related to culture. In those societies where it is generally expected that pregnant women will experience morning sickness many women do, but in those where it is not, only a few women do.

The way in which we perceive the world around us is also affected by our culture, as this determines how we categorize our experience. A clear illustration of the point was provided by the results of a study of colour perception among several groups of American Indians (Ray 1953). Different groups divided the spectrum into different categories with the number of basic colours ranging from three to eight. A wavelength, which in one culture was in the middle of one colour range, might be on the dividing line between two colours in another culture. The categories used by a particular culture to divide up the world often reflect what is of importance to that culture. For example, in one tribe where good skin is particularly valued and brings high bride prices, there is a very elaborate classification of skin diseases.

Culture has a pervasive impact on all levels of human functioning. Aspects of society such as the structure of the family and the complexity and bases of social stratification are related to culture. The beliefs, attitudes and ideas of the members of a society are the result of their culture as are everyday implements such as automobiles, television sets, tools, clay pottery, spears, etc. Furthermore Kluckhohn (1949) contends that

> In sum, the distinctive way of life that is handed down as the social heritage of a people does more than supply a set of skills for making a living and a set of blueprints for human relations. Each different way of life makes its own assumptions about the ends and purposes of human existence, about what human beings have a right to expect from each other and the gods, about what constitutes fulfillment or frustration. (p. 35–6).

Culture affects our entire world view; whether the earth is considered to be round or flat, at the centre of the universe or not, whether the cosmos is believed to be inhabited by one deity or many, by ghosts, demons or ancestral spirits is all determined by culture.

CULTURAL UNIFORMITY AND CULTURAL DIVERSITY

So far in our discussion we have emphasized **cultural diversity**, the vast variety of human beliefs and behaviour that can be found in different cultures. But are there similarities, are there ways in which all people everywhere are alike? The answer appears to be yes. There are a number of **cultural universals**, elements found in all known human societies.

Murdock (1945) provides us with the following partial list of elements,

> which occur, so far as the author's knowledge goes, in every culture known to history or ethnography: age-grading, athletic sports, bodily adornment, calendar, cleanliness training, community organization, cooking, cooperative labor, cosmology, courtship, dancing, decorative art, divination, division of labor, dream interpretation, education, eschatology, ethics, ethnobotany, etiquette, faith healing, family, feasting, fire making, folklore, food taboos, funeral rites, games, gestures, gift giving, government, greetings, hair styles, hospitality, housing, hygiene, incest taboos, inheritance rules, joking, kin-groups, kinship nomenclature, language, law, luck superstitions, magic, marriage, mealtimes, medicine, modesty concerning natural functions, mourning, music, mythology, numerals, obstetrics, penal sanctions, personal names, population policy, postnatal care, pregnancy usages, property rights, propitiation of supernatural beings, puberty customs, religious ritual, residence rules, sexual restrictions, soul concepts, status differentiation, surgery, tool making, trade, visiting, weaning and weather control. (p. 124).

When we consider the components of these elements we see even more uniformity. For instance, '... funeral rites always include expressions of grief, a means of disposing of the corpse, rituals designed to protect the participants from supernatural harm, and the like.' (p. 124).

It is the content of these specific forms that is diverse. All people have language but specific languages differ. All cultures have some form of medicine; in some it is based on the scientific method, in others it involves the supernatural. Hospitality appears to be universal, but in some cultures it is expressed by offering the visitor food and drink, while among some Eskimo groups it is expressed by offering him your wife for the night.

We should note at this point that we need not go so far afield to observe cultural diversity. Although the differences may not be as dramatic as some found in non-western societies, we can find cultural variation close at hand by comparing the many subcultures, such as ethnic groups, that exist within urban industrial society. These groups, to a greater or lesser extent, have their own distinct values, beliefs and patterns of behaviour which comprise their own particular culture.

CULTURAL VARIATION IN ILLNESS AND TREATMENT

CULTURE AND ILLNESS

The health of the members of a society is related to their cultural patterns. Obviously, dietary and hygiene practices can affect the risk of contracting certain diseases. But other cultural practices can affect risks as well: Susser and Watson (1971) note that 'It is scarcely suprising that *tetanus neonatorum* is common among those African peoples who apply a herbalist's mixture containing powdered dung to the cut cord of each newborn baby ...' (p. 70–1). Closer to home, Mechanic (1968) observes that our own culture is not without its particular health risks due to such factors as smoking, alcohol consumption, poorly designed automobiles, air pollution, etc.

Beyond the actual incidence of illness, culture to some degree determines how illness is perceived. 'To some extent the cultural context defines what conditions are recognized, the causes to be attributed to them, and which persons have legitimate authority to assess and define such conditions.' (Mechanic 1968, p. 52).

Examples of the effects of culture on perception of illness and reactions to it are not difficult to find. Many cultures have classification systems of illness that differ greatly from our own and which often include illnesses not recognized by western practitioners. Paul (1955) cites one culture in which there are five basic categories of illness, but only for two, 'obstruction of the gastro-intestinal tract' and 'undue exposure to heat or cold' are scientific doctors consulted. Popular medicine is used for the remaining three, and can also be used for the first two – 'exposure to "bad air" ', 'severe emotional upset', and 'contamination by ritually unclean persons'. Scientific medicine is not believed to be effective against these diseases. Unfortunately however tuberculosis is sometimes thought to be 'fright' and remains untreated by scientific doctors.

Similarly, Rubel (1960) in his study of a group of Mexican-Americans found that they defined four illnesses not recognized by medical practitioners. With two of these, '... *mal ojo* and *susto*, an essential part of the self of an individual is believed to be overcome or lost due to the power of a stronger alien force, eventuating in the loss of the individual's equilibrium. The loss of balance is manifested by somatic illness.' (p. 807). They believe that Anglo-Americans are not afflicted by these illnesses and that they are not understood and cannot be treated by doctors. Instead they are attended to by local curers. Belief in these illnesses persists despite the presence of scientific medicine. Rubel attributes this persistence (for three of the four diseases) to the function they serve in sustaining some of the dominant values of the culture.

Culture also can affect responses to symptoms. Mechanic (1968) notes that from the point of view of western medical practitioners, some African women over-react to abdominal pain due to gonococcal salpingitis. However, their response can be understood within the context of their culture which greatly emphasizes childbearing and disparages barrenness.

Perhaps the most dramatic example of the effects of culture on health can be found in accounts of death as a result of sorcery in individuals who believe in sorcery. Individuals who believe they have been so afflicted typically do not eat or drink and experience a high level of fear. Cannon (1942) attempted a physiological analysis of these occurrences: '... a persistent and profound emotional state may induce a disastrous fall in blood pressure, ending in death. Lack of food and drink would collaborate with the damaging emotional effects, to induce the fatal outcome.' (p. 179). Remember also our discussion of health changes in relation to feelings of helplessness, in Chapter 7.

CULTURE AND TREATMENT

The treatment prescribed for an illness follows from its perceived cause. If, as in our society, illness is believed to be caused by the presence of particular micro-organisms, a drug proved effective against these micro-organisms is administered. But not all cultures perceive illness to be the result of biological causes; some attribute illness to the supernatural.

The Azande, a tribe in Central Africa, (Evans-Pritchard 1937) attribute misfortune, including illness, to witchcraft. An Azande who stubs his toe while walking along a familiar path or who contracts tuberculosis, assumes the event to be caused by the attack of a witch. Witchcraft in this society, and in others like it, is a part of everyday life. The witch responsible is another member of the society who has some reason to wish the victim harm, and there are set procedures for identifying the witch and inducing the witch to end the attack.

The Azande will readily agree that tuberculosis is due to the presence of the tubercle bacillus. Western medicine, however, does not explain why a particular person at a particular time contracted the disease. Everyone is bitten by mosquitoes; the victim has been bitten before without contracting the disease; why did this particular occasion result in the disease? The answer is the action of a witch. Azande witchcraft explains the 'why' of causality. In our western society, the explanation for 'why me, now' is not nearly as satisfying; the event is usually attributed to chance, luck, or occasionally, the will of God. But for the Azande the answer is clear; the illness is caused by the attack of a witch and the victim is not expected to recover until the attack ceases.

The Azande belief in witchcraft, very much like our own belief in scientific medicine, is not refuted by its failure in any particular instance. If, despite the attempts of doctors, a patient does not recover, this failure does not lead us to question the whole system of scientific medicine. We explain the failure within the system by proposing scientific reasons for the lack of recovery. Similarly, in Azande society, if a person fails to recover, even though the procedures for identifying the witch and ending the attack have been followed, the Azande do not question their belief in witchcraft. Once again, the failure is explained within the system – the illness is due to the actions of more than one witch.

The Kwakuitl of western Canada believe that illness can be caused by the intrusion of a foreign object in the body, and the afflicted may seek the treatment of a shaman. The shaman, during a curing ceremony, pretends to extract a foreign object from the body of the patient.

> The shaman hides a little tuft of down in a corner of his mouth, and he throws it up, covered with blood, at the proper moment – after having bitten his tongue or made his gums bleed – and solemnly presents it to his patient and the onlookers as the pathological foreign body extracted as a result of his sucking and manipulations.
>
> (Lévi-Strauss 1958/1963, p. 175.)

The patient is presented with clear evidence of the cause of the illness and of the fact of the cure. Compare this treatment to that of western medicine, where the cause of the illness is often beyond the comprehension of the patient, if not the doctor, and evidence of a cure may be far less obvious.

In Sri Lanka, some groups use exorcism as a means of treatment for certain diseases (Kapferer, 1975). The patient is believed to be possessed by a demon and now believes demons to be superior to humans when in fact they are believed to be inferior by healthy members of the community. The exorcism itself is a long and elaborate ceremony which takes place in the vicinity of the patient's home. The ceremony not only involves the patient and the exorcist but also family and friends. In fact the whole community is present and to some extent participates in the exorcism. The social and physical setting of this treatment certainly differs from that of western medicine, where treatment takes place in the unfamiliar and alien environment of the hospital and in relative isolation from family and friends. The community actually witnesses the cure, and at the end of the ceremony is presented with a person who is now defined as well rather than ill. In effect, the role that the person plays in the community is changed, and both the person and the others in the community now expect that he or she will act like a well person.

Frank (1973) analyzes healing methods in non-western societies like those we have just discussed, as well as religious healing in western society (in particular the healing rituals at the Shrine of Lourdes), and emphasizes the similarities among these non-medical methods of treatment. He states that

> Chronic illness, especially, causes demoralization. Constant misery, forced relinquishment of the activities and roles that supported the patient's self-esteem and gave his life significance, the threat of suffering and death – all may generate feelings of anxiety and despair, which, in turn, may be intensified by reactions of anxiety, impatience, and progressive withdrawal in those close to him, especially when his illness threatens their security as well as his own. Thus illness often creates a vicious circle by evoking emotions that aggravate it. (p. 47).

These psychological and social aspects of illness have usually been ignored by western medicine. In contrast, non-medical techniques seem to function by fostering hope and an expectation of a cure and improving the patient's self image and relationship with the group.

> All forms of healing are based on a conceptual scheme consistent with the patient's assumptive world that prescribes a set of activities. The scheme helps him to make sense out of his inchoate feelings, thereby heightening his sense of mastery over them. Non-medical healing rituals are believed to

mobilize natural or supernatural healing forces on the patient's behalf. Often they include detailed confessions followed by atonement and reacceptance into the group. Many rituals also stress mutual service, which counteracts the patient's morbid self-preoccupation, strengthens his self-esteem by demonstrating that he can do something for others, and, like confession, cements the bonds between patient and group. Confession and mutual service contribute to the feeling that performance of the healing ritual confers merit in itself. If the patient is not cured, he nevertheless often feels more virtuous. If he is cured, this may be taken as a mark of divine favor, permanently enhancing his value in his own and the group's eyes. This may also help maintain the cure, for if he relapses he is letting the group down. Finally, in religious healing, relief of suffering is accompanied not only by a profound change in the patient's feelings about himself and others, but by a strengthening of previous assumptive systems or, sometimes, conversion to new ones.

(Frank, pp. 76 and 77.)

WESTERN MEDICINE IN NON-WESTERN CULTURES

Westerners, equipped with their ethnocentric belief that scientific medicine is the correct and best system of medicine, have often tried to introduce it to non-western cultures. Many of these attempts have been less than successful, because they have failed to take account of the culture of the people. Attempts to introduce changes in dietary or hygiene practices may be resisted because they conflict with important cultural values. In some cultures the orientation is towards the present rather than the future, and patients are unlikely to complete a long term course of treatment once immediate symptoms have disappeared. In one society, where the cure was believed to be related to the amount paid for the treatment, there was a lack of trust in cheaply available western medicine.

One need not travel outside the borders of western industrialized countries to find views of illness and treatment, and health care practices, that differ from those of scientific medicine. Subcultures within western societies may retain their traditional beliefs about health and illness, as well as associated health-related behaviour, to a greater or lesser extent. Weidman (1979) states that although the patient may perceive alternative health care systems (one of which is scientific medicine), the practitioner of scientific medicine usually perceives only one, and ignores the beliefs and practices of the patient associated with other systems. This failure to acknowledge the patient's interpretation of his illness can result in misunderstanding and alienation, and can interfere with the ultimate goal of health improvement. Weidmann contends that the provision of health care in such situations will be improved as scientific medicine adopts a transcultural approach; that is, the ability to perceive, but to maintain a degree of detachment from, these alternative cultural views.

SUMMARY

Culture, or 'the total life way of a people' (Kluckhohn 1949, p. 17), is learned and transmitted from one generation to the next. The belief that one's own culture is the natural or best one and that those which differ are inferior is known as ethnocentrism. Culture channels our biological needs, determines how we will categorize our experience, and influences our beliefs, values and view of the world. Despite the existence of cultural diversity, there are a number of elements that are found in all known cultures. Although all cultures have some form of medicine, they differ in their perceptions of illness and methods of treatment.

TERMS AND CONCEPTS

culture
ethnocentrism
cultural diversity
cultural universal

FOR DISCUSSION

1. Why do you think ethnocentrism exists? How do you think it can be decreased or eliminated?
2. Consider Murdock's list of the elements found in all known cultures. Why do you think that all cultures have these elements in common? How would you explain the great diversity of the beliefs and behaviour associated with any particular element, such as medicine?
3. Are there different sub-cultures in your community? How do they differ in their beliefs and behaviour?
4. What advice would you give to a medical student who intended to practice western medicine in a non-western culture?

330   *Behavioural Science in Medicine*

SUGGESTED READING

Frank, Chapter 3. Non-medical healing: Religious and secular. A compelling account of non-medical healing procedures.

Kluckhohn: a book written to explain anthropology to the layman.

Murdock: discussion of the commonalities among cultures.

REFERENCES

Cannon, W. G. 1942. 'Voodoo' death. *Amer. Anthropologist* **44,** 169–81.

Evans-Pritchard, E. E. 1937. *Witchcraft, Oracles and Magic among the Azande.* Oxford: Clarendon Press.

Frank, J. D. 1973. *Persuasion and Healing* (Rev. edn). Baltimore: The Johns Hopkins University Press.

Kapferer, B. 1975. Entertaining Demons. Comedy, interaction and meaning in a Sinhalese healing ritual. *Modern Ceylon Studies* **6,** 16–63.

Kluckhohn, C. 1949. *Mirror for Man.* New York: Whittlesey House.

Lévi-Strauss, C. 1963. (Original publication 1958, in French.) *Structural Anthropology.* (C. Jacobson and B. G. Schoepf trans.). New York: Basic Books, Inc.

Mead, M. 1957. *Male and Female.* New York: Mentor Books.

Mechanic, D. 1968. *Medical Sociology: A Selective View.* New York: The Free Press.

Murdock, G. P. 1945. The common denominator of cultures. In R. Linton (ed.) *The Science of Man in the World Crisis.* New York: Columbia University Press.

Paul, B. D. (ed.) 1955. *Health, Culture and Community.* New York: Russell Sage Foundation.

Ray, V. E., 1953. Human color perception and behavioral response. *Transactions of the New York Academy of Science* **16,** 98–104.

Rubel, A. J. 1960. Concepts of disease in Mexican-American Culture. *Amer. Anthropologist* **62,** 795–814.

Susser, M. W. and Watson, W. 1971. *Sociology in Medicine.* London: Oxford University Press.

Weidman, H. H. 1979. A transcultural view: Prerequisite to interethnic (intercultural) communication in medicine. *Soc. Sci. and Med.,* **13B,** 85–7.

First Author Index

Where papers are co-authored, only the first-named author has been indexed. The italicized page numbers indicate in each case where the full reference is to be found.

Subject Index

Accidents, 4, 152

Acupuncture, 54, 56

Adolescence, 147–9
  behavioural and medical disorders of, 149; cognition in, 65, 147; identity, 148–9; sexuality in, 147–8

Affectionless psychopathy, 132

Affiliation, 213–14
  and anxiety arousal, 214; and birth order, 214; and fear, 213–14; and sex, 214

Ageing, 4, 162
  disengagement, 153; disorders of 154; effects on IQ, 119–21; personality changes, 153–4; preparation for, 154

Aggression
  determinants, 101–2; relationship to anger, 102–3; treatment, 207; TV influences, 104; see also, Anger

Alcoholism, 4, 220
  control of, 91, 204–5; genetic predisposition, 39

Altruism, 221
  see also Helping behaviour

Amniocentesis, 39

Analysis of research data, 21–3
  computers and, 22; correlation, 22; probability level, 22; statistical significance, 22

Anger, 83
  and personal problems, 101; antecedents, 101–4, 167; consequences, 104–5

Animals
  behaviour, 28–9, 31–2; learning, 76, 82, 87; resemblances, and personality, 181

Anxiety
  and affiliation, 214; and anger, 104; and isolation, 213; and pain experience, 56, 57, 99; and pain tolerance, 55; and sex, 161; and thinking, 66; antecedents, 83, 98–9, 167; avoidance of as a reinforcer, 91, 98, 99; consequences, 99–101, 254; in children, 145; treatment, 205–6

Anorexia nervosa
  and body image, 61; treatment, 204

Anoxia, 41, 146

Aphasia, 68, 198

Arthritis, 54, 152

Assertiveness, 80, 104
  training, 101, 201, 203, 206

Associations
  and roles, 309, 312; as distinguished from primary groups, 308, 309; characteristics of, 311–13; formal organization of, 311–12; informal organization of, 312; scientific management vs. human relations approach, 312–13; the hospital as an example of, 313–14

Asthma, 77, 86

Attachment, 88, 130–9
  definition, 131; deprivations of, 30, 33, 133–4; disruptions of, 135–8; past infancy, 138–9, 162; supplementary figures, 134–5

Attitude change
  and cognitive dissonance, 249–52; and consistency, 249; and functions of attitudes, 248; and persuasive communication, 252–6; and reference groups, 234–5; and role playing, 255; and inoculation, 255; and the social environ-